The Art of Kim Hong-do

A Great Court Painter of 18th-Century Korea

The Art of Kim Hong-do

Oh Ju-seok

Art Media Resources

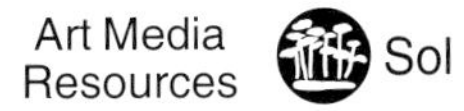

Sol

The Art of Kim Hong-Do
by Oh Ju-seok

First published in the USA by
Art Media Resources, Inc.
1507 South Michigan Avenue
Chicago, IL 60605 USA
Tel: 312-663-5351
Fax: 312-663-5177
info@artmediaresources.com
www.artmediaresources.com

Originally published in Korean as Danwon Kim Hong-do
단원檀園 김홍도金弘道 first published by Sol Publishing in 1998.

Translated by Lim Seon-young · Yang Ji-hyun, revised by Mark S. Turnoy for Sol Publishing and Art Media Resources with the support of the Korea Literature Translation Institute in commemoration of Korea being the Guest of Honor at the Frankfurt Book Fair 2005.

ISBN 1-58886-088-4

Printed in Korea

Library of Congress Cataloging-in-Publication Data

O, Chu-sæok, 1956-
[Tanwon Kim Hong-do. English]
The art of Kim Hong-do / by Oh Ju-seouk.
p. cm.
Includes bibliographical references and index.
ISBN 1-58886-088-4 (softcover : alk. paper)
1. Kim, Hong-do, 1745—-Criticism and interpretation. I. Title.

ND1069.K475O1713 2005
759.9519—dc22
2005024524

Table of Contents

Foreword

In the winter of 1995, the National Museum of Korea, Hoam Art Museum and Kansong Art Museum co-sponsored a special exhibition commemorating the 250th anniversary of Kim Hong-do's birth. I first proposed the exhibition when I was a guest research fellow at Hoam, and saw the exhibition through. One of the many tasks that occupied me during the two years of preparation for the exhibition was gathering sufficient material to write this book.

The exhibition's hectic schedule delayed the publication of the book until after the exhibition closed. Even at that, the book was only published in a collection of papers. People interested in Kim Hong-do barely knew of the book's existence, and the book was inaccessible to the general reader because it was a limited edition and unavailable in bookstores.

This book has a new cover and adds newly discovered details along with more than a hundred plates and descriptions. This edition also corrects some errors and omissions from the previous version. The book includes all known records of Kim Hong-do so that readers can review the details of his life. I have attempted to provide an easy-to-follow chronological narrative to portray Kim Hong-do as accurately and consistently as possible. I wanted the readers to encounter Kim Hong-do, the man as they read.

Kim was one of the most talented Korean painters, and more importantly, his personal charms gave additional weight to his artistic achievements. His skills go beyond painting as he also excelled in calligraphy, literature and music. The personality revealed between the lines of the records show a man who was at times amiable but at other times arrogant. Reflecting upon the works of such a man and following his footsteps was indeed a joyful task.

This book owes its publication to many people. Thanks go to Directors Jeong Yang-mo, Hong Ra-hui and Jeon Yeong-u of the National Museum of Korea, Hoam Art Museum and Kansong Art Museum, respectively, who agreed to co-sponsor the exhibition. In addition, Kang U-bang, the Research Director of the National Museum of Korea, Lee Jong-seon, Deputy Director of Hoam Art Museum, and Choi Wan-su, Research Director at Kansong Art Museum, taught me lessons on practical matters. I would also like to express my sincere gratitude to Lee Won-bok of the Art Department at the National Museum, Kim Jae-yeol, Research Director of Hoam Art Museum, and Jeong Byeong-sam, Chief Researcher at Kansong Art Museum.

I would also personally like to thank those who provided me with valuable sources of information on Kim Hong-do. These include Professor Yu Bong-hak of Hanshin University, Professor Kang Gwan-sik of Hanseong University, and Chinese literature experts Kang Gyeong-hun and Kim Yeong-jin. My thanks also go to art researcher Im Jae-wan of Hoam Art Museum, who helped me with the translation of Chinese passages.

I could not have completed this book alone. I availed myself of the abundant academic resources accumulated by scholars, including Go Yu-seop, that date back to the Japanese colonial era. Hoam Art Museum graciously agreed to republish the book, and I am extremely grateful to the museum staff at the National Museum of Korea for reprinting passages previously published in its Museum Newsletter.

I have added a brief, introductory summary, in hopes that it will help readers organize their thoughts about Kim Hong-do. I also tried to write this book in a manner that would make it accessible to the general reader.

I dedicate this book to Kim Hong-do.

Oh, Ju-seok

Spring 1998

Notes

1. The names of paintings in this book have all been put in italics, as have the titles of books, historical records, and albums.
2. The titles of poems are set in double quote marks and italics.
3. All the dates in this book follow the lunar calendar, unless stated otherwise.
4. The Joseon Dynasty adopted the Chinese method of counting years. Unlike many other calendars, the Chinese calendar does not count infinitely sequential years. Instead, years have specific names that repeat every 60 years. Within each 60-year cycle, each year is assigned name consisting of two components:

1.	gap	6.	gi
2.	eul	7.	gyeong
3.	byeong	8.	sin
4.	jeong	9.	im
5.	mu	10.	gye

The first component is a *Celestial Stem*. These words have no English equivalent:

The second component is a *Terrestrial Branch*. The names of the corresponding animals in the zodiac cycle of 12 animals are given in parentheses.

Each of the two components is used sequentially. Thus, the first year of the 60-year cycle becomes gap-ja, the 2nd year is eul-chuk, the 3rd year is byeong-in, etc. At the conclusion of a component, the cycle is repeated: The 10th year is gye-yu, the 11th year is gap-sul (restarting the Celestial Stem), the 12th year is eul-hae, and the 13tth year is byeong-ja (restarting the Terrestrial Branch). Finally, the 60th year becomes gye-hae.

1.	ja (rat)	7.	o (horse)
2.	chuk (ox)	8.	mi (sheep)
3.	in (tiger)	9.	sin (monkey)
4.	myo (hare, rabbit)	10.	yu (rooster)
5.	jin (dragon)	11.	sul (dog)
6.	sa (snake)	12.	hae (pig)

For example, the "eulmyo" in Kim Hong-do's *Eulmyonyeon Album* is a combination of "eul" and "myo." For readability's sake, however, the year "eulmyo" is written 1795, as are all other years. The days are named in a similar manner.

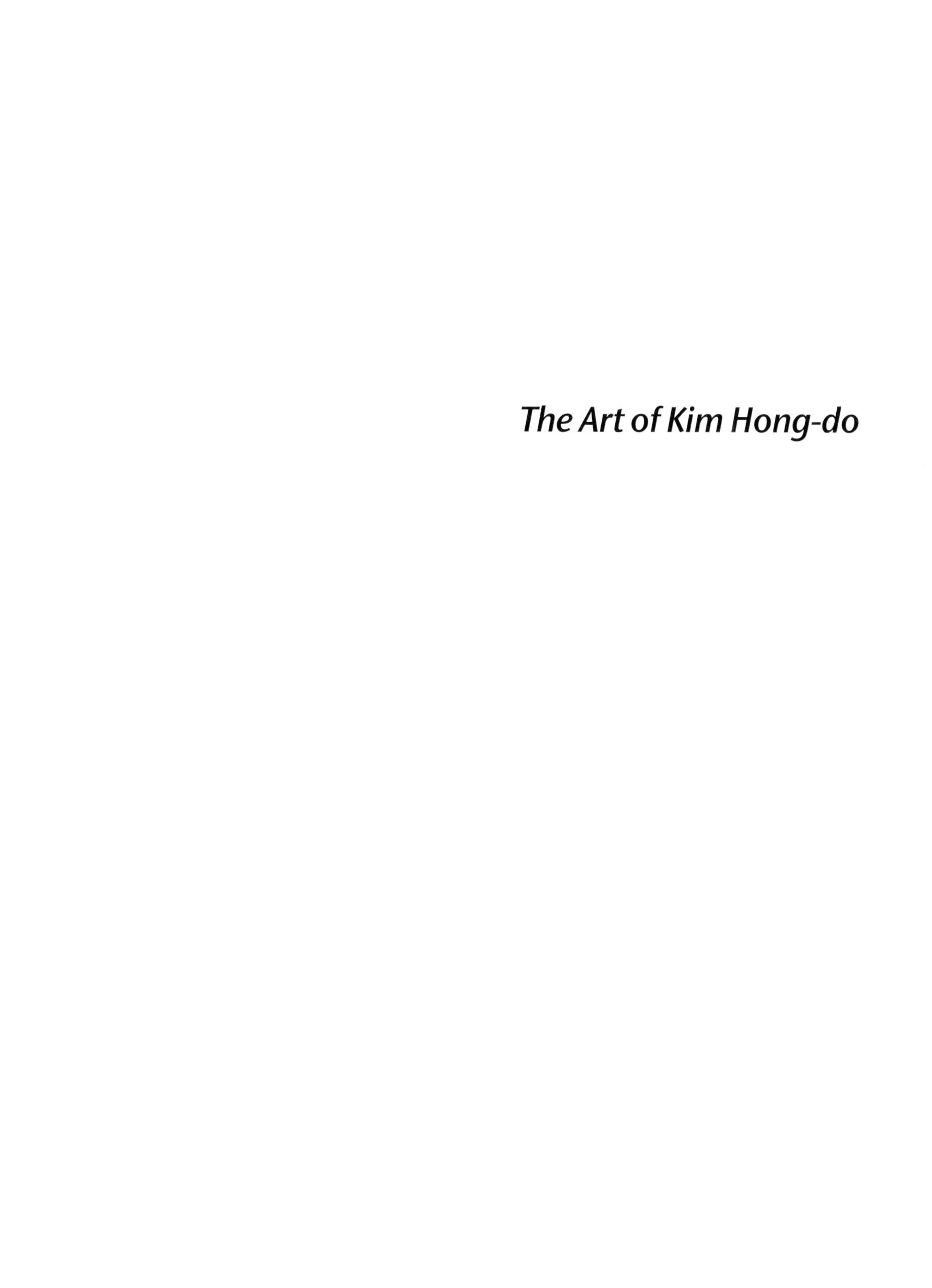

The Art of Kim Hong-do

Preface

Kim Hong-do (1745–ca.1806) was a court painter representative of the latter half of the Joseon Dynasty. He painted masterpieces in many genres, which encompassed the three mainstream trends of the time: realistic or 'true-view' landscape, genre painting, and Chinese painting, of the Southern School. In addition, he painted Taoist Immortals; figures from old Chinese stories, birds and animals against a background of flowers, grass and trees; the Four Gracious Plants (plum blossoms, orchids, chrysanthemums and bamboo); portraits; documentary paintings; and even Buddhist paintings and prints. Under the ardent support of King Jeongjo, he established the 'Kim Hong-do School,' with its strong Korean characteristics. By extending his individual style to the artistic mode of the times, Kim influenced both contemporaries and future artists.

Kim Hong-do is an important figure in the history of Korean art because his works contain a high level of artistic sophistication, creativity and a classically Korean sense of beauty. His works are also valuable to cultural historians because, whether it is his realistic landscapes, which captured the beauty of the Korean landscape from a unique perspective, or his genre paintings, which realistically depicted the lives of everyday Koreans with style, wit and comedy, the subject matter of his paintings is very modern. Furthermore, Kim was cultured in other areas—poetry, calligraphy, painting and music—and this was a decisive factor in upgrading the overall quality of his works. Contemporary painters still emulate the aforementioned characteristics of his paintings, and the paintings serve to inspire many.

What kind of painter was Kim Hong-do? He painted the portraits of kings three times—when painting a king's portrait was considered the highest honor for the court painters. He also painted a painting dedicated to Crown Prince Sado, the father of King Jeongjo, which hung behind the Buddha's statue in the main worship hall of Yongjusa Temple. He painted the legendary palace mural, masterpiece 'Sea Fairies.' He was the king's most favored artist, which was demonstrated by his being ordered to travel and sketch the scenes of four districts near Mount Geumgang. During his travels, the king gave special orders to the districts to treat Kim with the utmost respect. His esteem is also witnessed in the official public titles he held: *chalbang*[1] at Angi, and *hyeongam*[2] at Yeonpung. During his reign, King Jeongjo selected the ten most gifted painters from the circle of thirty court painters and named them *jabidaeryeong* court painters of the Gyujanggak, the royal library. Kim Hong-do was not one of them; having received special treatment, he was excused from daily court chores and his name was never directly mentioned in the *Gyujanggak Daily Journal*. In short, Kim was King Jeongjo's favorite *daejo* court painter.[3]

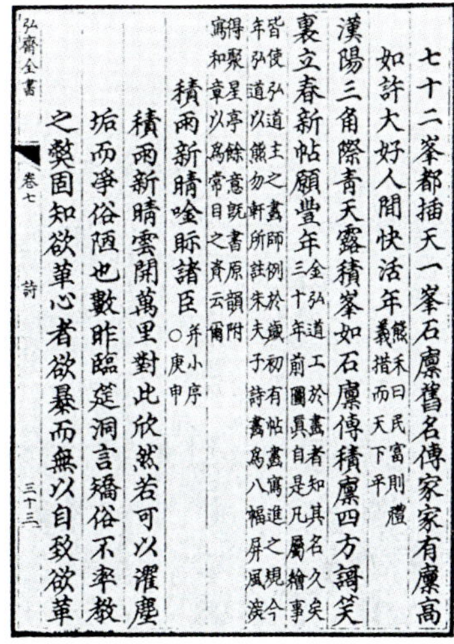

七十二峯都插天一峯石廩舊名傳家家有廩高
如許大好人間快活年熊禾曰民富則禮義措而天下平
漢陽三角際青天露積峯如石廩傳積廩四方謌笑
裏立春新帖願豐年金弘道工於畫者知其名久矣三十年前圖眞自是凡屬繪事
皆使弘道主之畫師例於歲初有帖畫寫進之規今年弘道以纖勿新所註朱夫子詩畫爲八幅屛風湊
得聚星亭餘意既書原韻附寫和章以爲常目之資云爾
積雨新晴唫眎諸臣并小序○庚申
積雨新晴雲開萬里對此欣然若可以濯塵
垢而爭俗陋也數昨臨筵洞言矯俗不率敎
之獘固知欲革心者欲暴而無以自致欲革

弘齋全書 卷七 詩 三十三

1 Text in *Hongjaejeonseo*
King Jeongjo s anthology amounts to 10 cases, 100 books and 184 volumes. The size of the anthology proves that he was a true philosopher-king. The king mentions Kim Hong-do s three-decade service as court painter and expresses his satisfaction with the paintings produced. The description is not lengthy, but the king s words succinctly yet comprehensively shed light on Kim s character and life. This sort of tribute is very rare in Confucian society.

Hongjaejeonseo [Hongjae is King Jeongjo's pen name], a collection of King Jeongjo's writings, shows the king's deep affection for Kim (Plate 1). The king composed eight poems in 1800 in response to the rhymes of Chu Hsi. At the end of the poems the following is written:

> Kim Hong-do is a skilled artist that I have known for a long time. He painted a portrait of me thirty years ago, and since then, I have ordered Kim to preside over all court paintings. Court painters are required by custom to draw and submit *cheophwa*[4] at the beginning of the year. This year Hong-do made an eight-

1 A magistrate of a small county.
2 A local officer in charge of transportation and communication.
3 A kind of secretarial court painter who had a different status from other Gyujanggak court painters and received orders directly from the king.

fold screen with Chu Hsi's poetry and included the commentaries of Mulheon Unghwa, and I was deeply touched by the teachings of Chu Hsi. In response to the original poem Kim wrote on the screen, I composed 8 poems. I will always look at the painting to remind myself of the teachings.

Go Yu-seop introduced the above writing half a century ago, but its significance for scholars and the general public does not seem to have sunk in. King Jeongjo's very concise writing summarizes the person and life of Kim Hong-do. In the quote, King Jeongjo recollected that he had known Kim Hong-do for a long time and that he had ordered Kim to preside over all court paintings for the past 30 years. Kim Hong-do was active as a painter from the end of King Yeongjo's reign to the early years of King Sunjo's reign, which encompassed King Jeongjo's 24-year reign. This means that most of Kim Hong-do's career, which started in the 1760s before King Jeongjo was on the throne, covered the splendid renaissance period of King Jeongjo's rule. Kim Hong-do supervised national painting assignments because the king especially favored him for 30 years, and that is how a mere court painter's name came to be mentioned in the king's anthology.

Even though Kim Hong-do's influence was overwhelming, as with the other court painters of the Joseon Dynasty there is neither sufficient nor detailed information about his life and work. It is not that Kim Hong-do as an artist or his world of art is not worth noting; presumably, it is because the *seongrihak*[5] of the time considered painting the basest of all skills and because Kim was a *jungin*[6]. The surviving works of Kim Hong-do are too few when one considers that he was a prolific painter. Furthermore, his most important pieces are lost. To begin with, the portraits of King Yeongjo and King Jeongjo, which Kim Hong-do had enthusiastically painted and which helped secure his reputation as a court painter, are missing. The long (40 to 50 meters wide), horizontal srolls of 'Mount Geumgang' that Kim painted with deep-colored pigments after spending 50 days visiting and observing the 12,000 peaks of Mount Geumgang on a royal assignment, are also miss-

4 A painting for inclusion in an album or a folding screen.
5 A philosophy of human nature and natural laws that originated in the Sung and Ming Dynasties.
6 A person who belonged to the middle class, and who was usually a professional technician or administrator.

ing. The legendary 'Sea Fairies' mural that Kim painted on a huge wall of Changdeok Palace with a few swift brush strokes was destroyed during a fire in the palace. Kim Hong-do had a seal that was as large as 12 square centimeters (Plate 2), which is also missing. A photograph of the seal tells us that the engraving on the seal read, "Family name: Kim. Given name: Hong-do. Courtesy name: Saneung. Pen name: Dangu. From Old Gaya Province." None of the paintings affixed with this seal survive.

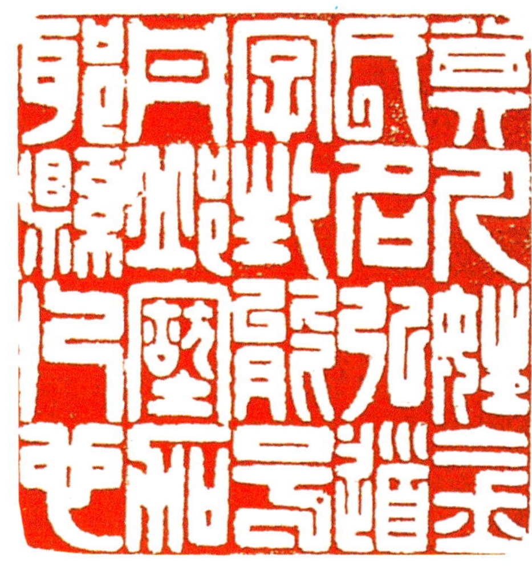

2 Kim Hong-do s seal
12 × 12cm.
The seal s magnitude permits solemn engraving of all the formalities: including name, pen name, courtesy name and family origin. The last character is a suffix expressing the honorific ending of a sentence. The size, style and inscription all lead to the conclusion that this seal was used on paintings submitted to the king. Unfortunately, however, the seal is lost, and no extant works bear its mark.

It is Kim Hong-do's personal tragedy that his masterpieces, the basic primary source materials that tell who the painter is, are lost. It is a tragedy for Koreans as well, because Kim's works are a reflection of the times that embody the spirit, style and life of his contemporaries. Of course, a considerable number of works survive, and, in fact, there are considerably more of Kim Hong-do's works than there are of many other Korean artists. This is probably because Kim Hong-do was able to devote himself to painting much of his art with enthusiastic support from the king. His works were preserved with the utmost care because he was such a well-known artist. There is no arguing, however, that he deserved to have more works preserved.

Today, no more than 300 of Kim Hong-do's paintings remain. This is too few to speak properly for his true world of art. Court painters of the Joseon Dynasty obediently, diligently and patiently performed their duties as painters, for beyond the imagination of today's artists. Unless they were portraits that required the utmost detail, paintings of Kim's era could be completed rather quickly once the artist had reached a certain skill level, due to the nature of the materials used. If the painters only painted one picture a day, it would amount to more than 300 a year. On the assumption that Kim Hong-do started his career in his twenties and continued to work for the next forty years, we can estimate that he painted more than 12,000

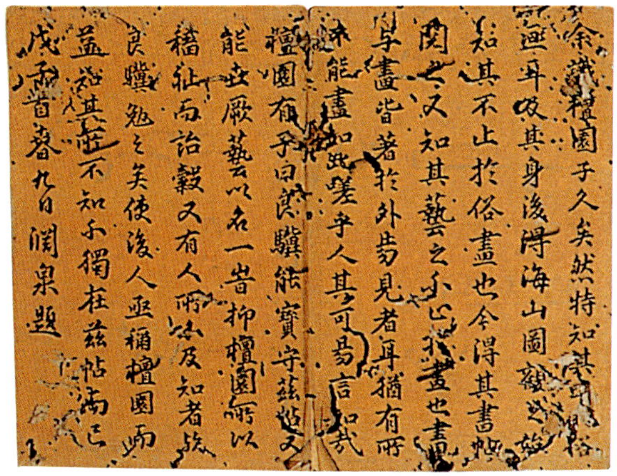
余識檀園子久矣然特知其[illegible][illegible]
畫耳及其身後得海山圖[illegible][illegible]
知其不止於俗畫也今得其書帖
閱之又知其藝之不止於畫也畫
與書皆著於外易見者耳猶有所
未能盡知此豈爭人其可易言知哉
檀園有子曰然驥能寶守茲帖又
能亟厲藝以名一世抑檀園所以
積[illegible]而詒穀又有人所以及知者[illegible]
良驥勉之矣使後人亟稱檀園而
益欽其德不知不獨在茲帖而已
戊辰首春九日淵泉題

3 Foreword by Hong Seok-ju to *Danwon s Posthumous Works*
Ink on paper. 33×44cm.
National Museum of Korea. The best-known scholar and writer of the time remembered Kim by his elegant nickname Danwonja. The foreword is included in the first draft of Hong s anthology Hakhae but excluded from *Master Yeoncheon s Anthology*, which was assembled by Hong s descendents, who thought it improper to include the foreword because it had appeared in the anthology of a middle-class court painter.

paintings during his lifetime.

Put this way, just like blind men touching an elephant, it is a frustrating and limiting experience trying to understand Kim Hong-do's world of art only through his remaining works. As luck would have it, at least Kim's album of writings and pictures in his own hand, *Danwon's Posthumous Works,* exists to shed some light on what kind of man he was (Plate 3). He wrote in a very natural manner, unmindful of others, and his numerous letters reveal glimpses of his personal life. Prefaces and postscripts written by numerous contemporary well-known figures help in understanding his life and work. But there are very few surviving works to use as primary source material.

The author deeply regrets the lack of preservation of Kim Hong-do's paintings and Korean paintings in general. The author is also skeptical of those who claim to know a great deal about a certain artist and his world of art based on a few remaining works and records. This does not mean, however, that we should forget about the life and art world of Kim Hong-do, who was by far one of the greatest artists in Korean history, simply because we lack detail. He is too precious a person to be dismissed. The author, therefore, intends to approach Kim Hong-do more closely by aggregating and re-interpreting the surviving records, correcting some obvious mistakes, and adding new information, however limited it may be.

This biography of Kim Hong-do and investigation into his world of art is by no means perfect. While this is due primarily to the author's shortcomings, it is also due to the wealth of materials that defy systematic organization. Neither is it the author's intention to distort the truth with assumptions; therefore, in certain parts of this book, only the materials are presented, however ambiguous they may be. The author seeks comfort in that this book is a complete collection of information on Kim Hong-do, and that for now it will serve as a comprehensive source of data on Kim.

Because of the gaps in our knowledge of Kim Hong-do's life, and because of the number of his works that are missing, readers should be as imaginative as possible in trying to feel the autumn in the air with merely the glimpse of a fallen leaf, and be as sensitive as possible in trying to guess what soup is in the pot with just one sip. Above all, any great piece of art contains in itself broad and profound implications that equal a thousand words. The author calls upon readers to find such meanings in the paintings themselves.

Chapter 1: The World of Kim Hong-do and the Social Status of the Artist

To understand Kim Hong-do's world of art, one must first understand what kind of life the man led. To do that, one must know something about the age in which he lived. He was born in the 21st year of King Yeongjo's rule (1745), lived through the 24 years of King Jeongjo's reign and died in the 6th year of King Sunjo's rule (1806). He lived his 62 years in a time of peace. In his *Eulogy to 'Eunam Gathering,'* a government official Kwon Sang-sin (1759–1824) wrote, "[he was] fortunately born in peaceful times and his paintings beautifully embody that sense of peace." Even though the passage is somewhat lengthy, it is reproduced here because it is relevant to Kim Hong-do's acquaintances.

> It is relatively easier to come across an agreeable season and place than to meet agreeable people, and even if one does meet such people, it is difficult for that meeting to take place in time of peace. That is why there have been very few meetings of taste and elegance recently. We are now in the 12th year of King Jeongjo's rule (1788). The government is fair. The country is peaceful. Crops are good every year. Farmers and merchants are happy. I told my friends, "We had fought a war many springs ago. The people of Hanyang [as Seoul was then known] have forgotten what war was like and are enjoying themselves and dancing to the beat of a drum in time of blessing. The villages in blossom and the creeks lined with willows resound with folk music. The

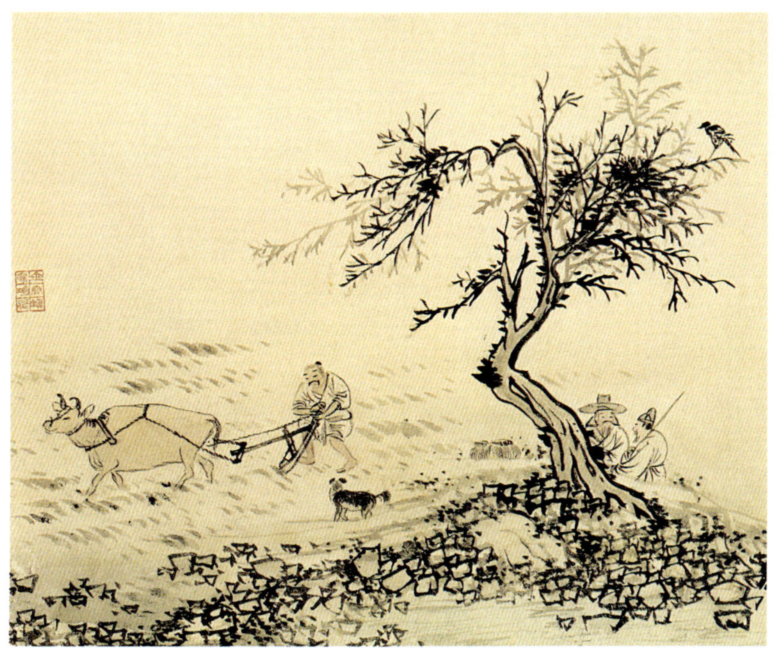

4 *Plowing the Field* from *Danwon-jeolsebo Album*
1796. Ink and color on paper. 26.7×31.6cm. Hoam Art Museum.
This scene was common throughout the country. The man, plowing the field with a yoked ox, has the posture and facial expression of a true farmer. The reliable dog watches over the hard-working ox. The pile of stones is done in various shapes and shades of ink and demonstrates Kim s skill. Under the bent tree, an old gentleman with a walking stick on his shoulder converses with another.

people are indebted to the king for his kindness. If we were to set the date for inviting noble friends to play at Chundangdae inside the Changgyeong Palace singing praise for the king, today must be it." On the first Day of the Snake in the 3rd lunar month, fourteen of us gathered at the Great Eunam with Gyeongsan Lee Han-jin present. Wine jars and glasses were scattered about, and dozens of poems and stories were recited. Half-drunk, Gyeongsan wrote in seal script, Yu Hwan-gyeong played the *geomungo*,[7] and Kim Hong-do painted birds, flowers and bamboo. Appreciation of the scenic beauty and the pleasure of enjoying ourselves were not easily abandoned. Only when the moonlight shone on our backs did we return home. Everyone was satisfied and agreed that there would never be another gathering quite like this one. I took the ink stone and said, "Today we all enjoyed Nanjeong's writing, Taehak's *geomungo*, and the poetry recited by the river frothing with water drops. But we never made a painting to tell the tale. What an immense loss it would be not to capture the beautiful moment in a painting so that our descendants can appreciate the same

7 A six-stringed Korean harp.

kind of elegance and serenity." With that, Danwon Kim Hong-do was commissioned to paint 'Eunam Gathering.'

As mentioned in the above excerpt, Kim Hong-do lived in a time of peace. No war or disturbance occurred between Lee In-jwa's uprising in 1728 and Hong Gyeong-rae's uprising in 1811. During their 52 and 24-year reigns, the wise rulers King Yeongjo and King Jeongjo devoted themselves to serving the people to solidify their weak hold on the monarchy. The country was prosperous and a variety of cultural developments ensued. The age is referred to as the Renaissance of the latter Joseon Dynasty. Kim Hong-do's paintings are a reflection of the times; they show the optimism and pride of the Joseon cultural heritage.

Kim Hong-do was active as a court painter from the end of King Yeongjo's reign and during King Jeongjo's 24-year reign. This chapter will mainly touch upon King Jeongjo, who was very fond of his court painter Kim Hong-do, the style of his regime, and the kind of life the middle class Kim Hong-do led.

During Kim Hong-do's lifetime, which extended from the end of the 17th century to the early 19th century, the three Northeast Asian dynasties, namely the Joseon Dynasty, the Ching Dynasty and the Tokugawa Shogunate, were at peace. Although Joseon was experiencing great internal changes such as the emergence of *silhak*,[8] *bukhak*[9] and Catholicism, the nation continued in its traditional way as a Confucian agricultural society based on seongrihak. All social relationships ranging from king and subject to master and slave were governed by *seongrihak*, as were moral values.

Lee Hwang established Joseon's *seongrihak* in the late 16th century, and Lee Yul-gok customized it to fit the Joseon society. Joseon *seongrihak* became the *de facto* national ideology as *seowon*[10] and *seodang* (village schoolhouse) spread nationwide. Even after the bitter Japanese invasion of Joseon in 1592 and the Manchu War in 1636, Joseon did not become a military state. It rather reinforced and encouraged the spread of *seongrihak*

8 A practical science that promoted agriculture.

9 A practical science that promoted commerce and trade that originated in the Ching Dynasty.

10 A lecture/memorial hall for Confucian scholars.

throughout society, which paved the road toward a cultural and ethical nation. In the 17th century, intellectual hermits were appointed government officials, and based on their beliefs and academic orientation they divided themselves up into cliques and began factional politics.

Against this backdrop, people thought that holding more stringently to traditional Chinese values would alleviate the social confusion caused by the two great wars. In the 17th century, this resulted in the emergence of two dialogues, "Attack North (Revenge on Ching)" and "Respect China (Loyalty to Ming)." As time passed, however, the "Attack North" dialogue became more about strengthening the inner self than fighting the barbarians, and "Respect China" became a cultural theory to solidify the identity of Joseon. The dichotomy between the pure and the barbarian Chinese dynasties helped maintain the overall peace, and the unique colors of Joseon culture became more pronounced.

Even before the 1592 Japanese invasion, Joseon sentiments were ex-

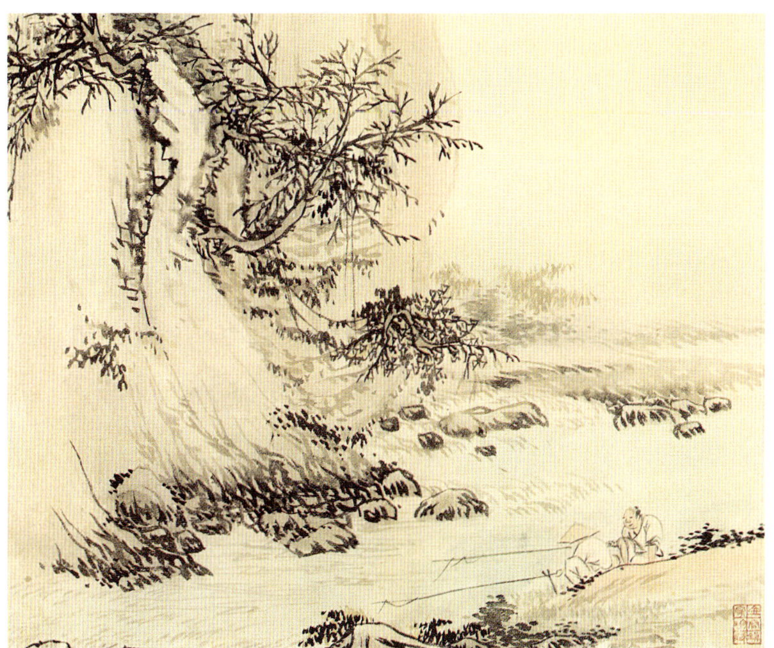

5 *Fishing Landscape* from *Danwon-jeolsebo Album*
1796. Ink and color on paper. 26.7×31.6cm. Hoam Art Museum.
Two men are fishing at a stream. The one wearing a wide hat is bent forward, and the wide-faced, bareheaded man seems to be making small talk. The stream flows from behind the cliff and joins a larger body of water. The observer can almost hear the lapping of the water. The left side of the painting is dense whereas the right side is sparse to give a sense of distance.

6 *Spring Magpies Herald Joy* from *Danwon-jeolsebo Album*
1796. Ink and color on paper. 26.7×31.6cm. Hoam Art Museum.
The peach flowers are in full blossom and magpies are chirping in the branches. The bluish tone on the bottom implies it is early morning. The magpie is an auspicious sign, and it is a good omen to see or hear a magpie in the morning. The two dashes in the line of the beaks are painted to indicate the sound of their cry. The magpies are all facing in one direction, making the painting dynamic.

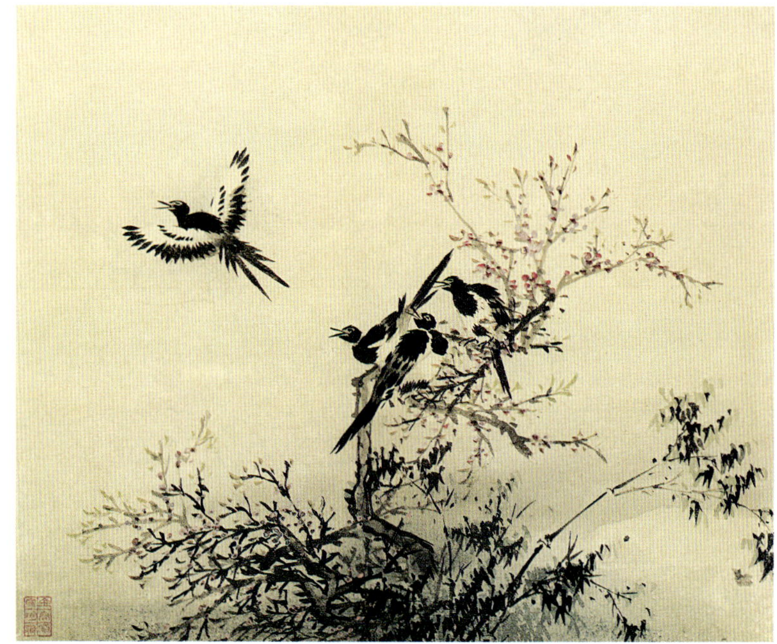

pressed in the indigenous literature of Jeong Cheol and Yun Seon-do, the Chinese literature of Choi Rip, the calligraphy of Han Seok-bong, and the paintings of Jo Sok. The early 18th century marked the establishment of Lee Byeong-yeon's poetry describing the scenery, Jeong Seon's true-view landscapes, and Yun Sun's 'donggukjinche' calligraphy. The latter half of the 18th century, when Kim Hong-do was active, marked the flowering of culture and the height of popularity for genre paintings and novels written in Korean. From the serene poetry, that sang about the scenery, and the realistic landscapes and genre paintings that depicted the peaceful and self-sufficient city along the Han River, where diverse commercial activities thrived along its banks, we can catch glimpses of the people-centered politics and the great harmonious relationship between the king and his people. The national stability and the high level of cultural sophistication of the day are easily observed in Hwaseong (more commonly referred to as Suwon Fortress), which was completed in 1796, and in the corresponding *uigwe*[11]

11 Records of important royal events or ceremonies.

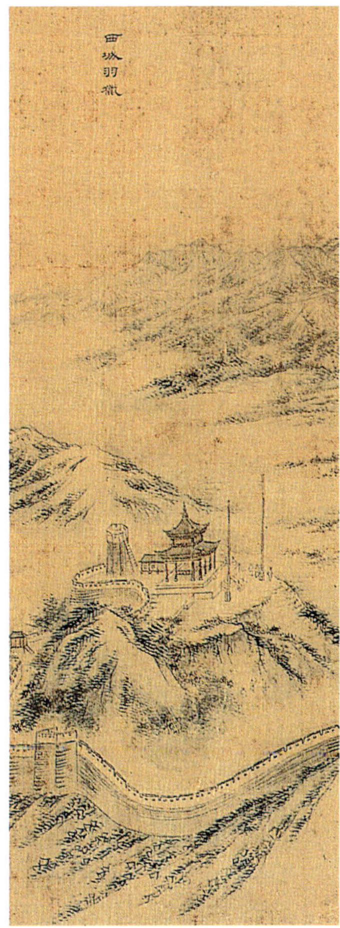

7 ***Bird Hunting in West Fortress*** **from the folding screen,** ***Eight Beautiful Scenes of Hwaseong in Spring and Fall***

Ink and color on silk. 97.7×41.3cm. Seoul National University Museum.

The West Fortress is the wall surrounding Hwaseo Gate. Outside, in the fields, people are hunting. Mount Gwanggyo lies far in the distance. In the middle stands Seojang Tower, Nodae Tower and tall flag posts. The aerial view is only imaginary.

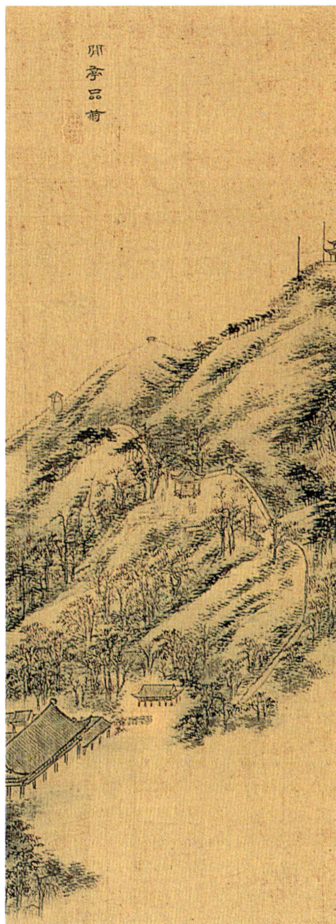

8 ***Appreciating Chrysanthemums in Hanjeong Pavilion*** **from the folding screen,** ***Eight Beautiful Scenes of Hwaseong in Spring and Fall***

Ink and color on silk. 97.7×41.3cm. Seoul National University Museum.

The large building on the bottom left is the Naknamheon of the secondary palace in Hwaseong. The painter was to the north of the spot looking up at Seojang Tower atop Mount Paldal. Inside the hexagonal building, the Miro Hanjeong Pavilion, some people are looking at chrysanthemums. The name of the pavilion means, relax before you get too old, and indicates King Jeongjo s intention to spend his last days in Hwaseong.

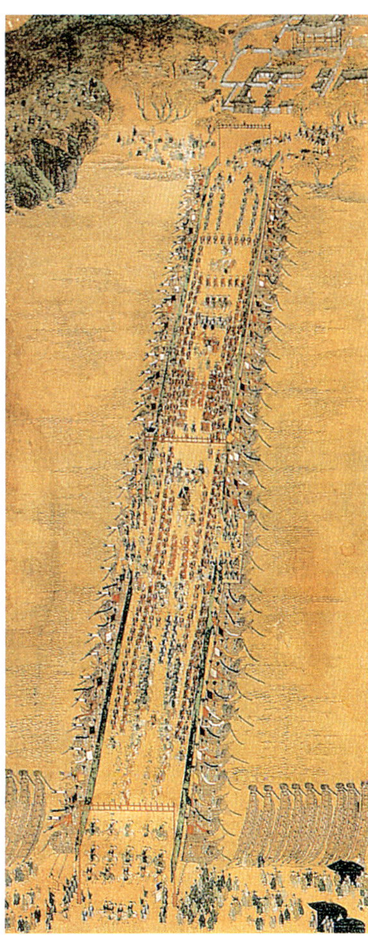

9 ***Crossing the Noryang Boat Bridge*** **from** ***Wonhaeng-eulmyo-uigwedo***

Color on silk. 142×62cm. Hoam Art Museum.

King Jeongjo s entourage returns to the palace on the 16th of the 2nd lunar leap-month of 1795 was painted as observed from Yongsan. At the very top is the Yongyangbongjeo (jumping dragon, flying phoenix) Pavilion in Noryangjin. King Jeongjo s mother, Lady Hong, heads the group; the pavilion is behind them. The bridge is made of thirty-six intertwined boats and has railings and three red spiked-top gates.

(records) on the fortress' construction that document in minute detail the materials used and the names of its masons. *Wonhaeng-eulmyo-jeongri-uigwe,* recording the royal procession to Hyeonryungwon and related events in 1795, also provides good evidence of the times. Kim Hong-do participated in the production of the above *uigwe*.

The 18th century, however, also witnessed many atrocities of *seongrihak*, which occurred because of the extended and prejudiced rule of the party in power coupled with the social changes and instability arising from the transition from an agricultural society to a commercial and industrial society. The two great wars further destabilized the social class system. The middle class and the *seo-eol* (the illegitimate sons of nobles) became restless and demanded more rights. As a countermeasure to the Confucian values that dominated society, the *namin* faction began the *silhak* school of thought. As agriculture-oriented reformers, they awakened the rural areas to the stark realities and criticized the land system and the local administrations. Beginning at the end of the 18th century, students under Lee Ik practiced their Christian beliefs, which threatened the legitimacy of *seongrihak* as the national ideology. King Jeongjo took a moderate and eclectic approach to dealing with these issues.

When Kim Hong-do was born in 1745, some from the ruling faction, *noron*, claimed Joseon needed to learn from the Ching Dynasty, and that the "Attack North" ideology was unrealistic. These proponents of *bukhak* were commerce-oriented individuals who recognized the existing set of values but emphasized nation building through commerce by the introduction of Ching technology. This unsettled the conservative establishment, who cherished the 'cause' of *seongrihak*. *Bukhak* contained numerous elements of bibliographical study of the Chinese classics that equated study with art and had a tremendous influence on contemporary culture. Kim Hong-do's painting behind the Buddha's statue in the main worship hall of Yongjusa Temple is an exemplary piece of work that evolved from the *bukhak* tradition. After Kim Hong-do died, during the early 19th century

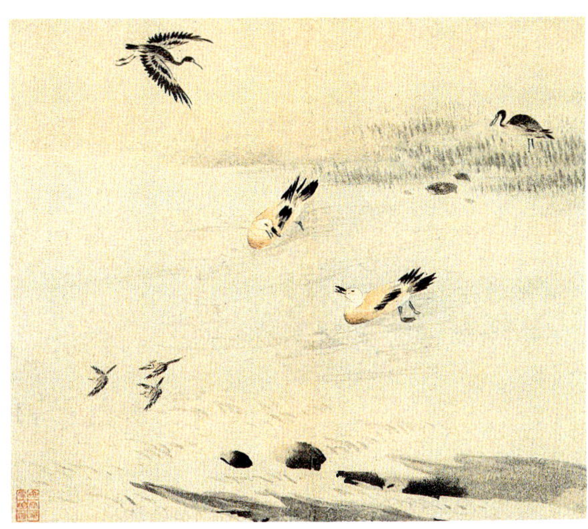

10 *Water Birds in the Stream* from *Danwon-jeolsebo Album*
1796. Ink and color on paper. 26.7×31.6cm. Hoam Art Museum.
Ducks, hooded cranes and other birds are playing by the water. The colors are pleasantly blurred. The painting is clean and looks as if it was washed, and nature seems warm and peaceful. The overhead perspective is something new. The birds are enjoying themselves and unaware that they are being painted. Despite the natural appearance, a close inspection shows that the ducks are enclosed in a tilted square.

bukhak spread among the middle class and became the fashion of the times. Kim Hong-do lived in an age when there were obvious signs of the disintegration of the feudal order as the transition to modern times evolved.

King Jeongjo (reign: 1777–1800), who was born in 1752, selectively embraced the merits of both *silhak* and *bukhak* but was wary of the *namin* Christian movement's and the *noron bukhak* movement's radicalism. The king also faced a political dilemma because he had to resolve these problems by working with the old ruling party, who had been hostile to his father, Crown Prince Sado. King Jeongjo opted for very complex measures, at the core of which were his principles of strengthening the royal authority, using the *Six Classics* of Confucius for reference and abiding by *seongrihak* standards. In 1792, his efforts at harmonization led to formation of the Literary Style Reform Movement, which denounced the newly emerging creative writing style. *Namin* adherents were admitted to public office, as were the illegitimate sons of nobles who belonged to the *bukhak* clique. The latter were appointed to work in Gyujanggak, the Royal Library.

As previously noted, King Jeongjo was especially fond of his court painter Kim Hong-do and mentioned Kim in his anthology, *Hongjaejeonseo*. Probing further into the king's character, policies and skills, we see that King Jeongjo rose to the throne despite the political handicap of being Sado's son, which underlines how capable and cultured the king was. His vast pool of knowledge, covering the *Thirteen Classics* of Confucius, coupled with his perfectionism and ceaseless efforts enabled him to achieve considerable success in national affairs; consequently, King Jeongjo is often likened to the early Joseon king, King Sejong. The concept of the philosopher-king is well-captured in the anthology, which itself serves as a documentary of the flourishing culture.

King Jeongjo implemented most of his policies through Gyujanggak, which he developed to organically link academics and politics and to nurture his supporters. After 1781, the Royal Library kept more faithful to its founding philosophy: 'academic-oriented politics' and 'growth through learning.' 'Academic-oriented politics' focused on civil administration and the civilized state through the publication of numerous books. As a result, during the second half of King Jeongjo's reign, Joseon published the most sophisticated books, and consequently it banned the import of books from China. The books of the time even went as far as rewriting the erroneous history (which were asserted to have been written by barbarians) of the Sung and Ming Dynasties. Socially, knowledge spread because of an increasing literacy rate and the publication of more books, and the illiteracy rate was reduced because of the spread of novels written in Korean. The population was controlled and appeased through an education system that prioritized loyalty, filial piety and fidelity.

The intent of 'growth through learning' was to nurture talented individuals. The king himself screened, lectured and evaluated young civil servants at Gyujanggak. Previously, civil servants taught the king; King Jeongjo reversed the process. Even among the circle of court painters, the king selected ten of the thirty gifted court painters and named them the *jabidaeryeong* Court Painters of Gyujanggak. Each quarter, the king evaluated the artists himself. Such a hands-on system is evidence that King Jeongjo had considerable influence over the court painters' work, and later records reaffirmed this. Lee Won-sun (1772–1823), who was the grandson of Lee Gyu-sang and left a written record of Kim Hong-do, recorded the following about the court painters during King Jeongjo's time.

> However insignificant the talent they possessed, scholars served the king because the king appointed them to the appropriate offices. He established Gyu-

janggak, appointed talented people from good family background as officials and had them recommend scholars who were fit to study the Confucian books, calligraphy and painting, industrial arts, and who were well behaved. The king called for *ad-hoc* state examinations and many scholars passed the exam, which boosted their morale and at the same time shamed those with no particular academic or artistic skills. Praise the king who revived the beautiful practice of recommending talented servants in the Zhou Dynasty.

As confirmed in his works, King Jeongjo was an excellent calligrapher and painter, and was so artistically talented that he carved his own seal. The king's deep insight into the world of art did not stop at the personal level, but he used his insight to exercise considerable influence on the court painters. The following excerpt from *Hongjaejeonseo* is a striking example of how King Jeongjo directly involved himself with the work of the court painters.

> The king wished to test the skills of the court painters. One brandished a brush tipped with watery ink to capture not the form but the spirit of the object. The king said, "The Southern School landscape puts a great deal of emphasis on detail, but this painter painted with no discipline. This is a small matter, but I am uncomfortable with it." He ordered the painter to leave. (Written in 1791)

These facts indicate that King Jeongjo strongly influenced Kim Hong-do's world of art. King Jeongjo was an absolute monarch who enlightened his people to Confucian values. During his reign, there was peace, prosperity and a cultural maturity, none of which would have been possible were it not for the king's incessantly hard work. He made more sorties out of the palace than did any other Joseon king to see for himself the kind of life his people led. He left the palace under the pretext of visiting the gravesites of his ancestors, but his real intention was to be a leader with close ties to his people. He traversed the grounds outside the city walls of Hanyang and often visited

Gyeonggi Province. These processions helped develop and improve the petition system. Near the end of his reign, King Jeongjo's Confucian belief in 'politics for the people' culminated in his plan to reform the slave system, but his sudden death forestalled any action. His absolute monarchy facilitated numerous achievements in military, economic and cultural areas. It is no coincidence that later, in 1894, the farmers of the Donghak Peasants Revolution called for a return to the values of King Jeongjo's regime. Kim Hong-do was the favorite painter of the philosophical and artistic king. The subject matter or the theme of Kim's paintings may seem progressive, but they are relevant to the king's model.

Of course, not all was peace and harmony during King Jeongjo's reign. The rivalry between the king's and the ministers' authority dated back to the time of King Sukjong. That rivalry was somewhat ameliorated through the *tangpyeong* policy,[12] but it did not entirely resolve the problems. Against this setting, King Jeongjo claimed the authority to carry out national affairs as a philosopher-king. As a prerequisite, he cultivated his morals first. He realized the limitations of King Yeongjo's *tangpyeong* policy because King Yeongjo had sought only a superficial balance of power among the four main factions. King Jeongjo prioritized righteousness and integrity, and changed the political landscape to one of true checks and balances between the *sipa*[13] and *byeokpa* factions. The king tried to solidify the throne by moving *byeokpa* members into the *sipa* faction, but that did not reduce the *byeokpa's* power. Consequently, the king had a significant role in maintaining the balance, so it was only natural that after King Jeongjo's death, chaos arose. By King Sunjo's reign, the *byeokpa* held a monopoly, so the efforts of King Jeongjo were for naught, and Joseon politics continued to deteriorate. *Sedo* politics, in which the king entrusts another individual to govern the country, became the norm, and in 1811, Hong Gyeong-rae led an uprising in direct defiance of such politics.

King Jeongjo died on the 28th of the 6th lunar month in 1800 at the age of 49. His death had enormous political repercussions because the *byeokpa*

12 Tangpyeong was a fair appointment policy that originated with King Jeongjo s predecessor, King Yeongjo. It was designed to allow the appointment of public officials from diverse factions so that each faction held the other in check and, at the same time, strengthened the throne.

13 Most sipa members were from the namin faction and sympathetic to Crown Prince Sado.

seized much of the power and purged the opposition. It is uncertain how this changed Kim Hong-do's personal life, but apparently he suffered hardship after King Jeongjo's death.

During King Jeongjo's reign, the *namin* faction was a stabilizing force. Kang Se-hwang, who was Kim's mentor and supporter, and Jeong Beom-jo (1723–1801), who wrote a lengthy poem praising Kim, both belonged to the *namin* faction. Many of Kim's acquaintances were members of the *sipa* faction. After King Jeongjo's death, the *byeokpa* persecuted these individuals. Although the details are lost, the king's death and the ensuing political changes must have been a great shock to Kim Hong-do. Of course, Kim was no political leader, much less a nobleman. He was a mere court painter who served as *hyeongam*, but he was a special court painter who had received great attention from King Jeongjo.

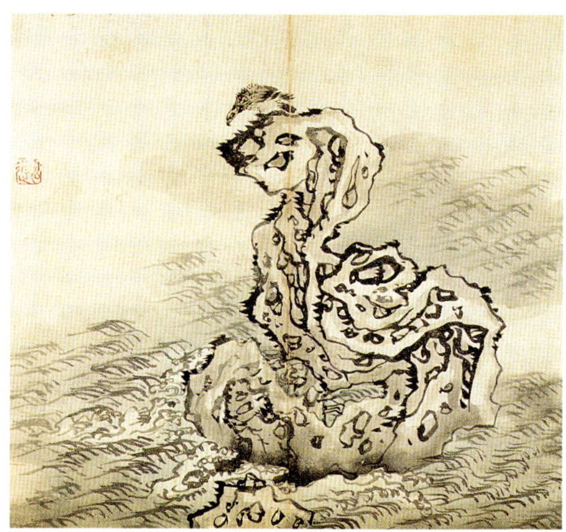

11 *A Brave Eagle on a Rock in the Sea* from *Eulmyonyeon Album*
1795. Ink and color on paper. 23.2×27.7cm. Private collection.
A strangely shaped rock emerges from nowhere in the vast sea, with a brave eagle perched on top. The composition is centered on the vertical axis in the middle to match the animating motif. The contours of the rock have been eroded by the wind and sea, as expressed by the different thicknesses of the lines. The dynamic-looking rock symbolizes the eagle s bravery.

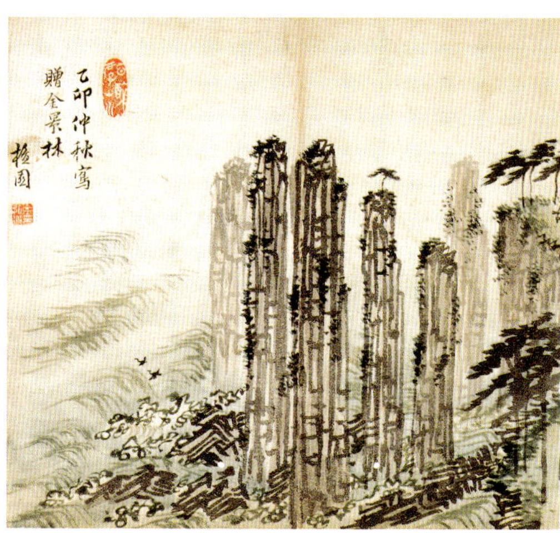

12 *Chongseokjeong* from *Eulmyonyeon Album*
1795. Ink and color on paper. 23.2×27.7cm. Private collection.
The viewer can feel the sense of infinite space and unique perspective from the small canvas on which this scene was painted. The difference in size between the pine trees in the front and back shows the distance. Two small waterfowls fly over the waves breaking against the cliff, expressing vast space and making the painting lively. This painting is poem-like.

Kim Hong-do was a low ranking official from the middle class. The class system was very rigid in the 17th century, and from then on, the middle class struggled to climb the social ladder. In the 1770s, a few illegitimate sons of nobles were allowed to hold public offices, and in 1779, illegitimately born *bukhak* scholars were appointed to work at Gyujanggak. The middle class generally lived in the northern and southern parts of Hanyang. The Songseokwon Literary Club of Mount Inwang, in the north, was composed of low ranking officials and was known as the *Okgye*, or *Seodae*. Affluent engineers gathered near the Gwanggyo Bridge in the south. The Songseokwon Literary Club, founded in the 6th lunar month of 1786 and which paved the way for commoners' literary clubs, produced the *Collection of Okgye Gathering* in 1791. *Pungyosokseon* (the Anthology of Native Songs) was first published in 1797 and updated until the 1820s. During this time, commoners began to publish individual collections of poems.

There were essentially three activities for the middle class: illegitimate sons were engaged in political movements that demanded their holding public offices; low ranking officials were involved in the commoners' literary movement, which was concerned with cultural issues; and engineers were involved in commerce. These activities led to an elevation of the social status of the middle class. Because he was a court painter, Kim Hong-do certainly belonged to the middle class, but he served as *hyeongam* by special request of the king. It is difficult to know precisely Kim's perceptions of class. At the time, the commoner poets shared a very strong bond and called each other by special names, but there is no information that Kim participated in that.

The commoners' literary movement, which started among the middle class and included minor officials in Hanyang, was led primarily by the officials working at Gyujanggak as a means of climbing the social ladder through intellectual activities. The officials had felt the need for such a movement, and it became possible because King Jeongjo permitted and encouraged it. It is worth noting that the middle class provided the most positive and proactive feedback on Kim Hong-do's art. It remains a future task to discover how middle class activities and thinking affected Kim.

As seen above, Kim Hong-do was most active from the end of the 18th century to the early 19th century when peace and traditional values still predominated. There were, however, numerous internal contradictions at the time. It was indeed a dynamic society and various factions provided their own solutions to issues. The society carefully weighed the consequences of the newly imported developments such as new culture and Christianity from the Ching Dynasty, but the problem of resolving conflicts that arose from the class system remained. No comprehensive study exists to precisely define the unique cultural climate of this era and the aesthetic taste that derived from it. We can only speculate what the overall atmosphere of the art circle was like by an extrapolation of the few remaining partial texts. We must await the progress of multi-disciplinary studies on the social and artistic climate of the time to understand more fully Kim Hong-do's life and his world of art.

In general, Kim Hong-do's era was a time when the nation was ruled wisely despite some hardships and conflicts. The cultural activities that centered on King Jeongjo's Gyujanggak represent the height of the latter part of the Joseon Dynasty. The magnitude of Kim Hong-do's art is attributable to his personal genius, to the favorable environment in which he worked and the support of King Jeongjo. Compared to the present era, Kim Hong-do's era placed a higher value on humanitarian issues, and the leaving as legacy of an honorable and good name was more important than accumulating additional wealth. In addition, the era was very proud of its traditional Joseon culture, while in contemporary times we have failed to establish our identity amidst a flood of Western culture. The frame of mind and the social conditions of Kim's era made the full blossoming of his art possible .

Chapter 2: Who Was Kim Hong-do and What Was His Art Like?

1. Kim Hong-do's Family Tree

The Kim Hong-do family tree that was based on a genealogy of the Gimhae Kim family is too careless and inaccurate to rely on. A more detailed version is found in the *Record of Family Name Sources*.

Before examining the records, we need to first identify Kim's family origins. According to the *Geunyeokseohwajing*,[14] Kim's family originated in Gimhae, yet his name was not cited among the existing registers of the Gimhae Kim clan. Some recent analysis suggests that his family origin was incorrectly reported. However, there are at least three reasons to support Kim's Gimhae origins. First, the engraving on the large seal that Kim Hong-do owned read, "Family name: Kim. Given name: Hong-do. Courtesy name: Saneung. Pen name: Dangu. From Old Gaya Province." Old Gaya Province probably indicates Gimhae. Second, O Se-chang, a calligrapher and independence leader against the Japanese colonial rule in the early 20th century wrote, "I am a third generation descendant of Danwon on my mother's side. My wife's uncle is a descendant of Yeongwon." Although O was mistaken in estimating the year of Kim Hong-do's birth, he would not have confused his mother's family origins. Third, the name 'Hong-do' may not be his given name but rather a professional name; therefore, it does not appear in the genealogy.

According to the genealogy, Kim Hong-do's great-great-great grandfa-

14 Geunyeokseohwajing is a record of Korean calligraphers and painters that stretches from ancient to modern times and first published in 1928.

ther was Kim Deuk-nam, who was one of the Royal Guards. His great-great grandfather was Kim Jung-hyeon, who served the king *pro bono* as *byeolje*. His great grandfather was Kim Jin-chang, a military officer. His grandfather's name was Kim Su-seong and his father's name was Kim Seok-mu, but there is no record of their official titles. The misconception that Kim Hong-do's maternal grandfather is Jang Pil-ju, from the Jang family of In-dong, who was famous for producing a number of court painters, occurs from a misreading of Mun Pil-ju. His great grandfather Jin-chang was supposedly a hero of the 1592 Japanese invasion, but this also proves in error if the chronology is checked. Kim probably did have an ancestor who fought against the Japanese at the end of the 16th century as O Se-chang notes, but it is unlikely to be Jin-chang.

Kim Hong-do's great-great-great grandfather, Deuk-nam, served as a Royal Guard, but we do not know whether his rank was *jong 6 pum* (a grade of hierarchy) or *jong 9 pum*. At any rate, the Royal Guards were selected from the middle class and nobles' illegitimate sons, so it is certain that the family was not of noble blood. Kim Hong-do was a tall man, which may explain why a number of his ancestors were in the military. The description of his career mentions that apparently he was appointed *hyeongam* because of his ancestral heritage. However, this is not entirely true. *Yangban* were sometimes appointed public officials without taking the government exam due to their ancestors' achievements, but since Kim was a *jungin* this did not apply. It means that King Jeongjo's affection for him allowed him to forego the official examination to become *hyeongam*. The names of Kim's second cousins are Gwang-tae and Hang-tae. Hong-do does not share the generational 'tae' suffix, so it is possible that 'Hong-do' was an official title or professional name.

To further probe the genealogy of the Kim family, let us examine the marriage of his ancestors. Kim Hong-do's great grandmother was Lee of Wansan. Her father went by the name of Lee Jin-hyeong, whose family descended from the Prince Wanchang sect. From the time of Lee Jeong, the family produced many interpreters including Lee Chun-on and Lee Man-jin. The three Lee brothers (Chung-il, Seong-il and Sin-il) and the other two Lee brothers (Su-min and Gu-min) were accountants. Lee Jin-hyeong took the interpretation examination and worked as *bongsa* at an administration office that orchestrated the friendly relationships between relatives of the royal family.

Kim Hong-do's grandfathers Su-seong and Su-gyeon took wives from one of the Park families of Milyang, which descended from the sect of His Highness Gyujeong. In this sect's genealogical table, however, there is no mention of Park Dong-sik and his descendants. Park Dong-sik began work as an interpreter, but later became a *jubu* at a tax office; the Park family, however, continued to produce interpreters. Kim Hong-do's grandfathers Su-seong and Su-gyeon married daughters of the cousins Park Jam and Park Jing. Both Parks served as *jeolchung* and *sayong*.

Kim Hong-do's father Seok-mu was married to Mun of Jangdam. The Mun family descended from the sect of His Highness Chung-seon of the Mun of Nampyeong clan, but Mujo and his descendants do not appear in the genealogical table. That is probably why the Muns adopted a new family origin, Jangdam, and dropped the old Nampyeong. Few of Kim's maternal ancestors were in public service. In short, Kim's ancestors married middle class families who produced interpreters, accountants and low ranking officials. What is noteworthy is that there are no court painters among Kim's close relatives. Let us examine the Lee of Wansan family tree to see whom their daughters married.

Kim Hong-do's great grandfather was Kim Jin-chang, whose daughter married Lee In-bang. He was a military man and served as *chalbang*. Kim Hong-do's family tree tells us that Kim's great-uncle Su-gyeon had a son-in-law, Lee Yu-bang (Lee of Wansan), who was the younger brother of Lee In-bang. This would mean that Kim Hong-do's aunt and great-aunt both married the Lee brothers; however, that must be a mistake. The family tree of Kim Hong-do indicates that Lee Yu-bang's maternal grandfather went by the name of Bang Pil-je. The Lee of Wansan family tree, however, says that Lee Yu-bang's wife was the daughter of Bang Pil-je. This is another contradiction. If we compare that with the Bang of Onyang family tree, we find that Bang Pil-je's daughter married Lee Gun-seok, who was Lee Yu-bang's father. Thus, the record of Lee of Wansan was in error and the record of Kim of Gimhae was correct. At any rate, Lee Yu-bang's daughter married Han Eok-rin, who was the link that brought the families of Kim Hong-do and Lee In-mun together. Han Eok-rin appears on the family tree of Han of Cheongju.

The Han family also produced numerous interpreters and accountants. An important detail is that Han Eok-rin's grandmother was Lee Yu-yeon of Haeju's daughter and Lee Seok-beon's younger sister. Seok-beon was Lee In-mun's grandfather. Han Hu-gi was Han Eok-rin's grandfather, and therefore Lee In-mun's great-uncle. Kim Hong-do's great-uncle had a granddaughter who married Han Eok-rin, whom we have seen is Lee In-mun's great-uncle's grandson. Consequently, Kim Hong-do and Lee In-mun were distant relatives; nevertheless, they were close. Among the Han of Cheongju family, Han Seon-guk, Han Si-gak, and his son-in-law, Lee Myeong-uk, were famous court painters.

An examination of Kim Hong-do's genealogy produces nothing that would indicate that Kim would become a court painter. The same is true for Lee In-mun. Compared to other court painters who basked in the reflected glory of their families, Kim and Lee made it in the world of art solely on their skills and talents. Kang Se-hwang said, "Kim Hong-do was known for his superior artistic ability and was far ahead of the often mentioned Jin, Park, Byeon and Jang of Dohwawon."[15] The author believes that Kang was trying to bring to light Kim's exceptional skills, which shone far more brightly than the established court painters' traditional way of painting.

15 The Office of Painting; also known as Dohwaseo.

2. Analysis of His Name, Courtesy Name, Pen Name and Studio Name

Kim's name is included in this discussion because of the possibility that 'Kim Hong-do' may not have been his real name but rather an official title or professional name, because, according to the *Record of Family Name Sources*, all his second cousins' names have the 'tae' suffix. If indeed Hong-do is not his real name, then it must have a special meaning. A father's friend or a teacher often gives a courtesy name at the coming-of-age ceremony, and the name usually reflects the person's character and future career. Pen names and studio names are also given in consideration of the person's career, place of residence or the current circumstances. Analyzing a person's name, courtesy name and pen name helps to understand the individual's character.

Kim Hong-do used two courtesy names—Hamjang and Saneung. He had many pen names: Seoho, Chwihwasa, Cheopchwiong, Danwon, Danno, Danong, Dangu, Nonghan, Nongsaong and Gomyeongeosa. Possible studio names are Daeuam and Osudang, and there is a letter signed 'Sorimkimwoo.'

When taken together, the Chinese characters of 'hong' (弘) and 'do' (道) literally mean 'expand the way.' In Book 15, *Wei Ling Kung*, of *The Analects*, Confucius said, "A man can enlarge the principles *which he follows*; those principles do not enlarge the man."[16] In other words, principles make a man stand, and the man embodies the principles; therefore, the two are inseparable. However, principles cannot be bought, and they only exist in the man who abides by them. Therefore, only the man can expand the principles; the principles cannot expand the man. Chapter 49 of Sima Qian's *Records of the Grand Historian* says, "Men can expand the way, but what of God's will?" Ban Gu's *Book of Han* also says, "It is only the sage who can return to his heart and expand the way from there." Therefore, the name 'Hong-do' or the act of 'expanding the way' (or 'enlarging the principles,' as Confucius puts it) indicates the attainment of a certain level

16 Confucian Analects, The Great Learning and The Doctrine of the Mean, trans. by James Legge (New York: Dover Publications, 1971) 302.

through independent and proactive effort.

A Korean pen name is often closely related to the person's name. In that sense, Kim Hong-do's pen name 'Hamjang' is very significant. The Chinese characters 'hamjang' (含章) mean 'hold beauty inside one's heart' or 'hide virtue within.' Hamjang appears in the *khwăn* hexagram in *The Book of Changes*. Paragraph 3 says, "The third line, divided, (shows its subject) keeping his excellence under restraint, but firmly maintaining it (*hamjang-gajeong*; 含章可貞). If he should have occasion to engage in the king's service, though he will not claim the success (for himself), he will bring affairs to a good issue."[17]

The commentary on the third paragraph explains that "keeping his excellence under restraint, but firmly maintaining it" indicates that sometimes the excellence is portrayed outwardly, and an "occasion to engage in the king's service" may arise because of the person's vast knowledge. In conclusion, the commentary implies that every person has the potential to serve in public office. The type of public office is well explained in an appendix to *The Book of Changes*. The phrase is structured *hamjanggajeong* because, even though the third line is on top of the second plate, no one doubts that it is Yang. *Jang* (章) is beauty (美). It is already on top of Yin, so that the person does not elevate himself and knows enough to take a step back, does not rush into things, keeps excellent and beautiful Tao (道) within, waits for orders, and obtains what is right; thus, the phrase, "keeping his excellence under restraint, but firmly maintaining it (*hamjanggajeong*)."

The above explanation is interesting because it is relevant to Kim Hong-do as a *jungin*, or a member of the middle class. *The Book of Changes* Section II, which is the appendix to the *khwăn* hexagram, reads,

> Although (the subject of) this divided line has excellent qualities, he (does not display them, but) keeps them under restraint. 'If he engages them in the service of the king, and is successful, he will not claim that success for himself'—this is the way of the earth, of a wife, of a minister. The way of the

17 The I Ching; The Book of Changes, trans. by James Legge (New York: Dover Publications, 1963) 60.

earth is 'not to claim the merit of achievement,' but on behalf (of heaven) to bring things to their proper issue.[18]

Hamjang, therefore, was a pen name given to Kim Hong-do with the expectation that he would use his skills and virtues to wholeheartedly serve the king and do so with humility. In the *khwˇan* hexagram, it is written, "The fifth *line*, divided, (shows) the yellow lower garment. There will be great good fortune,"[19] because there are beautiful patterns (*munchae*, 文采). The character *jang* together with the character *mun* (文) forms the word *munjang*, which means 'writing.' It is uncertain how seriously Kim Hong-do thought about his pen name, but it closely matches his life as we know it. Like a true artist whose pen name included the character *jang*, which was later used to create the word 'writing,' Kim was an excellent writer.

Another of Kim's pen names, 'Saneung' (士能) was quite popular at the time and means 'only the refined scholar can do it.' *The King Hui of Liang* section in *Mencius* reads, "They are only men of education, who, without a certain livelihood, are able to maintain a fixed heart,"[20] which contains the word *saneung*. The meaning becomes clearer further in the text.

> As to the people, if they have not a certain livelihood, it follows that they will not have a fixed heart. And if they have not a fixed heart, there is nothing which they will not do, in the way of self-abandonment, of moral deflection, of depravity, and of wild license. When they thus have been involved in crime, to follow them up and punish them; this is to entrap the people. How can such a thing as entrapping the people be done under the rule of a benevolent man?[21]

In other words, *saneung* means a respectful person who is unmoved by materialistic concerns and is different from the average person. Anecdotes about Kim Hong-do and the class and leisurely subjects of his paintings prove that his pen name was quite appropriate.

The name Hong-do, and the pen names 'Hamjang' and 'Saneung,' all add

18 Legge, The Book of Changes, 420.
19 Legge, The Book of Changes, 60.
20 The Works of Mencius, trans. by James Legge (New York: Dover Publications, 1970) 147.
21 Legge, Mencius, 147-148.

up to the definition of someone who is able to improve his skills and serve his country, and at the same time, know his place and act with humility. In this context, it is worth noting that one of Kim's seals read, "Of essential use." The pen names Hamjang and Saneung were mainly applied to works Kim produced before he turned forty. Pen names were almost the same as a name and were used as an expression of modesty before the person had made his reputation, but at the same time, they were also an expression of ambition.

'Seoho,' Kim Hong-do's pen name during his earlier years, may be interpreted in many ways. China has numerous lakes named Seoho, the best known of which, West Lake, is to the west of Hangzhou in Zhejiang Province. During the Sung Dynasty, Su Shi spent his leisure time there. Nearby in seclusion lived a famous poet, Lin Bu; Su referred to him as the "retired gentleman of Seoho." Lin was a favorite subject of many artists, and he appears in some of Kim Hong-do's paintings. Kim also inscribed Lin's poetry on his paintings, so Kim's pen name possibly relates to Seoho of China or to Lin Bu.

More likely, however, Kim's pen name refers to the Seoho of the Han River in Korea. *Ho* usually means lake, but it was sometimes used to describe flowing water. The riverside near the present Yanghwa Bridge was called Yangho; Dumopo (a riverside area near the present-day Oksu-dong in Seongdong-gu) was called Duho; and the riverside area near the present-day Dongho Bridge was named Dongho. Seoho referred to the area that encompasses the present-day Yongsan, Mapo, Bamseom, Seonyubong, Noryangjin and Mount Ujam; the scenery at the time was thought to have been extremely beautiful. Joseon anthologies often sing of Seoho, and there are two poems about the area in Book 1 of the *Bomanjae Anthology* by Seo Myeong-eung (1716–1787). One poem describes ten beautiful scenes in the area: the morning tide in Baekseok, the evening atmosphere on Mount Cheonggye, plowing the fields after the rain in Bamseom, a sailboat docked like a cloud at Mapo, the evening haze and weeping willows in Saeseom, the fine, clean sand under the Banghak Bridge, the moon reflected on the water at Seonyubong, the Han River lapping the rocks in front of Bamseom, fishing at Noryangjin, and the collecting of firewood on Mount Wau (Mount Ujam). Book 2 of the *Bomanjae Anthology* describes eight scenes around the Yongsan area of present-day Seoul. Kim Hong-do probably adopted the pen name Seoho to connect with both the neighborhood he resided in and the famous Seoho of China. Seo Yu-bon, grandson of Seo Myeong-eung and Kim's contemporary, published the *Jwasosan Anthology*, and it includes a poem whose rhyme follows *The Poem about the 10 Beautiful Scenes of Seoho*.

Kang Se-hwang notes in his *Danwongi* that Kim Hong-do's most famous pen name, Danwon, derived from Li Liufang's pen name. Li (1575–1629) was a well-known Ming-dynasty *literati* painter. Danno or Danong are variations of Danwon that Kim used when he grew older. Kang stated that Kim used Li's pen name as a token of admiration. Kang then refers to the historical event in which Su Shi evaluated Bai Juyi and Han Yu, and then concludes by analogy that Kim Hong-do was superior to Li Liufang.

It is unclear how Kim Hong-do came to hear of Li and what it was that he admired. Li Yu wrote the prologue to *Jieziyuan Huazhuan* (*Mustard Seed Garden Painting Manual*), in which he claimed that Li Liufang drew the rough sketches in the manual. Other than that, the author has discovered little information. Furthermore, it could not be ascertained if Li's paintings were ever brought directly to Joseon, or whether there were contemporary records about him. Possibly, Kim Hong-do was in awe of *Jieziyuan Huazhuan* because it was the authoritative work of the Southern landscape school, and he admired Li Liufang because Li drew the sketches in the book. However, a recent study has revealed that Li Liufang did not draw the sketches in the manual and that Li Yu had lied in his prologue. At any rate, Hong Won-seop's poem contains a line that reads, "This is what I heard about: That Danwon learned the Chinese painting of the Southern School," which indicates that Kim's name was renowned in that particular genre.

Kim also went by the pen name Chwihwasa. The suffix 'sa' was variously written: 史 (history), 士 (person who is devoted to the work), and 師 (skilled person). Regardless of the spelling, the pen name can be translated as 'drunken painter.' This is similar to yet another of his pen names, Cheopchwiong (輒醉翁), which means 'old man who gets drunk easily.' Ouyang Xiu, a writer of the North Sung Dynasty, wrote in *Zuiweng* (醉翁) *ting ji* (*The Pavilion of the Old Drunkard*) "only a small amount of wine is enough to get me drunk." Ouyang Xiu said that the Zuiweng pavilion was named for his pen name, so Kim Hong-do, who was fond of reading his poetry, must have been aware of it.

The pen name Cheopchwiong reminds the author of the court painter Chwiong Kim Myeong-guk who, in the mid-Joseon Dynasty, painted excellent Taoist hermits and landscapes. Kim Myeong-guk is considered the most good-natured man in the history of Joseon painting. A Joseon poet, Jeong Rae-gyo, described his character as follows:

> He did not follow the conventions of painting, but followed his heart. He was exceptional in painting men, water and stones, and especially in capturing their style, mystical atmosphere, spirit and personality. He was generous, witty and a heavy drinker. Most of his excellent works were painted when he was drunk.

There is a striking resemblance between the two Kims. In their paintings of Taoist hermits, both painters drew orchid leaves with a light and cheerful touch. We can gather that Kim Hong-do was familiar with Kim Myeong-guk's work and may have been conscious of his influence.

Another of Kim Hong-do's pen names was Gomyeongeosa. Kim wrote this on a tablet in Chehwajeong in Andong after he finished his term as *chalbang* in Angi in the 5th lunar month in 1786. *Gomyeon* means sleeping comfortably on a high pillow, and *geosa* indicates a civilized person who does not seek public office and instead leads a leisurely life. Of course, this is just a figure of speech.

In his later years, Kim Hong-do used the pen name Dangu, which was written either as 丹丘 or 丹邱. The original meaning is "a place which is bright, day and night, because of the Taoist Immortals' presence." Chapter 5, *Yuan You* (Travel Afar) of *Chu ci* (The Songs of the South) reads, "Lead the Taoist Immortal to Danqiu[22] and have him stay at an immortal village." The commentary explains, "Danqiu is always bright whether it is night or day." A Taoist hermit from the Sui Dynasty named Danqiuzi lived near the end of the Kaihuang reign under Emperor Wendi; his other names were Yuan Danqiu and Danqiushen. The poet Li Bai wrote in the poem *Bringing in the Wine*, "...To the old master, Tsen, and the young scholar, Danqiu; bring in the wine, let your cups never rest!"[23] Danqiu is also the pen name of Yan Yu, a famous critic in the Sung Dynasty, known for his *Ts'anglang's Remarks on Poetry*. Ke Jiusi, *literati* painter of the Yuan Dynasty, had the sobriquet Danqiushen.

Anthologies from the latter Joseon Dynasty indicate that Dangu was a common pen name. People with this name probably had a connection with Danyang in Chungcheong Province since the county seat was named Dangubaek. The place was so beautiful that it was named the Mount Geumgang of the south. Perhaps people used the pen name Dangu because it implied a beautiful place with style. Kim Hong-do was *hyeongam* at Yeonpung, which was not far from Danyang. According to Han Jin-ho's *Dodam Travel Log*, Kim Hong-do received a special order to paint the beautiful scenery of Danyang, Cheongpung, Yeongwol and Jecheon. From this we can conjecture why Kim painted many realistic landscapes of the Danyang area in his later years (for example, in the *Danwon-jeolsebo Album*), how much his work as *hyeongam* involved painting, and the origin of his pen name Dangu.

Kim assumed other pen names, such as Nonghan and Nongsaong, which both appear in *Danwon's Posthumous Works* and mean 'farmer' or 'old farmer.' We can catch glimpses of his peaceful days in retirement in the beginning of King Sunjo's reign. The studio name Daeuam was recently dis-

22 Dangu is pronounced Danqiu in Chinese.

23 Poetry and Prose of the Tang and Sung, trans. by Xianyi Yang and Gladys Yang (Beijing: Panda Books, 1984)

covered, and the record *Daeuamgi*, which explained the meaning, was written by the best writer of the time, Lee Yong-hyu (1708–1782).

A Higher Being gave birth to everything on earth, and the ways of the Divine were captured in shapes and figures. The holiest and most wondrous ways were put into words and taught amongst the people, which is the canon. Since the words had to be written down, the ancient Emperor Huang Di (2697–2597 BC) ordered his historian Can Ji to establish a writing system for China. He invented pictographs, but there was only so much that could be expressed. The Emperor ordered the historian to paint pictures as well, and only when the writing was coupled with pictures was the meaning complete. As time passed, the writing system became more stable, but the pictures sometimes stood out and sometimes did not. After the Airs of Bin (豳風), Book of Songs (Shijing) and Chapter 7 of The Lost Book of Zhou (Yizhou shu), there were fewer traces of pictures.

Some time later, a man of exceptional skills painted flowers, bamboo, birds and animals. His pictures were in harmony with nature and pleasing to the eyes and hearts of many. This was no small feat. Saneung Kim Hong-do acquired wisdom without a teacher and willed his brush to paint what was on his mind like no other man. His brush strokes were steady, accurate and never missed even by a hair's width. The color combinations of blue, gold, red and white were so splendid, precise, exquisite and marvelous that it was understandable that he said, "Woe to those who went before me, for they never saw me." Despite his pride, he was not careless with the ink, which shows that he was a man of character and a poet with style. He did not let his skills suffer the fate of being merely toyed with or being reduced to gossip.

As writing is likened to a person's name, painting can be likened to his face. If you knew a person only by name even if you were sitting across from him, you would not recognize him. Painting and writing share the same origin, and both strive to be truthful. The world, however, elevates writing above painting, and some think that anyone can paint. Kim Hong-do wrote the characters 'Daeu' (對右), framed it, and hung it on the wall in his house. It means 'face to face with respect.' The Chinese characters come from the phrase "look down on painting and respect writing (左圖右書)." Painting and writing have been separated for a long time, but now they are reunited. It is time that they were in accord and respected each other.

Since Lee Yong-hyu died in 1782, presumably this piece was written before Kim Hong-do was 38, so even when he was young, Kim was a man of character and a stylish poet who took pride in his art and did not want it treated merely as a commodity. His character is clearly stated in his pen name Daeu. The academic circle generally believes that Kim became a refined scholar after he turned 50, but the above writing tells us that the change occurred much earlier.

The text also shows that Kim's earlier works were precise, elaborate and splendid paintings of people, flowers and birds. Throughout the text, Lee Yong-hyu mentioned the historical, innate nature of the "complementary" relationship between writing and painting and stressed that Kim was good at both. A detailed evaluation of Kim's calligraphic skills by his contemporaries will be covered in the conclusion of this book. Let me just mention here that such skills were achieved very early in his career.

Finally, we cannot fail to notice that *Daeuamgi* was written by the best writer of the time, Lee Yong-hyu. It is significant that we were able to ascertain the relationship between the elite Hyehwan Lee Yong-hyu and the painter Kim Hong-do, and this will be dealt with in another section. Lee wrote *Daeuamgi* for Kim and the following maxim, Daeuam-myeong, for Kim's studio, Daeuam.

During Fuxi's reign, a horse with the head of a dragon appeared from the river, and the shape of the entangled mane was later called Hetu (河圖). During Emperor Yu's reign, a divine turtle appeared near a waterfall, and the shapes on its back are called Luoshu(洛書). These two writing systems combined to manifest the wonders of the world and open a new page of human civilization. But some are outside the boundary of odd and even numbers in the *Book of*

Changes, and some are not expressed by xiangsu (images and numbers, 象數). If you are in doubt, go ask the old man of no bounds.

Lee Yong-hyu cites Hetu and Luoshu, which are core elements of the *Book of Changes*, which in turn is the foundation of Asian philosophy. As in *Daeuamgi*, Lee emphasizes that painting and writing share the same historical origin. Considering that the word for book (doseo, 圖書), came from the characters, Hetu and Luoshu, the above excerpt has the following implications. Painting and writing are not merely basic skills but originate from Hetu and Luoshu, on which Asian humanities are based, and at the same time are important subjects that deal with very critical aspects of traditional culture. To be more specific, painting creates a concrete form of innate natural beauty (related to Hetu) and acquired lifestyles (related to Luoshu) within the framework of the humanities. However, the painting should never be entrapped within the metaphysical, but rather allowed to express objects freely with unlimited flexibility and fresh liveliness, just as the truth is both absolute and timeless.

Another name for his studio is Osudang, which appears in *Danwon's Posthumous Works*. It means 'house for a nap,' and Kim Hong-do probably used it in his later years, but there are no specific details. Page 33 of the album mentions another nickname, Sorimkimwoo, but there is no confirmation of what Sorim is.

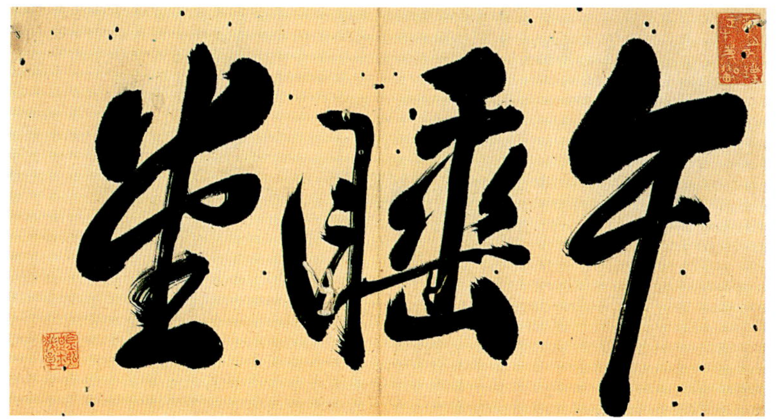

13 *Osudang*
Ink on paper. 24.4×44.4cm. National Museum of Korea.
One of Kim Hong-do s rare, large-character calligraphies that shows his bold strokes. The seal on the bottom reads, By Kim Hong-do, Saneung.

3. Kim Hong-do, a Man and His Art

All forms of art, but especially painting, are reflections of the painter. Understanding an artist's life, therefore, is a certain way of accessing his art. This section will discover Kim Hong-do's appearance, character and religion by introducing comments about his art that are found in literature, and a few incidents in his life that illustrate the characteristics of his works. There will also be some brief comments about his mentor, Kang Se-hwang.

First, we shall examine *Eulogy to Daeuam Kim Hong-do*, which Lee Yong-hyu wrote while looking at the portrait of young Kim Hong-do, which is no longer extant.

> If you have someone else paint a portrait, it is objective; but if you paint yourself, it is subjective. For this reason, Kim Hong-do had Sin paint his portrait. This is similar to the conventional practice of writers having another write the preface to their book and of famous people not writing their own biography. Just as the world regards Kim as precious for his art, I, too, cherish him for his art. Now that I have laid eyes on his portrait, there is the sheen of jade and the scent of orchid. He is better looking than rumors have it, and he has the looks of a true man of virtue. Kim Yun-seo and Jeong Sa-hyeon told me, "If you chance to see Kim Hong-do in person, feel his presence and listen to his voice, you will realize the portrait is only telling seventy percent of the truth."

Lee Yong-hyu compared Kim to writers and famous people and described him as "a true man of virtue" whose appearance was more attractive than rumored. When the eulogy was written Lee probably had not met Kim. The interpreters Kim Yun-seo and Jeong Sa-hyeon were likely to have introduced the two. As we will see later, Jeong Sa-hyeon was fond of paintings and owned Bokheon Kim Eung-hwan's 'Landscape.' According to the records, Kim Hong-do saw this painting in 1788, and this shows that Jeong Sa-hyeon and Kim Hong-do maintained their acquaintances. This is the first revelation of Kim Yun-seo and Kim Hong-do's relationship, and the

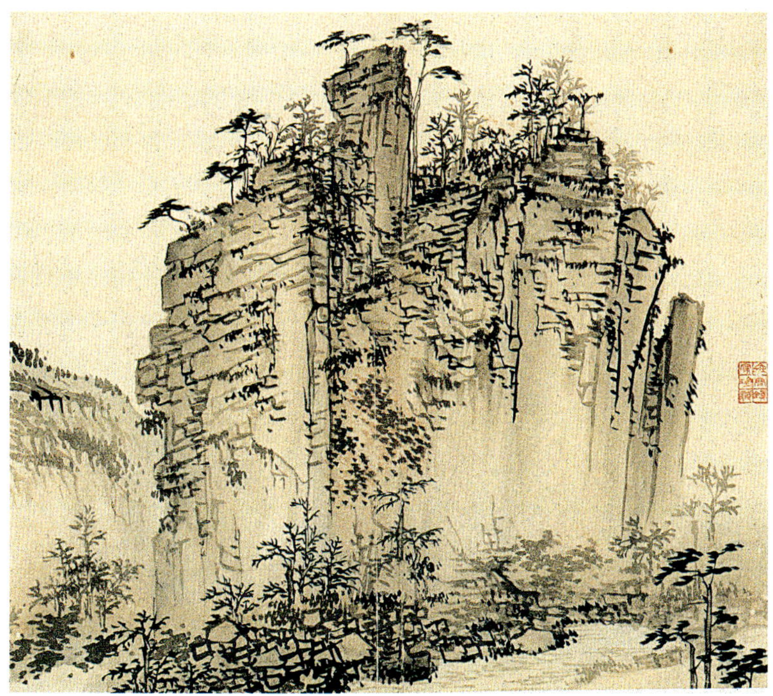

14 *Sainam Rock* from *Danwon-jeolsebo Album*
1796. Ink and color on paper. 26.7×31.6cm. Hoam Art Museum.
Sainam Rock, the cliffs that shoot up from the stream, cover the whole canvas, but the scene in the far distance is laid out on the left side to give the painting more depth. The lines describing the texture of the rocks are of different thickness and ink shade, and the gradation is indicated. The elegant distribution of the trees on top of the rocks pleases the eye. The bottom portion is blurry because the artist was looking up from very close to the rocks.

author looks forward to more supporting documentation in the future. At any rate, Kim Yun-seo and Jeong Sa-hyeon both knew Danwon very well, and they both spoke highly of him.

The famous Jo Hui-ryong (1789–1866) commented that Kim Hong-do's personality was equal to his great works.

> In his words of praise, Jo Hui-ryong said that Ni Zan's pictures washed away the traces left by those who went before him. His pictures depicted clear and beautiful scenes. People living in the southern part of the Yangtze River Delta judged others by whether they possessed Ni Zan's pictures or not. The Yuan Dynasty boasted of many great artists, but of those Ni Zan was the most prominent because of his virtuous character. Why do you think Danwon stood out among Geungjae, Hosaenggwan and Gosongyusugwan? [Geungjae is the pen name of Kim Deuk-sin, Hosaenggwan of Choi Buk and Gosongyusugwan of

15 *Dodam Sambong* from *Danwon-jeolsebo Album*
1796. Ink and color on paper. 26.7×31.6cm. Hoam Art Museum.
Three stone islands are neatly lined up like a bowstring in the middle of a meandering river. The islands are placed symmetrically, but the shores are painted diagonally to make the composition dynamic. The distant mountains take on simple contours and a refreshing gradation. Floating in the back, the mountains create additional liveliness in the painting. The area between the ferryman rowing the boat and the travelers waiting on the shore is filled with the expectations of both parties.

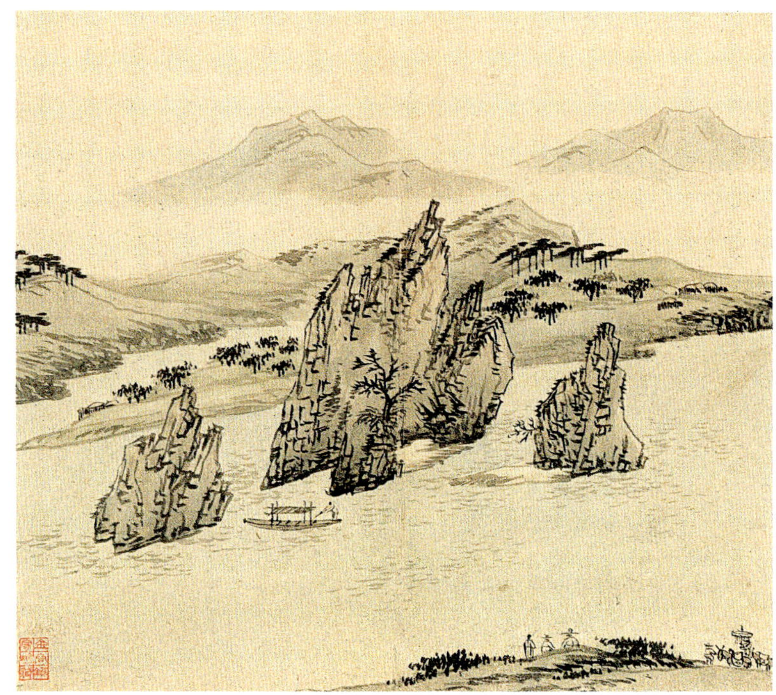

> Lee In-mun. They all made their names known alongside Danwon.] The more refined the person, the more refined the brush.

Kim Hong-do's mentor, Kang Se-hwang, who had known Kim since he was young, said the following:

> Kim Hong-do, who holds the title of *chalbang*, has a pen name, Saneung. He used to come by my house when he was young. His eyes shone brightly. He was good-looking. He had the air of a Taoist hermit about him, as if he did not belong in this world.

Hong Sin-yu (1722–ca. 1785), who also knew young Kim Hong-do, wrote in the epilogue to his *Poem on Mount Geumgang*, "He was very tall and handsome. He did not look like a mortal; that is also true of his paintings. I was as fond of him and his paintings as he was of my poems and writing." This reinforces the idea that Kim was very tall and good looking, as do words of praise written in Hosan Jo Hui-ryong's records. "He is a man of high stature and a big heart. Little things do not tie him down. People referred to him as a Taoist hermit." His appearance was so striking that people thought of a Taoist hermit when they saw Kim Hong-do. Of course, in late Joseon, 'Taoist hermit' was a cliché to describe people who enjoyed writing and living a life of integrity; however, it is noteworthy that people used the expression to describe Kim. In another piece Kang Se-hwang wrote,

> When one looks at Saneung, one knows that he has a good face and a good heart. Everyone understands that he is a man of virtue, is above this secular world and is unlike the common folk. He loved refined music such as the *geomungo* and *daegeum*[24]. Under the moonlit blossoms, he would play a tune or two to entertain himself. His skills were so exceptional that he rivaled his ancestors, and his appearance and spirit were so superb that he could find a true counterpart in learned scholars of the Qin or the Sung Dynasty.

Kang emphasized in this writing that Kim was a man of high character and that he loved refined music. Another of his documents backs this up.

> Saneung was well versed in music and was remarkable with the *geomungo* and flute as well as poetry and prose. He was a man of taste. Every time he felt like strumming an instrument and singing a sad song, he could not help shedding a few tears. How can anyone dare understand what he goes through? People say that in his house, the desk is well organized and the stairs and yard are so spacious that even when one is inside the house he feels separated from the outside world. Clumsy and narrow-minded people may exchange jokes with Kim Hong-do, but they will never realize the depth of his soul.

24 A Korean flute.

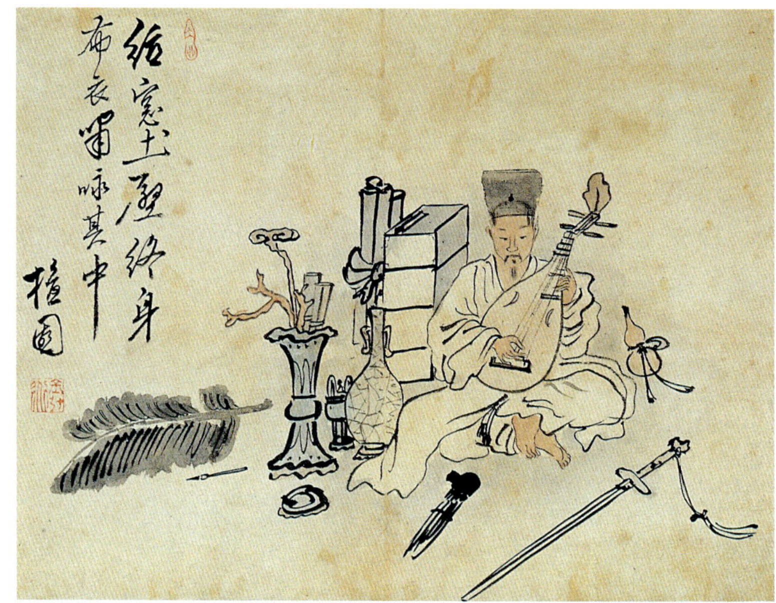

16 ***An Idyllic Life of a Scholar without a Government Office***
Ink and color on paper. 27.9 ×37cm. Private collection.
The inscription, As long as I can plaster paper on the window and mud on the wall, until my body wastes away, I shall recite poems without serving in a government office sounds like an autobiographical statement. Books, rolls of paper, a reed instrument, a Korean mandolin, chinaware and bronze-ware for appreciation, a gourd bottle with, wine inside, and a plantain leaf to write poetry with all show the man s character. Even though the man is wearing a hat, he is barefoot, indicating his casual manner.

As such, Kim enjoyed refined music, and he led an orderly life of which many were unaware. Throughout his life, there were numerous anecdotes about his attachment to music. We should pay careful attention to the parts that indicate he was well versed in poetry and prose and that he was a man of taste. Some of his extemporaneous Chinese poems are extant, and we shall look at them later. For the moment, let us examine the two Korean verses (*shijo*) that he left behind and are evidence of his poetic, musical and artistic talents. *Cheongguyeongeon* (*Collection of Ancient Shijo*), edited by Lee Han-jin (1732–1815) contains two verses by Kim Hong-do.

Set a boat afloat on the water in the spring
Below the water is the sky; above the sky is the water
The flower that catches the old man's eyes must be in the haze.

Did the rooster crow afar, darling in my arms is about to leave.
If she goes then I have half the night all to myself

She shall stay and we will make love.

By Kim Hong-do.

The first is about the scenery and the second is a type of love poem. The love poem gives us a glimpse of his romantic tastes, but that is all we can assume. The first verse was probably written when he was older since the last line refers to "the old man's eyes," but we do not have to rely on the direct hint of "the old man's eyes." The poetry sings about the horizon where the sky meets the water and where the distinction blurs amidst the haze. This automatically reminds us of the spacious margin and poetic sentiment contained in Kim's descriptive paintings of scenery, mountains and rivers in his older days.

One of Kim Hong-do's paintings, 'Looking at Plum Blossoms from a Boat,' (Plate 17: private collection), is an exact match to the above verse. At the bottom left of the picture, a boat floats by the rim of a mountain. A master and a young boy are sitting across from each other at a drink-laden table in the boat, and beyond the foggy water, hills and flowering trees are reflected in the sunlight. The focal point of the painting is the blank space, not the objects; or, rather it is the subtle melding of the objects and blank spaces into one another. This poetic space sense was typical of Kim's later paintings. Kim Hong-do wrote as an inscription, "Flower to the old man's eyes seems to be buried in the haze." This phrase appears in a poem by Du Fu (712–770) written just before he died at the age of 59.

Written in a boat on the day before Hansik[25]

I forced myself to drink and eat thinking the day was good, but rather it was cold.
Sit away from the table, feeling lonely. I wear the crown of a hermit.
A boat on spring water seems to be sitting on top of the sky
Flower to the old man's eyes seems to be buried in the haze.

Fluttering butterfly passes by a lazy curtain

25 The 105th day after the winter solstice.

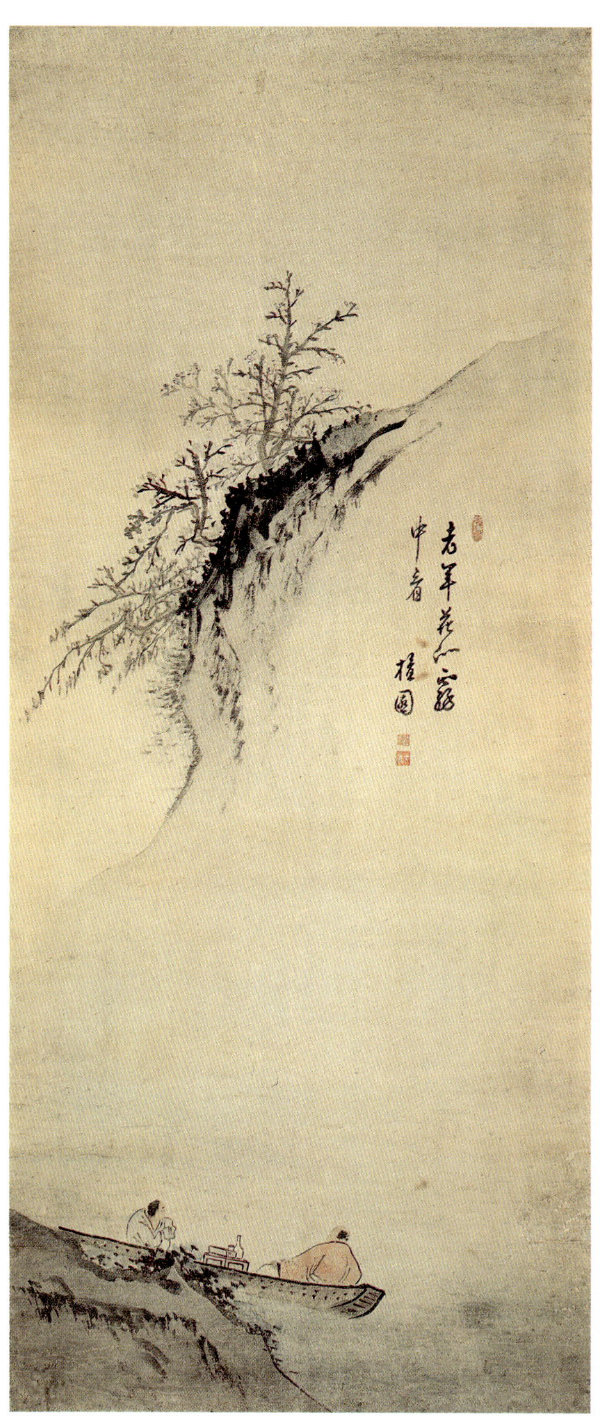

17 *Looking at Plum Trees from a Boat*

Ink and color on paper. 164×76cm. Private collection.

Far up the haze is a steep cliff on which there are a few flower trees. The center of the cliff is very dark and well focused, but the sides are blurred. The artist released his force on the brush as he moved away from the center, on the boundary between to-be and not-to-be, and the ink has faded away naturally. This is a subjective view through the eyes of the old man sitting in the boat, but the viewer gets to see the old man as well. Danwon s empathy with the old man is so complete that the boat is painted as if the artist were looking up from the surface of the water.

Light-winged gull lands softly on the rapids

Clouds are white, mountains green, and the road I need to travel far, far away

Turn northward and wonder if Chang'an lies in that direction.

The poem was a source for Kim Hong-do's *shijo*. "Flower to the old man's eyes seems to be buried in the haze" directly relates to the last line of the *shijo*, and "Boat on spring water seems to be sitting on top of the sky" is the background to the first and second lines. In poetry, this is known as *jeomhwa* (點化) and it is a Chinese rhetorical device used to transpose another's poetic expression into one's own work. It is not an exact copy but a seamless reconstruction of the words. We know that painting also employs this *jeomhwa* technique, such as in imitation. Kim's *shijo* reads, "Below the water is the sky; above the sky is the water," which shows that he was able to detach himself from the source material and create his own sense of space. Thus, Kim sublimated his inspiration from Du Fu's poem into a painting and a *shijo*, which is quite extraordinary because the poetry and painting are two different genres.

The discovery of the two *shijo* by Kim Hong-do is twice as thrilling because they are examples of the most Joseon form of literature composed by the most Joseon painter. *Shijo* are often the lyrics to traditional songs or *shijochang*, and his composing them is further evidence of Kim's musical talent. Kim's spelling of *hanneul*, the Korean word for sky, is intriguing from the perspective of eighteenth century Hangeul orthography, and thus Kim has inadvertently shed light on earlier Korean writing. As seen above, Kim Hong-do was cultured in diverse areas such as music and literature. In that sense, he is different from the other court painters who merely painted good pictures of objects that they saw. Kim's paintings always entail comments about his unique style. The following was written by Kang Se-hwang.

Painters then and now were exceptional in only one aspect and were not skilled in multiple disciplines. Kim Saneung, however, had studied painting since he was young and could draw anything. His paintings of people, landscapes, Taoist hermits, Buddhism, flowers, flowering plants, birds, insects, fish and crabs were all superb. No great artist of the past could challenge him. He was especially talented in Taoist hermit and bird and flower paintings. The current generation is mesmerized by his art; the repercussions will also be felt by the next generation. He is also good with genre paintings, and he very well captured the scenes of refined scholars diligently studying, merchants on their way to market and women rearing silkworms. The way he painted travelers on the road, farmers in the field, women's boudoirs, big houses and heavy gates, rugged mountains, fields and water showed that he paid careful attention to every detail. His paintings were faithful to the original shape and form and did not distort them, which was unprecedented at the time.

Most painters learn how to paint by recopying the paintings of their predecessors. Kim, however, acquired creativity all on his own and was able to steal the harmony of nature on to the canvas. This gift from heaven transcends the secular world. There is an old saying that it is difficult to draw chickens and dogs and easy to draw ghosts. This means one has to draw carefully what everyone else can see, for others are not easily deceived.

What Kang emphasized in this commentary is that Kim Hong-do was different from painters before his time in that he was a master of many genres. He also drew accurate pictures of everyday objects. Kang did not think that such skill could be learned through training and believed that Kim was born with the talent. Kang stresses this point elsewhere.

The who's who of Dohwawon-Jin, Park, Byeon and Jang–fell short of Kim Hong-do's performance. In painting towers, landscapes, people, flowering plants, insects, fish and birds, the resemblance was so striking that Kim seemed to be stealing the harmony of nature on to the canvas. It is accurate to say that he was the first to achieve this feat in the 400 years of court painting. He was also good at depicting daily lives and common customs. When his brush drew

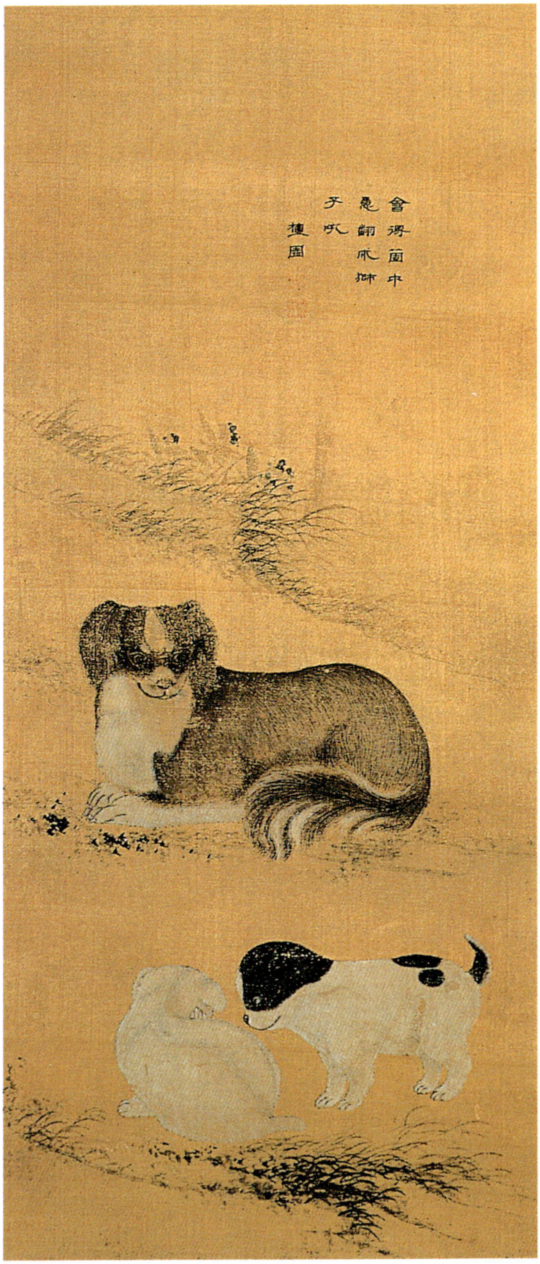

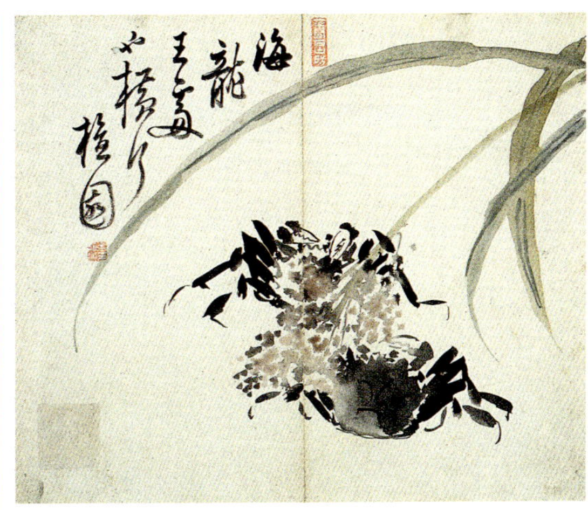

18 *A Mother Dog and Two Puppies*

Ink and color on silk. 90.7×39.6cm. Kansong Art Museum.

A mother dog looks fondly at her two puppies playing. The inscription reads, grow up to be good dogs. The dogs have cute plump bodies and short legs and tails. This painting is an exemplary piece of endearing animal painting that is unique to Korean tradition.

19 *Crabs Devouring Reed Flowers*

Ink and color on paper. 23.1×27.5cm. Kansong Art Museum.

The motif, two crabs with reed flowers in their mouths, traditionally means, pass the national examination twice and eat the food given by the king. However, the inscription reads, They even walk sideways in the presence of the Dragon God, which seems to mean a lot more. The reed leaves and crabs are painted with swift strokes with no contour outlining for a liberal, dynamic and lively look.

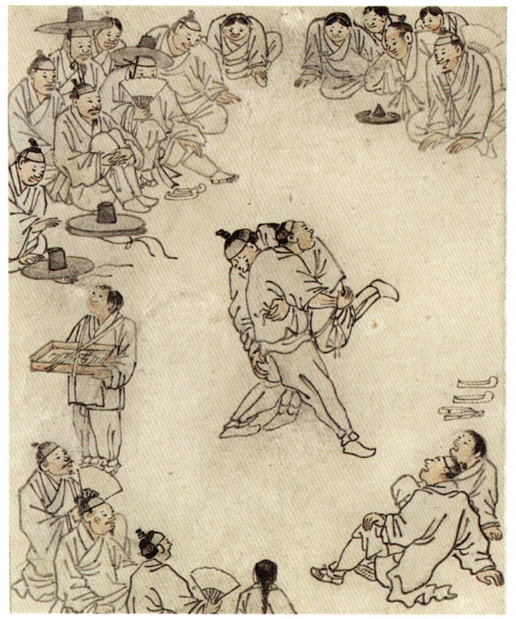

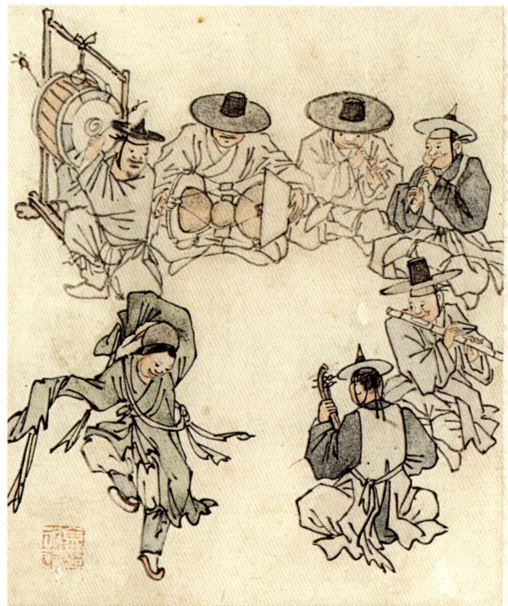

20-23 From *Danwon Genre Paintings*
Ink and color on paper. 27×22.7cm each. National Museum of Korea.

20 *Wrestling*
The wrestlers with their bodies twisted are placed in the center while spectators facing them and a peddler facing the other way form a circle, giving the picture a sense of unity. The excitement from the ring can be felt from the spectators facial expressions and postures and from the composition, which places more spectators at the top than on the bottom.

21 *A Dancing Boy*
A pretty boy is dancing to a tune played by drums, flute, fiddle and clarinet. The flute player has sore lips from playing so long. Lines of different thickness outline the boy s clothes, thereby making the dance more dynamic, whereas consistent contours outline the musicians clothes; but different ink shades express the distance.

streets, ferries, shops and open markets, exam centers and playgrounds, everyone clapped their hands and marveled at the paintings' realism. This is the "genre painting of Kim Saneung" that everyone talks of. How is it possible unless he has learned the way of the universe with his divine soul and wisdom?

This quote is redundant, but it further emphasizes the "genre painting of Kim Saneung." The author's guess is that everyone had heard of "Kim Saneung's genre painting." Seo Yu-gu (1764–1845) vividly describes the common people's response to the painting in the following comment.

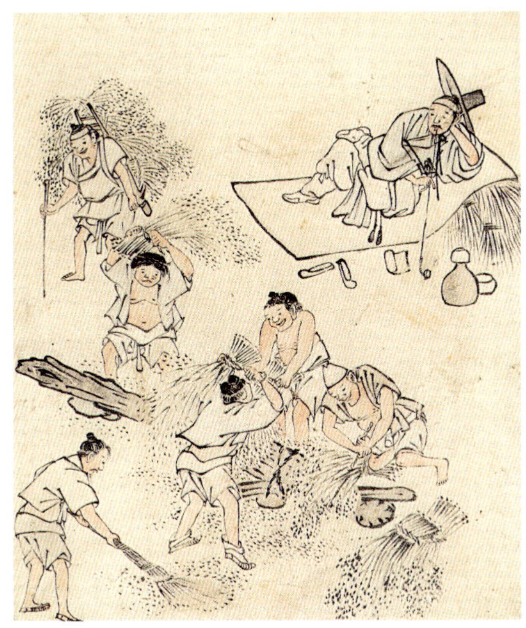

22 *Rice Threshing*
A moment of joy is captured in the dynamic X-shaped composition. A sheaf of rice is carried on an A-frame. Several workers thresh rice on a log. Another man sweeps the grain on one side. Everyone looks busy. In contrast, the supervisor is at leisure lying on a straw mat with his head perched on top of a sheaf of straw and smoking a long pipe. He also seems to have had some wine as well.

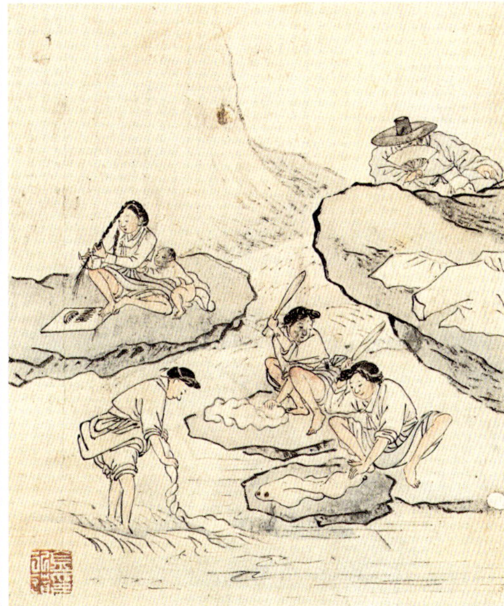

23 *Laundry*
A passer-by is sneaking a peek at women washing their clothes and bathing in a stream. The women have their skirts and underpants rolled up to their thighs, showing their flesh. They are rinsing the laundry in the water and beating it dry with clubs, or washing and brushing their hair, too busy to notice the intruder. The passer-by displays the same mental age as the little boy who is begging his mother for milk.

> Kim Hong-do painted the common people's everyday life in a colorful manner, depicting travelers in the street markets, pleasure quarters, or inns; people selling firewood and cucumbers; male and female Buddhist monks; Buddhists, porters and beggars. Women and children broke into laughter whenever they saw his paintings; this is a first for any painter.

Lee Gyu-sang (1727–1799) wrote the following about Kim Hong-do in his *Hwajurok*,[26] "His painting follows the rules of painting, but the spirit is alive." Kim earned his reputation through his keen eye, accurate sketching

26 *Summary of Late Joseon Painters.*

skills and unique approach to painting. Jo Hui-ryong's record summarizes this point nicely.

> Kim Hong-do worked wonders when he drew landscapes, people, flowering plants, birds and animals. He was very gifted at painting Taoist figures. The silhouette, color spread [blot] and the drape of the robe were all expressed in an original manner, and he did not follow anyone else's methodology. Mystical meanings were portrayed clearly and cheerfully, elating everyone. He was an artist of special taste in the art circle.

This commentary is also focused on Kim's being capable in all kinds of genres and that he painted paintings that were original and had a living spirit. He may have drawn Chinese motifs, but his works revealed his strengths very plainly. The famous 'The Gathering in the Western Garden' (Plate 37) has the following postscript written by Kang Se-hwang.

> He must have gained this talent through either a spiritual awakening or a gift from God. Kim Hong-do's painting is much better than Chou Ying's fragile work and is on a par with Li Gonglin's original. Joseon is lucky to have such a magnificent painter. My writing falls short of that of Mi Fu, and I only damn Kim with faint praise. I cannot escape the blame of others.

Kang Se-hwang said that while his own writing did not match that of his Chinese counterparts, Kim Hong-do's work was worthy of the original Chinese work. This may be rhetoric, but such words of praise were not easily given to all other artists. Seo Yu-gu cannot but exclaim over the painting of Taoist Immortals that Kim had copied.

> Mi Fu's *Shu Shih* talks about the 'Five Stars' of Zhou Fang. People of the Tang and Sung Dynasties drew five stars or three stars to celebrate birthdays. I saw a Chinese painting 'Three Stars' in which an old man with bushy eyebrows

> and hair down to his waist was bent over a walking stick. Another man was wearing jade accessories and a golden crown. He had a large forehead, lean body and a dignified look. The other man was wearing a hat and a green summer jacket. He had a mild and auspicious look about his forehead and eyes. Many works have come from China, and they all look so similar because they are all copies of an older version. Kim Hong-do once imitated a masterpiece on a silk measuring 8 *ja*[27] in length and width. The colors were splendid, the beauty mesmerizing, the brush strokes accurate and without a hair's width trace of unsteadiness. The color combinations of blue, gold, red and white were wonderful. It truly belongs in the palace.

As such, Kim Hong-do even brought new life to copies of original Chinese paintings. Some uninformed people think that paintings of Taoist hermits and the gathering in the Western Garden have themes that originated in China and thus lack the Korean sense of beauty. People averse to typical Chinese-style landscapes and paintings of old Chinese stories should remember that European paintings are not criticized for copying Jewish and Greek paintings. Europe, which extends from the United Kingdom to Russia, has been creating art for a long time. Most paintings are either Judeo-Christian in nature or figure paintings depicting Greek or Roman mythologies. Should then the pictures of the Holy Mother and Jesus, or of Aphrodite, Dionysus and Zeus, drawn by Italian, French and German painters be castigated as second best in comparison to Jewish and Greek paintings? The art of the Joseon Dynasty contains many Chinese elements such as folklore, motifs and clothing, but this should not matter. As seen from the previous chapter, during Kim Hong-do's time, Joseon intellectuals prided themselves on being traditional and not following the ways of the barbarian Ching Dynasty. They believed themselves to be the final fortress in the defense of authentic Chinese culture and tradition. It was a cultural, not a nationalistic issue.

Kim Hong-do's imitations of Chinese paintings amazed viewers because

27 A unit of length.

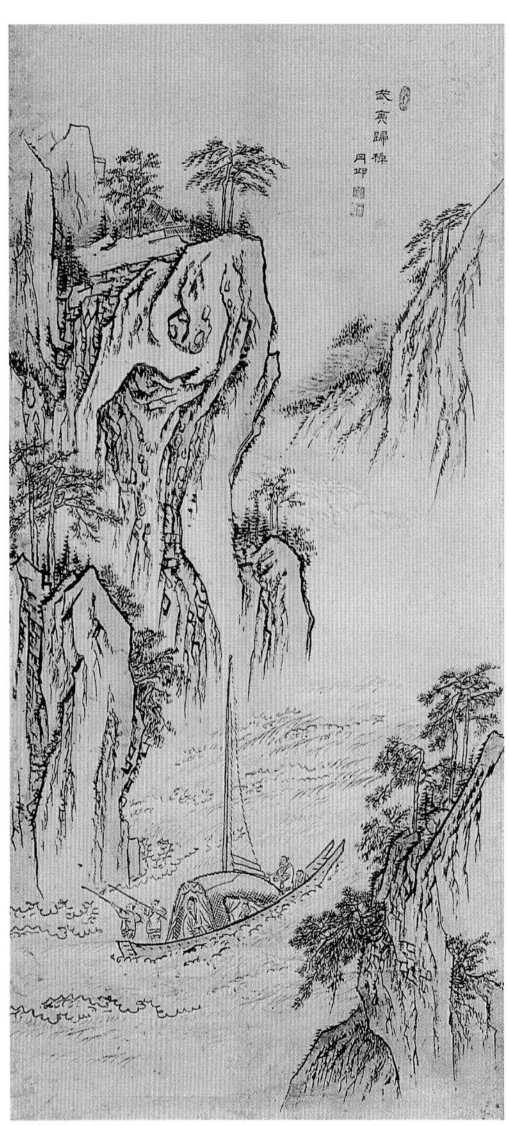

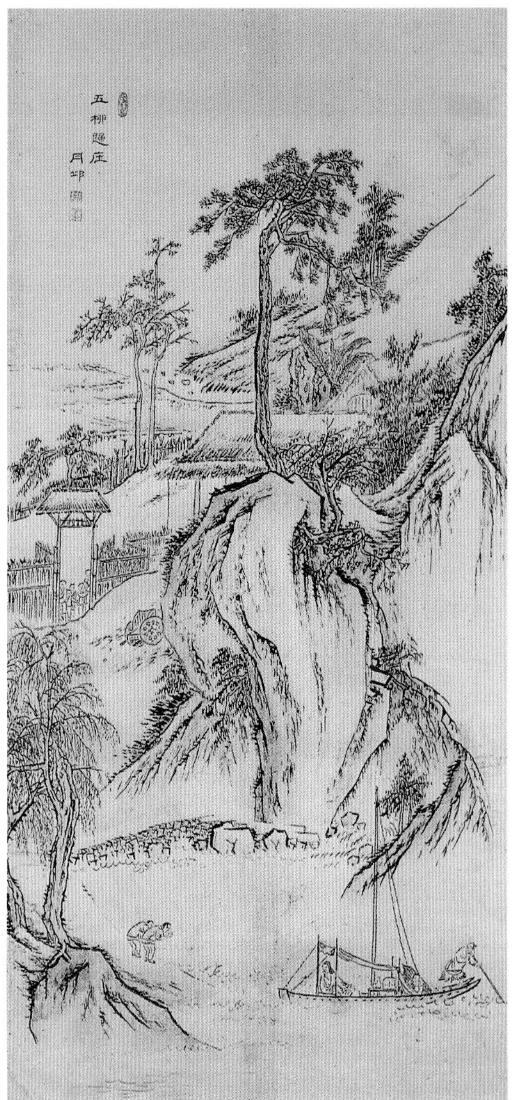

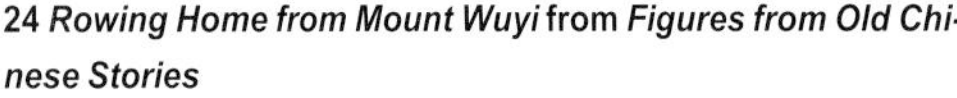

24 *Rowing Home from Mount Wuyi* from *Figures from Old Chinese Stories*

Ink and color on paper. 111.9×52.6cm. Kansong Art Museum.

Mount Wuyi in Fujian Province in China was famous for its beautiful scenery, but even more famous as a place where Chu Hsi used to stay. The currents run rapidly under the steep cliffs. The people in the boat are quickly folding their sails and steering the boat with poles so they can enjoy the scenery. The background and the people are typically Joseon style.

25 *Five Willows Coming Home* from *Figures from Old Chinese Stories*

Ink and color on paper. 111.9×52.6cm. Kansong Art Museum.

The reclusive poet Tao Yuanming was also called Five Willows because he had so many trees at home. While serving as a petty official, his boss demanded a bribe from him; however, Tao refused and boarded a boat for home. His family looks pitiful as they wait for him at the gate, but the poet, like a big rock or handsome pine, never loses his composure.

he had a unique sense of form and stubborn artisanship. This is most clearly seen in the following episode that occurred in 1791 when King Jeongjo had his portrait painted. According to the entry dated 28th of the 9th lunar month of 1791 in *The Diaries of the Royal Secretariat,* the king, ministers, Kim Hong-do and Lee Myeong-gi looked at three first drafts and made comments.

> The king came to Seohyanggak, an annex of Gyujanggak. He ordered the ministers to look at the first drafts of the portrait. The drafts had already been hung on the eastern wall of Seohyanggak. In one of the portraits, the king was wearing his morning attire of a *wonyu* crown and a *gangsa* robe, and the painting was mounted and hung in the center of the wall. The other two were drawn on oil-coated paper, and the king was wearing a *yeongeo* robe. The paintings were placed to the east and west of the mounted picture. The king told the ministers, "Please look at these drafts and tell me what you think. Those who are to attend the royal ceremony are advised to come in threes and look."
>
> Chae Je-gong (1720–1799) said, "It is better to look at the paintings from a distance than up close. If I were to step too close to the paintings, then my eyes catch every detail down to a single hair, and that may distort the truth of the work." He raised his hand to point to the painting on the oil-coated paper to the west of the mounted one and said, "To my humble eyes, this one is the best of the three." The king said, "I agree with you. The sketches were done a dozen times before the picture was painted. I do not like the one hung to the east of the mounted picture because it was hastily drawn this morning to be ready to show to the ministers."
>
> Hong Nak-seong said, "I think the mounted picture was painted very well, except that the face is too pale. I think the painting would leave nothing to be desired if the color were a little brighter." The king said, "The color of my face changes often during the day. It's different when I am just out of bed from when I wear my crown after combing my hair. It's different between morning and afternoon. It's different between afternoon and evening. It is very difficult to know which time of day to choose for my face color. That is why I told Lee Myeong-gi

that I didn't think it was a good picture. I am afraid that the painter's hand may betray my true appearance. This version happened to be slightly better."

Chae Je-gong said, "Your Highness, the mounted picture is not as good as the oil-coated paper painting." The king said, "I agree," and he asked the opinions of others. O Jae-sun, Seo Ho-su, Park U-won, Jeong Dong-jun, Seo Jeong-su, Lee Man-su, Yun Haeng-im, Seo Yong-bo, Seo Yeong-bo, Kim Mun-sun, Jeong Hwa-jin, Kim Jeong-jin and others said, "We think the mounted picture is better." Gu Ik said, "The oil-coated paper painting to the west of the mounted picture is much better in my opinion, but the mounted picture is good, too." Hwang In-jeom said, "The mounted picture is most verisimilar." Hong Eok said, "The facial color is better on the mounted picture." The king asked another minister, "What do you think?" Jeong Chang-sun said, "I also like the mounted picture."

Chae Je-gong said, "Both are good, but of the two the painting done on the oil-coated paper hung on the west is better. Many ministers think that the mounted painting is better because the attire is familiar. If the painting were reproduced on silk and if you wear the same attire as you wore for the mounted picture, then it would be very true to life." Hong Nak-seong said, "I don't think the oil-coated paper painting is better. I think it would be better to make the colors brighter on the mounted picture."

The king said, "I agree with Chae Je-gong. The oil-coated paper version in the west is better than the mounted picture. Since the ministers disagree, however, let's call forth Lee Myeong-gi and Kim Hong-do." The king rose from his chair and walked to the center of the building, asking their opinions. Lee said, "From the beginning, I thought the oil-coated paper painting on the west was better." Kim said, "The oil-coated paper painting hung to the east of the mounted picture is good. If it is complemented with the mounted picture and reproduced on silk, it would be very good."

The king said, "When you are to judge a portrait, you first have to look at the pupils. I cannot look at my face objectively, but the picture hung to the west of the mounted painting has eyes that shine very brightly. Why don't you think the oil-coated paper version hung to the west is better? The oil-coated paper version hung to the east of the mounted picture was painted in a hurry. It's not even worth mentioning." Seo Ho-su said, "Ministers looked up at the paintings under the column, and we think that the mounted picture is good. The oil-coated paper painting hung to its west has a full chin that is a bit exaggerated. Which one would you choose as the one to be reproduced on silk?" The king said, "In that case, have the mounted picture reproduced on silk. Let the coloring and mounting jobs be done quickly so that it is complete by the second day of the next month."

There is no way of telling what those three first drafts were. What is certain, however, is that at first King Jeongjo, Chae Je-gong and Lee Myeong-gi preferred the picture hung to the west because of the shine in the eyes. Hong Nak-seong and other ministers suggested brightening the colors of the mounted picture in the center in which the king was wearing familiar attire. However, Kim Hong-do's opinion was quite unexpected because he recommended selecting the picture hung to the east and using the mounted picture as reference. The painting on the oil-coated paper hung in the east was hastily drawn that morning, and King Jeongjo disregarded it from the very beginning. Neither did the other ministers mention it. Unfortunately, Kim had not elaborated on his opinions; King Jeongjo probably cut him short because he did not like the painting. Since the picture Kim liked best was hurriedly painted that morning, it probably lacked ingenuity, but it must have looked lively and dynamic. Since we have nothing to refer to, there is no way of confirming our assumptions. It is, however, quite impressive that Kim Hong-do spoke his mind in front of the king and the ministers even though he was not supported.

Kim Hong-do could express his opinion on the king's portrait in front of such a royal gathering because he was an excellent painter himself. Being cultured in every way, he had the confidence to speak his mind. He was especially talented in calligraphy, as we will later see.

Finally, in discussing Kim's character, we cannot ignore the sense of humor witnessed in his work. It is needless to explain further since it is so well known. Park Yun-muk (1771–1849), who is supposed to have watched the process of Kim Hong-do's painting, wrote the following poem.

> When he was about to paint
> He would take off his coat
> His breath reeked of alcohol
> Jokes would escape his mouth
> Nothing seemed to be on his mind
> But his brushstroke told the truth.

We can speculate where the sense of humor in his paintings comes from by reading the poem about his painting in a drunken state, and making jokes now and then. This is another point of contrast between Kim and Hyewon Sin Yun-bok, who was also good at genre paintings. Kim Hong-do immersed himself into the paintings by empathizing with his characters' actions and emotions, whereas Sin detached himself from his objects and dispassionately described them, slowly and objectively observing them. Their lives are a direct reflection of their differences. What little material there is on Kim Hong-do's life indicates the kind of person he was, whereas Sin's life is hidden behind a veil like the characters in his paintings, whose expressions and thoughts are difficult to read.

Kim Hong-do's open-mindedness and drollery matched those of his mentor, Kang Se-hwang, as Kang may have even influenced his student. Kang was the ninth child of a 64-year-old father, and received all the love from his family. His cheerful and humorous character is often witnessed in the inscriptions and postscripts to Kim Hong-do's work. In his 'Self-portrait' (Plate 26) drawn at the age of 70, Kang is wearing *yabok* and *osamo*, the typical attire of a hermit, trying to look serious, but the portrait produces a rather comical effect. In praising the work of art, he wrote, "I painted it for

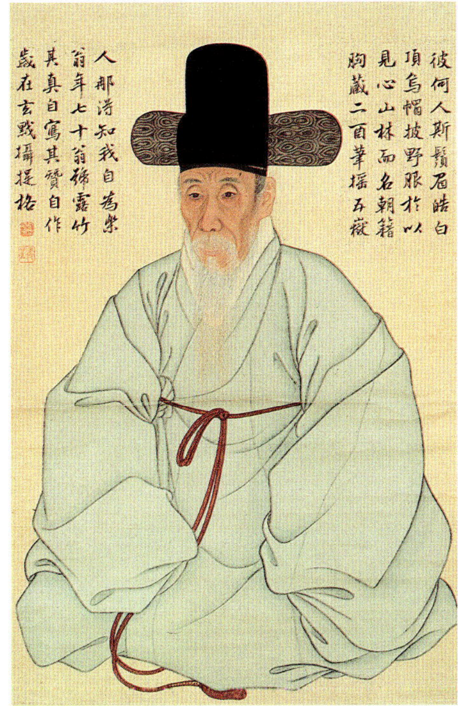

26 Kang Se-hwang. *Self-portrait*
1782. Color on silk. 88.7×51cm. Private collection.
Kang Se-hwang emulated many painters/ writers that came after Wang Xizhi and left many self-portraits. The wit and pride in this one is extraordinary. The inscription reads, Who is that man? His beard and eyebrows are white, but he is wearing a black silk hat and a common robe. This shows his mind is at leisure as if he were in the countryside, but his name is written in the list of government officials. He has memorized one thousand books, and his brush is strong enough to shake from the bottom the five great mountains of the world, but how could other people know?

personal enjoyment. I painted myself, and I wrote the eulogy myself." Lee Gyu-sang wrote the following about Kang.

> Kang Se-hwang is very optimistic and easy-going, but at the same time is a man of integrity and obstinacy. He would politely indulge requests for a painting even if they came from a poor old man or a farmer. All the houses in Joseon decorated their folding screens and walls with his calligraphy.

Mentor and student alike were optimistic and easy-going, and that is why they were able to get along so well despite the 32-year age difference. According to newly discovered material, Kang's brother-in-law, Yu Gyeong-jong (1714–1784), wrote a poem after he watched the mentor and the student each paint a tiger.

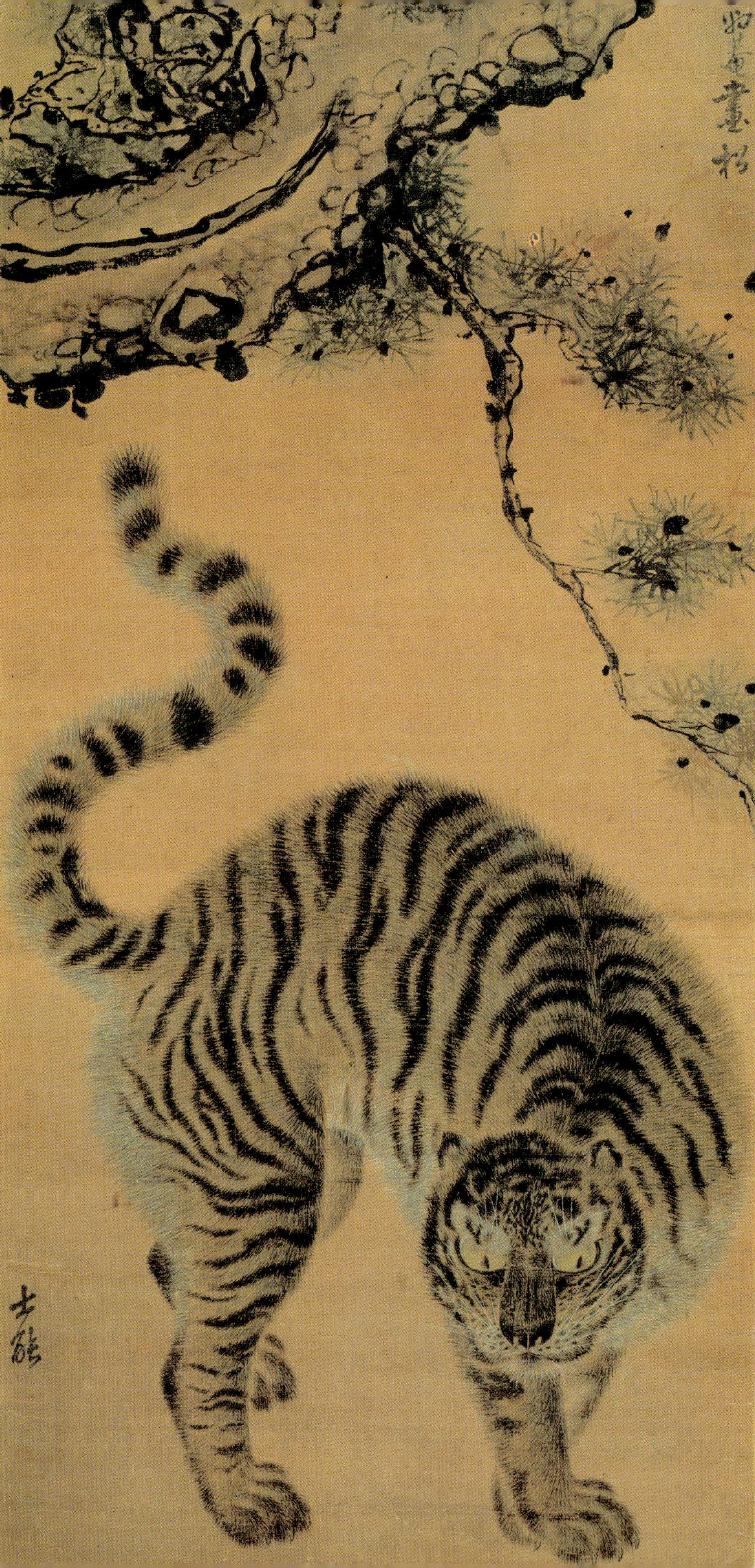
豹菴畫松
士能

Two men are painting a tiger each
Whose tiger will be more realistic?
If they paint well, they are both good painters
If not, their skills prove worthless.

Wang Anshi is supposed to have been a great painter
Now there is Kang Se-hwang and Kim Hong-do.
Watching the paintings, a poem naturally comes to mind
Who will follow their footsteps?
It seems beneath the pine trees
Cool breeze is actually blowing in the late summer season.

The tiger's stripes look threatening
I fear it may eat up the dogs in the neighborhood and cause concern.
The two tigers may fight each other
Goea is already scared. [Goea: Kang Se-hwang's grandson]

27 Kim Hong-do and Lee In-mun. *A Brave Tiger under the Pine Tree*
Color on silk. 90.4×43.8cm. Hoam Art Museum.
The stealthy tiger has suddenly become aware of something and quickly turned its face forward. The fur and the stripes look surprisingly natural; they were painted with thousands of detailed brush strokes. At the same time, the observer can feel the heaviness, agility and flexibility of the tiger.

In a very convivial environment in his brother-in-law and grandson's presence, Kang Se-hwang drew pictures with his student. He summarized his lifelong friendship with Kim Hong-do as follows.

> Friendship with Saneung went through three phases. The first was when Saneung visited me when he was young, and I would compliment him on his skills or teach him how to draw certain things. The second phase occurred when we were in the same government office together and saw each other every morning and evening. In the final phase, we belonged to the art circle and felt like old friends. There is a reason why Saneung insists on getting the inscriptions on his paintings from me.

Finally, let us examine Kim Hong-do's Buddhism. In 1790, the king ordered Kim to paint the platform painting in the main worship hall of

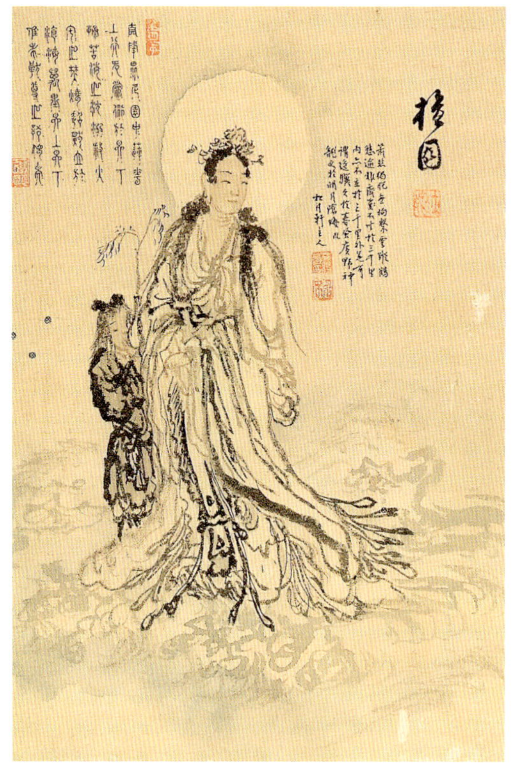

28 *Avalokitesvara (Guanyin) in the South Sea*
Ink and color on silk. 30.6×20.6cm. Kansong Art Museum.
Avalokitesvara stands with her hands clasped together and her robes flowing against the background of the ocean waves. Highlighted with a crown on her head, her braids on her shoulders and the halo in back, her face looks beautiful and kind. The child is shyly hiding behind Guanyin, half of his face covered by a vase of willows. This picture presents a typical mother and son in the Joseon period.

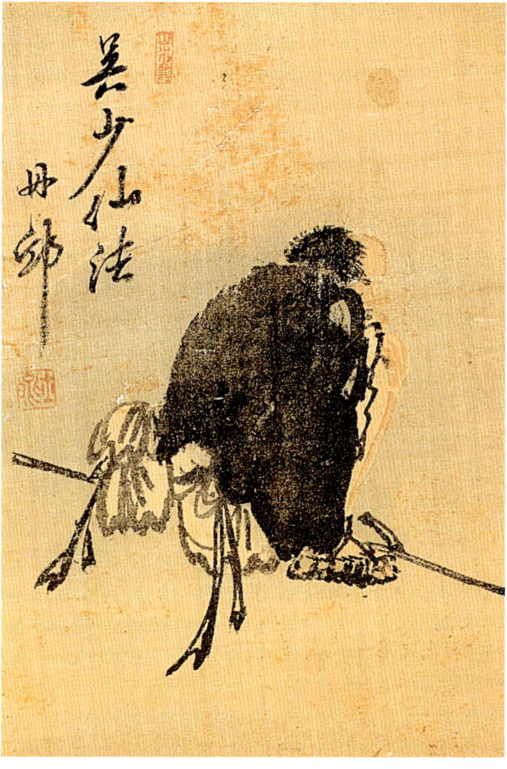

29 *Monk Shide*
Ink and color on silk. 21.5×15.2cm. Kansong Art Museum.
A balding man in beggar s clothes is squatting. He is wearing loosely woven straw shoes, and a small package is dangling from his stick. He looks like an itinerant monk and invokes the image of the Tang Dynasty monk, Shide who helped the poor. Swift, rough brushstrokes and a bold ink touch entrance observers.

Yongjusa Temple. To paint a Buddhist painting, one must follow a religious ritual, so Kim in one way or another must have been involved in the religion. Jo Su-sam's records tell us that Kim had drawn the 12-leaf *Danwon's Album of Buddhist Paintings* already in 1786; however, this work was merely for appreciation. The record, *Restoration of Sangamsa Temple located on Mount Gongjeong in Yeonpung County* is concrete evidence that

Kim was a Buddhist. Hyeongam Kim Hong-do went up Mount Joryeong to pray for rain in his village, which was suffering from a lengthy drought. He noticed how clean and neat the temple was and concluded it was the right place for prayers. He offered a sacrifice from his own salary. With that money, the faded Buddhist statue was newly gilded and torn portraits and paintings were restored and recolored. Further evidence of Kim's Buddhism is found further along in the record, which said, "[He] did not have a son until he was very old, and after praying to the spirits in the mountain, he had a son." In his later years, he painted masterpieces such as 'Avalokitesvara in the South Sea' (Plate 28), 'Old Monk Chanting' and 'Monk Shide' (Plate 29), which were inspired by religious devotion. However, one report, which was written to the king in 1795 by Hong Dae-hyeop, mentions that Kim went hunting. We cannot verify the details at this stage.

4. The True Picture of Kim Hong-do's Daily Life

It would be interesting to glimpse Kim Hong-do's daily life, but that is of course difficult to do. Occasionally, misunderstanding facts leads to erroneous conclusions. Previously, Kim's stature and character, resembling that of a Taoist hermit, were introduced. One revealing and well-known episode is the *Story of Plum Blossom and Wine*, told by Jo Hui-ryong.

> He rose to the position of *hyeongam* of Yeonpung due to his ancestors' past deeds, but he was poor and sometimes skipped meals. One day, a man was selling a pot containing a unique plum flower, but Kim did not have the money to buy it. As luck would have it, his patron had paid three thousand won in advance for a painting. Kim paid two thousand for the flower, spent eight hundred on liquor and invited his friends for a party commemorating the flower. The remaining two hundred was for rice and firewood, which did not even last a day. Kim was such a heedless fellow.

The episode is introduced here is because it portrays Kim's character better than any other does and because it led to the misconception that he spent his days in poverty. This anecdote must have been quite impressive, for it is often quoted in literature written in later years. Yu Jae-geon's *A Record of Personal Experience in Foreign Regions*, Kang Hyo-seok's *A Collection of Biographies and Anecdotes on Figures of the Joseon Dynasty* and Jang Ji-yeon's *Biographies of People from All Walks of Life* mention it, and it became the *de facto* most famous story of Kim Hong-do. All modern literature written about the painter also includes it. If we were to judge him by today's standards, he would be an irresponsible head of the family leading a romantic life and meeting the disapproval of everyone. However, not so long ago, such a nonchalant lifestyle must have been refreshing enough to readers to relieve their minds of their routine even for a short while.

The following poem is evidence that indirectly supports the hypothesis that Kim was a poor painter (Plate 30).

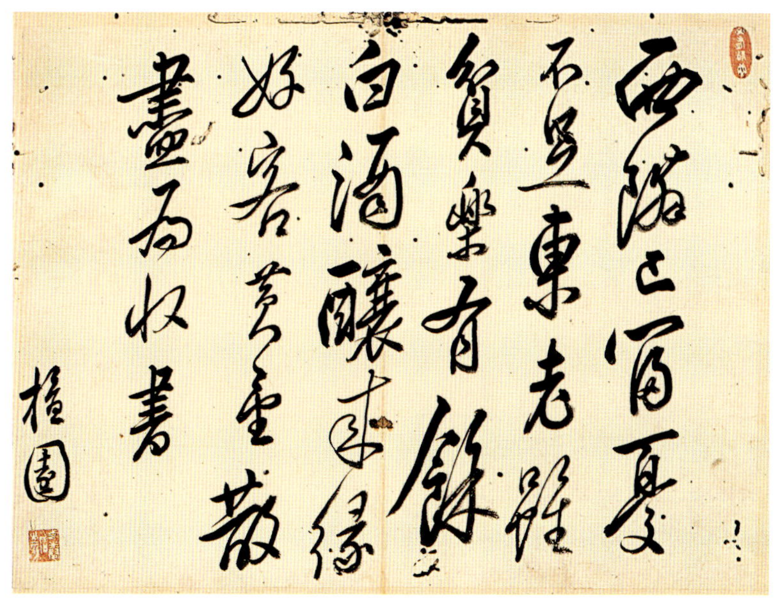

30 *Hui Daoren s Poem* from *Danwon s Posthumous Works*
Ink on paper. 33×44cm. National Museum of Korea.
The poem describes a nonchalant life, and the characters are written in a free and lively manner. They are long and lean, and tilt upwards to the right, which reinforces the effect. Calligraphy is supposed to mirror one s soul, and this shows Kim Hong-do s reflection of himself being tied down to nothing.

Neighbor in the west, though a wealthy man, worries that he has not enough.
Neighbor in the east, though a poor man, is happy for he has enough.
He buys wine to please his guests
And spends all the gold to buy good books.
Danwon

The poem is in the beginning of *Danwon's Posthumous Works*, the anthology published by Kim Hong-do's son Kim Yang-gi, who collected his father's writings. The poem is in Kim Hong-do's handwriting and it has the inscription and seal, Danwon, so everyone took it for granted that it was Kim's work. Quoted in later literature, the poem best represented Kim's lifestyle. People thought that the poem epitomized Kim's philosophy of life. However, the above poem was written by a Taoist hermit in China named Hui Daoren (Taoist Hui; real name, Lu Dongbin). The following is a summary of relevant information found in the works of a famous writer, Su Shi.

> A man named Shen Si, who was also called Dong Lao (old man living in Donglin), lived a secluded life in Donglin in Huzhou. He made very good *shiba xian baijiu* [white wine of eighteen notables]. One day Hui Daoren came over, said hello and asked for a sip of the wine, for he heard that it was well fermented. Shen Si realized that this was no ordinary man from the way his eyes shone brightly and how he looked at people with a penetrating stare. He took out the wine, and they drank together. From noon to evening, they finished many a bottle. Hui Daoren peeled a tangerine and with it wrote a poem on the wall. It is the poem written above.

Some people may say that even though the poem is Chinese, Kim Hong-do liked it very much, and the poem may represent his lifestyle, at least his ideals. While it is true that Kim liked the poem and the theme of leisure amidst poverty may be relevant, the love of good wine and books is not a luxury afforded by the poor. They cannot afford to have kegs of wine at home; it is just a rhetorical device. This poem was most favored at young noblemen's and royal descendants' summerhouses. *Imhapilgi* of Lee Yu-won (1814–1888) contains an article which says the following:

> According to Su Dongpo's book of poems, a Taoist who called himself Hui Shan Ren stopped by Shen Si's house, drank wine and wrote a Chinese quatrain on the wall with a pomegranate peel. The poem became widely known, and if young noblemen or royal descendants did not frame and hang it in their summer homes, they were considered unsophisticated. The source of the original text was unknown until Hong Yang-ho found it amongst a bunch of dirty and worn paper.

Even such a learned man as Lee Yu-won did not know the poem's origin. It was introduced to the public as something new and quickly caught on. In fact, Hong Yang-ho (1724–1802) had found it amidst wrinkled paper and spread it among people. Hong Yang-ho had received the fan-painting 'Bamboo in Ink,' and afterward wrote the inscription in which he likened

Danwon to Gu Kaizhi.

As you may have guessed, Kim Hong-do wrote few, if any, of the Chinese poems in *Danwon's Posthumous Works*. The poem on page 9 is by Choi Chi-won, and the ensuing ten-part *Nonggajeuksa* is written about the leisurely life of the rural areas. Many people understand it to be the life Kim led when he grew old, but the ten-part poem was actually written by a young poet named Byeokokran, which was the pen name of Lee Yu-gyeom, who grew up in a wealthy family. Lee Deok-mu (1741–1793) wrote a preface in Lee Yu-gyeom's *Byeokokransigo*. In the many forewords and epilogues of *Danwon's Posthumous Works*, people complimented Kim's painting and calligraphy but not a word was mentioned about the poetry. The following is a poem on page 13.

> Petty officials collecting tax money are passing by the village
> No one in sight; only the sound of the mill
> A year of hard work does not amount to much
> How can we afford to send our children off to marriage?

Reading the poem, we cannot readily conclude that it is proof of Kim's critique of the social structure or love for the common people. Of course, something must have inspired him to copy the poem in his own handwriting, but we cannot speculate beyond that. Since Du Fu and Bai Juyi's time, social or political satire has a long history in Chinese literature. Satirical poetry forms a genre of its own, and anyone from the noble and learned family would write and recite such poems.

Kim Hong-do led a very busy life as a court painter and he was well off. The following records from Nam Gong-cheol (1760–1840) tell the tale.

> *Painting of Later Han Dynasty's Kuang Wu Ti Drying His Clothes in the Fire*
>
> Under the painting of Kuang Wu Ti drying his clothes in the fire the follow-

ing comments are recorded:

> "This painting was done by Wu Daozi of the Tang Dynasty. My friend Jeongsu got it from Monk Jeomgang in Sinan. Jeongsu is a learned scholar whose courtesy name was Mokcheon. He was good at poetry, calligraphy and painting, and he liked to own famous works of art. This painting has some divine meaning to it. There are eight men and one horse ... [continues to explain the details of the painting]"
>
> I wanted to have Kim Hong-do draw another set according to the description, but regrettably, he did not have enough time. I was not able to see the original writing or the painting. I had to rely on records to create an epilogue and use it as reference. I am sure that the learned scholars will approve of the methodology I used.

There is a famous tale about Mingdi of the Later Han Dynasty building a platform in the South Palace and placing in it the portraits of twenty-eight generals such as Deng Yu and Feng Yi. The aforementioned painting is about the meritorious retainers of the Later Han Dynasty. Nam Gong-cheol traced back through research the content of the original Chinese painting and the measurements of the generals. He wanted to have a copy of his own. Nam was from a renowned family and his father had been one of young King Jeongjo's teachers. Despite being such a powerful person, even he could not receive a favor from Kim Hong-do. This shows that Kim was busily engaged in the painting of works for royal inspection. It is easy to imagine how the common people would want to own a painting by Kim, who was always occupied with painting for the king.

As seen previously, the poems that Kim Hong-do 'included' in *Danwon's Posthumous Works* serve as a reference and provide only secondary information rather than a glimpse of his real life. In comparison, Kim's letters are a direct reflection of his life and character. For example, the letter on page 22 of *Danwon's Posthumous Works* tells a lot about Kim Hong-do's status among the public officials.

How are you? I send my words of comfort from afar. My daughter, who recently became a widow, is still sick in bed, and I am worried about her. How is Dangheon? The thing I mentioned separately must be discussed between you two and carried out prudently. I had asked the question concerning the permanent appointment of a public official to a *siljik*, and you can refer to *Jeondongji*.

Dangheon, the provincial governor's office, is another name for Seonhwadang, and so in the letter Kim Hong-do is really asking after the provincial governor's health. The letter recipient must be working under a provincial governor. The matter about which he wrote separately and confidentially and which is to be discussed by the two men is about the *yeongbujigwa* of a government official, which was permanent appointment to a *siljik* under the king's special orders. This may mean that Kim Hong-do had some kind of influence on court painters' appointments, which were of great interest. The above letter also shows that Kim had a bedridden, widowed daughter. Another letter continues on page 23.

It's been a long time since we last corresponded. I was worried because there was no deliveryman. Just then, the mail arrived, and I learned that you were doing well. I send words of comfort from afar. I must have nine lives, but as this year draws to a close, endless pain haunts me. I received the things you sent me. Your kindness does not stop at words. They are essentials for the memorial service, and I thank you for your warm and caring heart. Did you plant the pine seedlings I sent you? It is a bit strange receiving two brushes, ink and a calendar from you. I cannot thank you enough for the other things.

The bamboo mat you sent me this year is of good quality. Since my room is spacious, could you send me a longer and tightly woven larger mat next spring?

The 23rd of the 12th lunar month, Year of eul, from Hayang

The year *eul* is one of the following years: 1765, 1775, 1785, 1795 or

1805. Given that he used the expressions "endless pain" and "essentials for the memorial service," it seems that Kim Hong-do was in mourning. The two letters that follow also seem to have been written while Kim was in mourning, and the three were probably written about the same time. Kim's activities in 1775 remain a mystery, and there are only traces of what he did in the other four years. We can assume that he was in mourning in 1775 when he was 31 years old. The way he addressed a younger friend shows he was very sentimental, and the manner in which he asked for another mat was so amiable that his friend could not have refused. His personality is shown much better in the following letter on page 24.

> I am in my three-year mourning period. I say this with my head bowed. I wondered this morning how you were. I am sad and share your loss. The pot of plum blossoms that I sent you was very rare, and I am sorry to hear that it is too small to fit. The thing you are asking for is no different from the last one. What shall I do? The red stamping ink is too light and dry. I am sorry to bother you but could you send me some more ink? I hope that you can borrow *Baekhacheop* from nearby.
>
> The first snow in the 12th lunar month is so lovely I want to hold it in my hand. Do you read books by the brightly lit window in front of your quiet desk while burning incense? Do you watch your daughter play? The pine tree by the windowsill has snow piled on its branches. Thinking of you made me smile. I must leave you in haste.

The letter shows Kim Hong-do as a warm-hearted man–even more so toward its conclusion. The subsequent letter mentions Lee Han-jin, and this will be examined later. It seems that Kim Hong-do was not in the best of health. The letter related to Lee Han-jin said, "While I was in mourning, my disease became worse and I almost died. I only just got better. What more can I say?" The letter on page 26, which was written in 1799, also said, "The disease I have is tormenting me still. What more can I say?" Signs of the disease are seen in the letter on page 27.

> I hope your body and mind are well in this winter season. Congratulations to your son for passing the official government examination; however, due to the state of my health, which has been this way for several months now, I cannot congratulate you in person. We have known each other for so long; I hope you understand. I am sorry for not being able to tend to other things because of my ailment.
>
> From Kim Hong-do

The letter on page 28 is a departure from the above letters in that Kim is leading a leisurely life, and living up to his pen names of Nonghan and Nongsaong (which mean 'leading a leisurely life in the countryside').

> I go fishing at night and plough the fields under the clouds. Such is the life of a man enjoying his leisure. I plant crops and weed the vegetable plots. Such is the life of an old farmer. Under a tall tree that almost touches the sky, there is a tall house and nearby is a stream. I call it the home of a Taoist hermit. A long day spent in poetry and wine feels like a year. The crops were good this year.
>
> Saying farewell made me uneasy, but now that I received your letter, I know that you are fine. The ailment persists, and I have worries on my mind. Hong-do is a pathetic person eating up all the rice, and there is not much else to say. Thank you for the two things you sent me. A friend of Baek's had asked me for two scrolls to hang on the wall. I was planning to send them via bang-nangcheong, but friend Seol comes over to my house every day and goes through my things. Our friendship grew more intimate, which is a good thing. When do you think that a man from the countryside and a man from the city can meet each other? I will tell you more when we meet. Good-bye.

The following are excerpts from *Danwon's Posthumous Works* and reflect similar feelings to the above letter.

Writing what comes to mind living in the mountains

Writing may catch the world by surprise, but can only be troublesome.
Wealth may hit the skies, but accumulating it is tiring.
Nothing can compare to a silent night in the mountains
Silently listening to the wind in the pine trees, smelling the incense.

I rub the ink stick, and the scent fills the room.
I pour water on the ink stone, and my face is reflected.

Birds visit my home every day not because of a special appointment
Wild flowers send off fragrances not because I planted them
Old man Danwon.

Look at a plum tree
Flowers are in blossom on the banks of the Han River.
I was not aware spring was already close by
Reminds me of a beautiful woman teasing beads.

What appointment hurries you into the green shades of the mountain?

These poems are all about distancing oneself from a hectic daily schedule and enjoying serene life as an old man.

The *yulsi* (eight-lined poem) on page 29 is probably Kim's own work.

Even when we were apart for a short while I missed you
But a true farewell tears up my heart inside.
The sunlight shines brightly upon us
A beautifully saddled horse awaits your departure to your chalbang office.
It will only be right to congratulate you on your way to Cheongha
But the place of farewell on the eastern fortress is very gloomy.
Upon your arrival, don't think too much about your parents who passed

away

Making your name as a competent officer will make them proud.

The reason the author mentioned that the above poem was probably written by Kim Hong-do himself is because of the words *chalbang* and Cheongha. *Chalbang* was the most common post awarded to the middle class, the class to which the court painters belonged. Kim mentions the parents who passed away whom he seems to have known when they were alive, and there are signs that he made corrections as he went along. We do not yet know to whom he was referring in the poem.

In this chapter we have looked at the writings in *Danwon's Posthumous Works*, but are still unable to gain an accurate picture of Kim Hong-do's life other than to conjecture that he led a busy life producing paintings for royal inspection. Naturally, he must have been affluent enough to support his refined lifestyle. Kim may also have influenced the appointments of his acquaintances. In his later years, he was likely to have lived peacefully in the countryside and distanced himself from his previously hectic lifestyle. Among the various aspects of his life, we were able to witness his sentimentality and failing health.

Chapter 3: Chronicle of the Life and Works of Kim Hong-do (1745– ca.1806)

The information on Kim Hong-do found to date is insufficient for vividly and concretely reconstructing his life, thoughts and emotions as an artist. He has no remaining *haengjang*[28] as is usually found for nobles. However, although the data about Kim is insufficient, there is more information about Kim Hong-do than for any other Joseon painter. This allows us to organize a rather detailed chronicle, which in turn indicates that Kim Hong-do was one of the greatest artists of the time.

1. Early Life – The Genius Court Painter

Kim Hong-do was born in 1745. According to Kang Se-hwang's *Danwongi*, Kim learned to paint from Kang when he was young. However, there is no record of how Kim came under the guidance of the noble, Kang Se-hwang. Nevertheless, since it is clear that Kang taught Kim, Kang's views on painting must have influenced Kim Hong-do, as is attested to in the aforementioned *Danwongi* and in *Danwongiuilbon*. Although it is believed that Kang Se-hwang helped Kim Hong-do to gain fame as a painter, Kim was already a highly renowned painter before 1773 when Kang began his career as a government official. Therefore, it is unlikely that Kang directly helped Kim advance his career as an artist.

28 A composition about the life and accomplishments of a deceased person.

The first record of Kim Hong-do's public life after he became an adult appears in 1765, when he was 21. It mentions that he painted 'Gyeonghyeon-dangsujakdo.' Originally, the painting was on a folding screen, but the painting was lost and only the script from two sides of the screen remains, now in the National Museum of Korea. The script on one of the two remaining sides reads:

> In 1765 when the king turned 72, His Majesty accepted a cup at Gyeonghyeondang on the 11th of the 10th lunar month...the king was sitting high on the throne, and his subjects were standing below in a line to honor the king. They enjoyed the food and drinks, the music of the banquet, and a dance to pray for longevity of the king. If this scene were not painted in color, the boundless respect paid to the king by his subjects and descendents, and their wishes for the king's longevity would be forgotten today. Since this auspicious occasion can be relived through this painting as if one were actually present, it proves that paintings are indispensable for such historic events. It is pointless to emphasize the importance of this since it is already a custom to make folding screens with paintings for national events... Therefore, the names of the painter and the calligrapher are recorded below, so that future generations can appreciate this occasion and gain detailed information.... The writing is the work of Kim Sang-bok, the sesonbu, and the painting is the work of Kim Hong-do, a court painter.

This text concerns King Yeongjo's Gyeonghyeon-dangsujak event on the 11th of the 10th lunar month of 1765 and appears in the record for the same day in *Yeongjosillok*.[29] In 1764, one year prior to this event, the 40th year of King Yeongjo's rule had coincided with the king's *mangpal*, seventy-first birthday celebration in expectation of the king reaching eighty years of age. The then Crown Prince (later, King Jeongjo) and high-ranking government officers had asked the king's permission several times to hold an event to mark the auspicious occasion. The Gyeonghyeondangsujak was particularly important, especially for the Crown Prince's political standing. The king had been asked five times before he agreed to the banquet. That Kim Hong-

29 The chronicle of King Yeongjo s reign.

do painted such an important painting for royal record when he was only 21 proves that he had been a highly regarded painter early in his career. This event was the first occasion that Kim painted for the future King Jeongjo.

In the spring of 1772, when Kim Hong-do turned 28, Bokheon Kim Eung-hwan, a senior painter, painted a small 'Full-view Painting of Mount Geumgang' for him. This painting is included in the preamble to *Bokheon and Baekhwa's Album*, an album of Hong Sin-yu (1722–ca. 1785). O Sechang wrote the following epilogue to the album.

> One day, Yu Ja-hu brought me this album in his sleeve. The 'Full-view Painting of Mount Geumgang' in the preamble was painted by Bokheon for Danwon, and the *Poem on Mount Geumgang* on the next page was written by Baekhwaja Hong Sin-yu at the request of Saneung. On the last page, there is another landscape painting, to which Bokheon added an inscription. This album brought me so much pleasure and I loved it so much that I was unable to close the book. The only painting of Bokheon that I have is a landscape painted on a folding fan, and it now flits through my mind like a shimmering cloud. Why do art lovers of the world know only Danwon Kim Hong-do but are in the dark about Bokheon Kim Eung-hwan, who was Kim Hong-do's teacher? People have seen only a few of Bokheon's works because he did not leave many paintings behind. He died before he turned 50.
>
> When Danwon was young, his pen name was Seoho, and Bokheon's other pen name was Damjoldang. As Seoho learned from Damjoldang, and his paintings were the equal of Chowon(焦園) Kim Seok-sin (1758–?), Damjoldang's son, he became known as Danwon (檀園), which became a highly renowned name later on. 'Full-view Painting of Mount Geumgang' is an extraordinary gem because it relates to the secret of painting, where the two great artists inspired each other. In addition, in 1788, during King Jeongjo's rule, 16 years after 1772, Bokheon implemented a royal order to paint a full view of Mount Geumgang. Later, Danwon also obeyed a royal instruction to paint a full view of Mount Geumgang. Considering their bond, this small work is an original

work of the two masterpieces. How precious this is! I asked Yu to give me the landscape painting attached at the end, and he obliged with pleasure. I hung it on the wall; I was deeply touched because my humble house suddenly became bright. Brief biographies of Baekhwa Hong Sin-yu, Bokheon Kim Eung-hwan and Danwon Kim Hong-do are included in *Geunyeokseohwajing*, an unworthy work of mine. As one can refer to it, I will not add details here.

> Wichang O Se-chang, a sick old man, writes on the 13th of the 5th lunar month in 1931.

This epilogue was written in 1931 at the request of Yu Ja-hu, a folklorist who owned the album at the time. However, the comments that Kim Hong-do was a disciple of Kim Eung-hwan and that the name Danwon was assumed by Kim Hong-do because his painting matched that of Kim Eung-hwan's son, Chowon Kim Seok-sin, are inaccurate. The problem seems to have arisen from O Se-chang's mistaken belief that Kim Hong-do was born in 1760. Since we now know that Kim was born in 1745, there is a 13-year age difference between Kim Hong-do and Kim Seok-sin, and only three years between Kim Hong-do and Kim Eung-hwan. This makes it hard to prove a master-disciple relationship between them. O Se-chang quoted *Genealogy of the Kims*, copies of which are not extant today, and commented:

> Kim Eung-hwan was famous for his paintings. In 1788, the twelfth year of King Jeongjo's rule, he obeyed a royal order to travel across Mount Geumgang and return with a painting of the mountain. The following year, he received another royal order to go to Japan and secretly draw a map, but he died in Busan at the age of 48. The young Kim Hong-do, who was accompanying him during the travel, handled the funeral, went to Tsushima Island alone, drew the map and returned to present it to the king.

The passage mentions "the young Kim Hong-do"; again, this arises from believing that Kim Hong-do was born in 1760. Another problem is the statement that Kim Eung-hwan first painted 'Full-view Painting of Mount Geumgang' by royal order in 1788 and that Kim Hong-do later obeyed a royal command to paint Mount Geumgang. According to revised data, the two artists went to paint Mount Geumgang together. Although there are some problems with the record, these are just a couple of the errors that stem from mistaking the year of Kim Hong-do's birth. Therefore, one cannot entirely dismiss the assertion that Kim Eung-hwan was Kim Hong-do's teacher, or that the two were to go to Tsushima Island in Japan through the southeastern part of Korea. This requires more study.

According to the *Imunjil* of the *Uigwe Record on Restoration Work of Yeonghuijeon* on the 28th of the 6th lunar month in the same year, Kim Hong-do and other painters are rewarded for their painting during the restoration work at Yeonghuijeon.

> On the 28th of the 6th lunar month in 1772, hojo[30] should make a report on this matter. [The king] ordered the relevant office to distribute rice and cloth to the workers and artisans who worked on the restoration work. According to the king's written command, the names and numbers of the workers and artisans should be put into a book. … There were 15 court painters including Kim Hong-do.

Kim Hong-do conducted similar general duties as a court painter with other court painters. The expression, "15 court painters including Kim Hong-do" implies that Kim Hong-do was the outstanding artist among court painters.

According to *King Hyeonjong-chujonho King Yeongjosajonho Sang-hodogam*[31] *uigwe*, Kim Hong-do worked with Byeon Sang-byeok, Kim Hu-sin, Kim Gwang-baek, Kim Deok-seong, Kim Eung-wi and Kim Kwan-sin on the 18th of the 11th lunar month. At the time, Kim Hong-do was the *busagwa*, who served as a court painter under the direction of the *ilbang*. He was rewarded with rice and cloth for his work. A *banchado*[32]

30 The Ministry of Finance.
31 A temporary office for naming posthumous titles for kings and queens.
32 A painting of the ceremonies and events in the court.

for the king was usually painted by the *ilbang*, who was in charge of recording important court ceremonies. It is assumed that Kim Hong-do was assigned to paint the *banchado*.

However, the last entry mentioning Kim Hong-do's name in the *uigwe* records related to the construction of buildings or events in the court appears in 1776, when he was 32. There is no extant data after that period. Although a future *uigwe* record may prove otherwise, one can surmise that from the time King Jeongjo ascended the throne in 1777, Kim Hong-do was exempt from many of the general court painter duties in recognition of his outstanding ability.

From the 7th to 22nd of the 1st lunar month in 1773, at the age of 29, Kim Hong-do participated in painting portraits of King Yeongjo, and King Jeongjo, who was the eldest grandson of King Yeongjo. The *gamjogwan*[33] was Kim Du-yeol, the chief painter was Byeon Sang-byeok, the associate painter was Kim Hong-do and the assistant painters were Sin Han-pyeong, Kim Hu-sin, Kim Gwan-sin and Jin Eung-bok. Kim Hong-do was promoted to *byeolje* of Saposeo[34] for his contribution. There is a related record in *The Diaries of the Royal Secretariat* on the 9th of the 1st lunar month in 1773:

> ... (The King) issued a royal ordinance. "...Let the painters Byeon Sang-byeok, Kim Hong-do, Sin Han-pyeong, Kim Hu-sin and Kim Gwan-sin be present today. Yesterday, I learned that Jin Jae-hae, previously recruited as a painter, has a son who is also a painter. Let Jin Eung-bok, a former *manho* [a military officer,] be present, too. Kim Gwan-sin and Jin Eung-bok shall be dressed in the official garb of military officers following the precedent of 1713.

On the 18th of the 1st lunar month in 1773,

> ...His Majesty said, "Allow in all officers and painters of Dogam."[35]...The painters, including Byeon Sang-byeok, Kim Hong-do, Kim Hu-sin, Jin Eung-

33 The same as *gamdongyeok* or *gamyeokgwan*; a temporary post given to an officer responsible for the timely completion of national projects or public works.

34 The office in charge of fruit and vegetable cultivation for the royal palace.

35 A temporary office governing royal events.

> bok and Sin Han-pyeong, entered one after another and prostrated themselves before His Majesty. ...Several painters finished painting a dragon on a mat...

On the 22nd of the 1st lunar month in 1773,

> ...His Majesty said, "Byeon Sang-byeok, who painted the king, shall be promoted according to custom. Without him, today's accomplishment would not have been possible. Because he served as *cheomsa*, he shall be appointed *suryeong* when the position becomes available. Kim Hu-sin is the son of Kim Hui-seong, who showed some accomplishment in 1748, and fortunately, participated in the work as an assistant painter. Since he already served as *chalbang*, he shall be promoted to *suryeong* following the example of Kim Hui-seong. Kim Hong-do, Sin Han-pyeong and Kim Gwan-sin shall be appointed as either civil or military officers when the positions become available. Whose son is Jin Eung-bok? Since he served as *manho*, he shall be appointed as *cheomsa* when the position is available. Deliver my order to the relevant office to distribute rice and cotton cloth to the workers and artisans.

In the 8th lunar month, Kim Hong-do painted 'A Taciturn Man (plate 31), his earliest extant dated painting. This painting has not survived in good condition. The uppermost inscription includes the comment: "Kang Se-hwang writes this for Jwacheongheon," who is none other than Haejwanoin Jeong Beom-jo—for Jwacheongheon is the name of his *jaesil*[36] in Dangu-li, Wonju.

In 1774, at the age of 30, Kim Hong-do was included in the record of personnel appointments dated 20th of the 5th lunar month, although he was not actually promoted.

> ...For the post of Uiyeonggo[37] *jubu*, Jojiseo[38] Byeolje Kang Hui-eon was nominated as the most qualified candidate, Binggo[39] Byeolje Lee U-chang was the second most qualified, and Jangwonseo[40] Byeolje Kim Hong-do was the third most qualified. The first candidate was appointed to the post....

36 A house where Confucian scholars studied or performed ancestral rites.
37 The office that supervised the procurement and management of cooking oil, honey, wheat, vegetable and pepper.
38 The office responsible for manufacturing paper.
39 The office responsible for storing and distributing ice.
40 The office that oversaw the royal gardens.

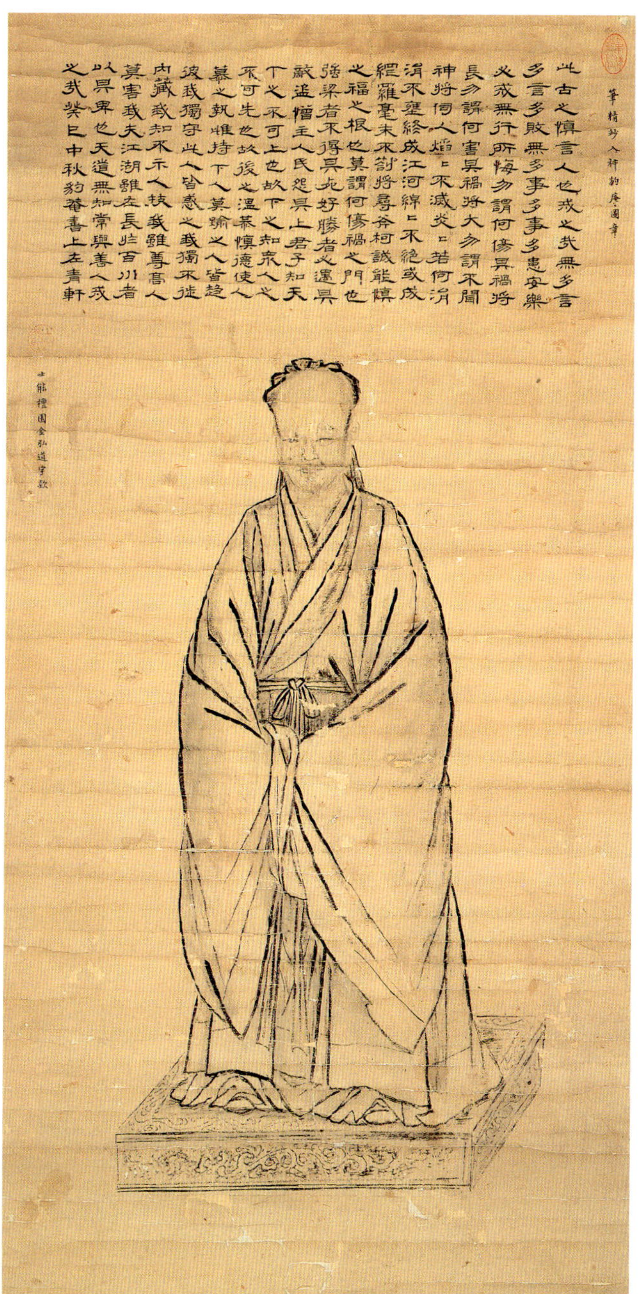

31 *A Taciturn Man*

1773. Ink on paper. 114.8×57.6cm. National Museum of Korea.

This is the earliest extant dated work by Kim Hong-do. The inscription by Kang Se-hwang is written in official script following the calligraphic style of the epitaph on the tombstone of Cao Quan, of the Han Dynasty. The figure standing on the platform is holding his own hands with his lips sealed. Since this painting depicts a verbally discreet man from an earlier time, the brush stroke was carefully done with dignity; a barely moist brush was moved slowly with some pressure, and there were no superfluous changes. Although both the painting and paper are in poor condition, the work is interesting, includes rare official scripts by Kang Se-hwang, and shows Kim s relationship with Jeong Beom-jo, the owner of the painting.

According to this record, Kang Hui-eon, the most qualified candidate, was appointed to the post, and Kim Hong-do at the time was Jangwonseo *byeolje*. The following record by Kang Se-hwang indicates that Kim was appointed to Saposeo as *byeolje* of *jong 6 pum* for his contribution to painting the royal portrait.

> Nearing the end of his reign, King Yeongjo ordered his portrait painted. Talented portrait painters were selected for the job, and Kim Hong-do was the right talent. When Kim was rewarded for his contribution, he was appointed to the post of supplying food to the royal court. As I was working as a government officer, we became colleagues. Although I once regarded him as a child, we were now on the same footing. However, I did not intend to make light of him, and Kim was deferentially polite to me and told me that he felt honored just to work with me. I admired his humility.

Recently, the dates when Kim Hong-do the student and Kang Se-hwang the teacher were appointed as Saposeo *byeolje* were confirmed. Kim Hong-do's appointment is recorded as of the 14th of the 10th lunar month, in 1774.

> ...For the post of Saposeo *byeolje*, Jangwonseo Byeolje Kim Hong-do was nominated as the most qualified candidate, Binggo Byeolje Kim Rak-jo was the second most qualified, and Waseo[41] Byeolje Park Chung-haeng was the third most qualified. The first candidate was appointed to the post. ...

Kang Se-hwang appears in the record of personnel appointments dated the 27th of the 12th lunar month in 1774, about two and a half months after Kim's appointment.

> ...For the post of Saposeo *byeolje*, Kang Se-hwang was nominated as the most qualified candidate, Lee Se-pil as the second most qualified, and Min Eun as the third most qualified. The first candidate was appointed to the post.

41 The office that procured the bricks and roofing tiles used in government construction projects.

By "a post of supplying food to the royal court," Kang Se-hwang meant that Saposeo was in charge of managing the farms and vegetable cultivation for the royal court. Kang Se-hwang's writing provides a glimpse of Kim Hong-do's everyday life with his teacher at Saposeo.

> I became a colleague of Kim's when I was a feeble old man at Saposeo. Kim went out of his way to do hard work for me out of compassion for my infirmity. This I will never forget. These days, those who get a hold of Kim's paintings come to me and ask for a couple of phrases for an inscription. Even some folding screens or scrolls in the royal court have my inscription on the back. One might say that Kim and I have a friendship that surpasses age and position.

This indicates that Kim Hong-do was a careful and courteous young man, and clearly explains why many of Kim's works bear the inscriptions by Kang.

While there is no record of Kim for 1775, in the spring of 1776, when Kim Hong-do turned 32, he painted an eight-paneled folding screen named 'Immortals' (Plate 32). This painting shows the young Kim's dynamic brushstrokes.

On the 5th of the 3rd lunar month in the same year, King Yeongjo died. For the national funeral of the king on the 6th of the 5th lunar month, Kim painted a decoration on the cloth, which covered the king's coffin.

> In addition, King Jeongjo issued a royal ordinance to Hong Guk-yeong to have Sin Han-pyeong, Kim Hong-do and Kim Hu-sin stand ready to paint the decoration on the cloth for His Majesty's coffin.

This is the first recorded instance of King Jeongjo assigning Kim Hong-do to participate in an official painting. On this occasion, Kim did not paint a full-scale picture, but painted only patterns including an ax-shaped one,

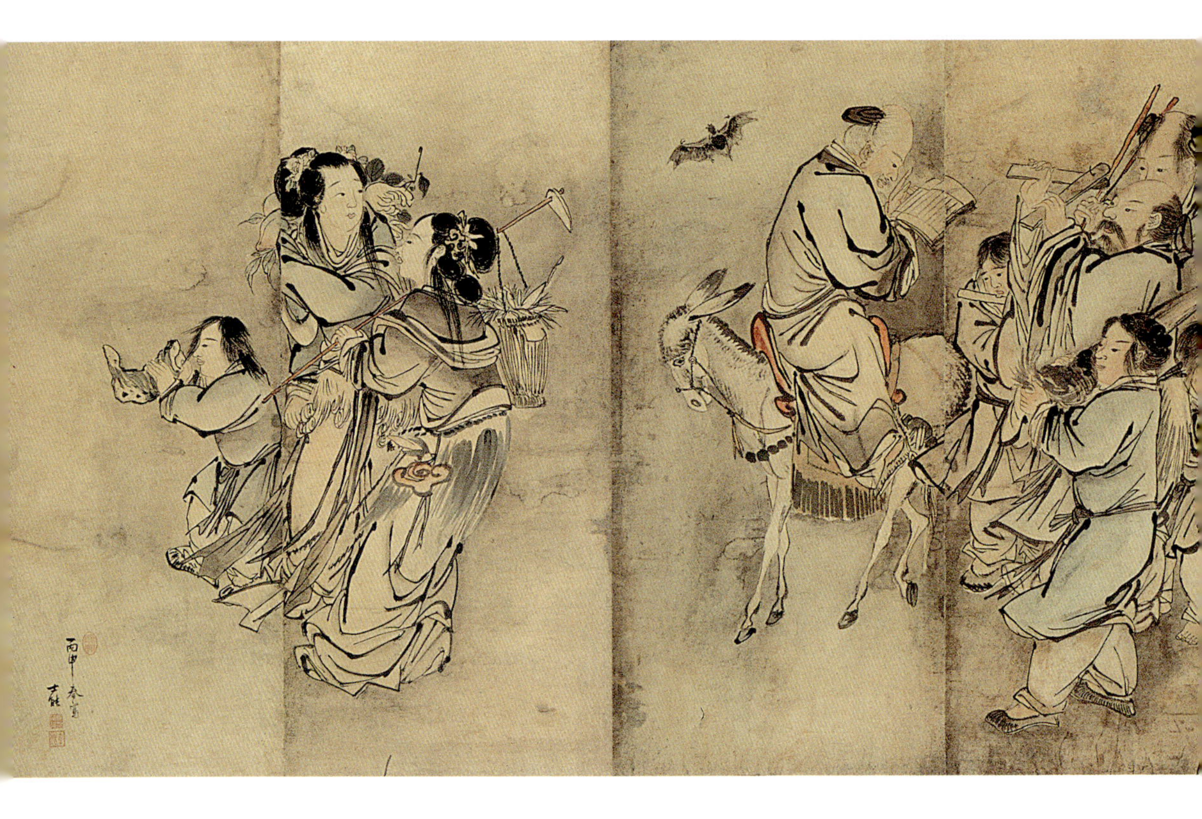

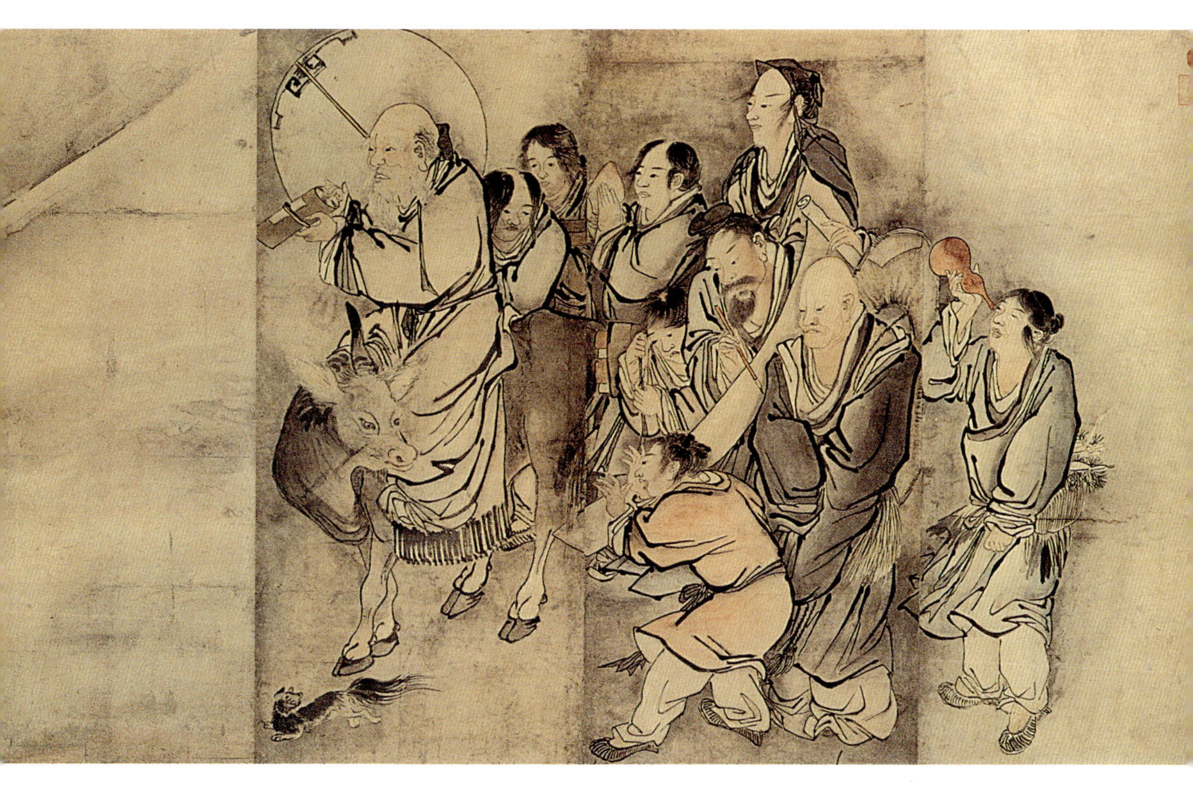

32 *Immortals*

1776. Ink and color on paper. 132.8×575.8cm. Hoam Art Museum.

The drawing depicts Taoist figures from ancient Chinese tales and includes the eight immortals (Li Tieguai, Zhongli Quan, Lan Caihe, Zhang Guolao, He Xianggu, Lu Dongbin, Han Xianzi and Cao Guojiu) with Laozi, Dongfangshuo and Wenchang on their way to a birthday banquet for Xi Wang Mu, the powerful Taoist goddess. The young Kim Hong-do s strength is felt at the points where the brush stroke starts, curves and ends.

33 *Gyujanggak*
1776. Ink and color on silk. 144.4×115.6cm. National Museum of Korea.
The large two-story building in the center consists of the Gyujanggak on the first floor and the Juhapru on the second floor. King Jeongjo ordered the construction of the Dogam just one day after ascending the throne in order to make Gyujanggak the center of academics and politics. The peak in the background is Eungbong, the mountain behind Changdeok Palace, and reflects the style of landscape painting of Gyeomjae Jeong Seon. Repaired many times, the elegance and dignity of the original painting have been considerably damaged.

symbolizing the king, on the cloth for the coffin. Kim Hong-do, Sin Han-pyeong and Kim Hu-sin had all participated in painting the king's portrait in 1773.

Around the 7th lunar month, Kim painted 'Gyujanggak' (Plate 33) at the direction of King Jeongjo. Immediately after ascending the throne on the 10th of the 3rd lunar month, King Jeongjo issued an ordinance to build Gyujanggak, a royal library, to house King Yeongjo's literary works. Based on the king's haste during a period of mourning, one can assume that King Jeongjo had built Gyujanggak according to his grand plan to use it as the central axis for conducting state affairs. The young Kim Hong-do's painting of Gyujanggak is further evidence of King Jeongjo's longstanding patronage of Kim Hong-do and Kim's status among court painters. In addition, the mountains in the picture hint at the influence of Gyeomjae Jeong Seon and reveal Kim's practice of techniques that he had used when he was younger.

Throughout the year of 1777, when Kim Hong-do was 33, he was commissioned to paint public and private paintings together with his colleagues Sin Han-pyeong, Kim Eung-hwan, Lee In-mun, Han Jong-il and Lee Jong-hyeon at Kang Hui-eon's house in Jungbudong. According to *A Record of a Life Time of Worries and Happiness* by Ma Seong-rin (1727–ca. 1798):

> In 1777, reputable painters, including Byeolje Kim Hong-do, Manho Sin Han-pyeong, Jubu Kim Eung-hwan, Jubu Lee In-mun, Jubu Han Jong-il and Jubu Lee Jong-hyeon gathered together at Mokgwan Kang Hui-eon's house to paint commissioned paintings, many of which were worthy of appreciation. As an art lover, I would visit the house from spring to winter to savor the pictures and write some inscriptions.

The aforementioned text confirms that, at the time, Kim Hong-do was *byeolje,* and that he was acquainted with Ma Seong-rin, who frequented the house to appreciate the paintings and write inscriptions. In addition, it is very interesting to note that court painters gathered at a house to work on

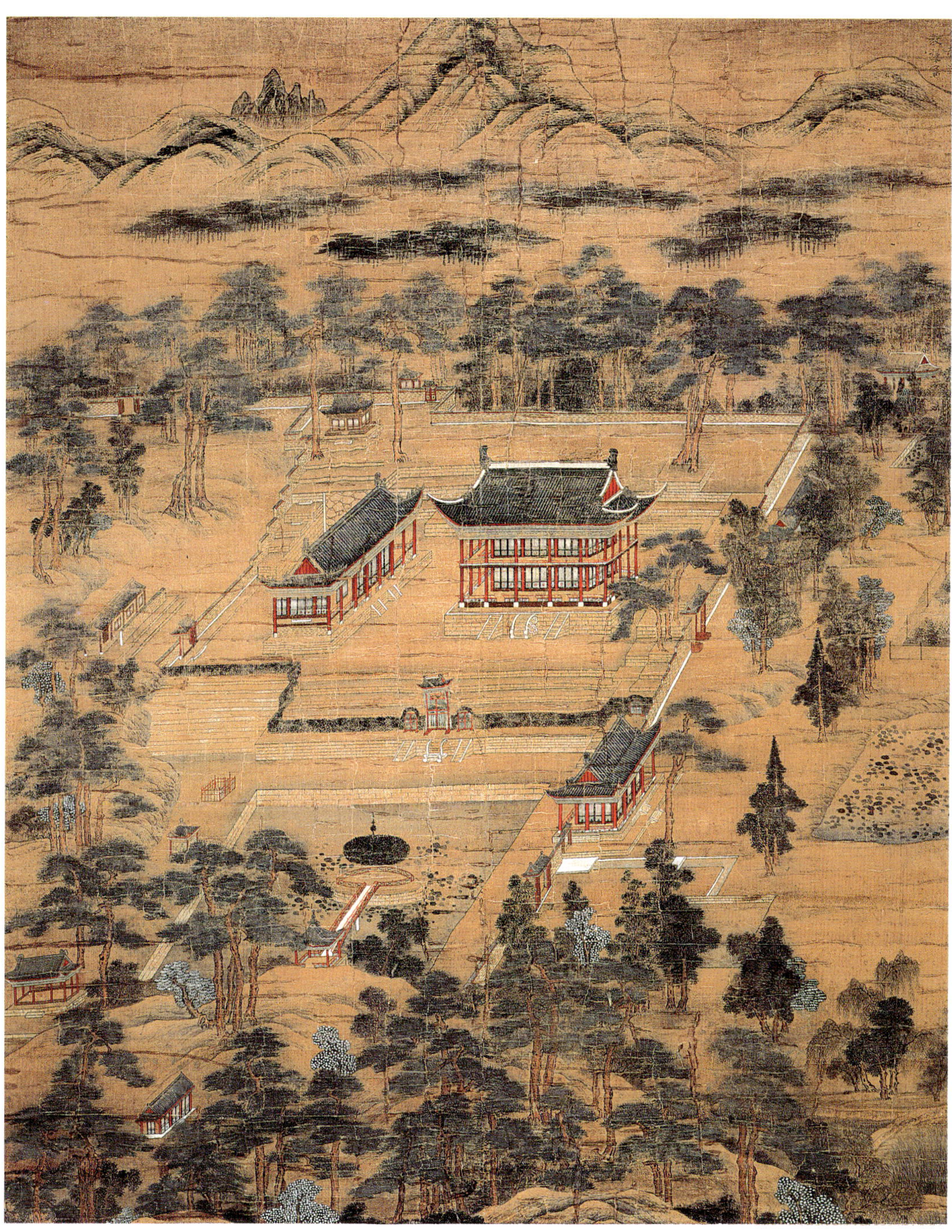

paintings. Significantly, the text indicates that there was a considerable demand for paintings because the court painters worked publicly and privately throughout the year. By working in the same place, they were probably able to learn from one another, compare the strengths and weaknesses of their paintings and exchange ideas on their works. The signature affixed to 'Haengryeopungsokdo,' which was painted the next year, reads "Painted by Saneung at Damjolheon in the 4th lunar month in 1778." This suggests that this gathering of the painters continued into early summer of the next year (Plate 34).

In the 4th lunar month in 1778, when Kim Hong-do was 34, he painted 'The Gathering of Four Taoist Immortals' on a folding fan for Ma Seong-rin, who had the following thoughts on the painting.

> There are three grades of supremacy in paintings: God-like, Masterly, and Talented. The landscape paintings of Gyeomjae Jeong Seon are rare works of God; the flower and bird paintings of Sim Sa-jeong reveal the masterly hand of the painter and are equal to those of the Tang Dynasty. In addition, Kim Saneung's Taoist, Buddhist, and genre paintings are lifelike; his talent is sent from above. In the spring of 1778, Saneung painted me a unique picture on a fan. Four Taoist hermits are together below a rough rock. One old hermit is sleeping against the rock and the remaining three face one another with their garments spread while a young monk's head droops because he is about to fall asleep. The other young monk is boiling tea and facing the steam from the teapot. The characters in the painting, old and young, show various poses. In the basket are mushrooms, and on the plate are peaches while a crane hovers near the steaming tea. This beautiful scene and its unique presentation place the painting at the summit of Kim's art world. I admired it so much that I attached it to a small folding screen so that I can spend my old age appreciating the picture while lying on my pillow.

The detailed description allows for vivid visualization of 'The Gathering of Four Taoist Immortals.' It is noteworthy that Ma cited Taoist, Buddhist,

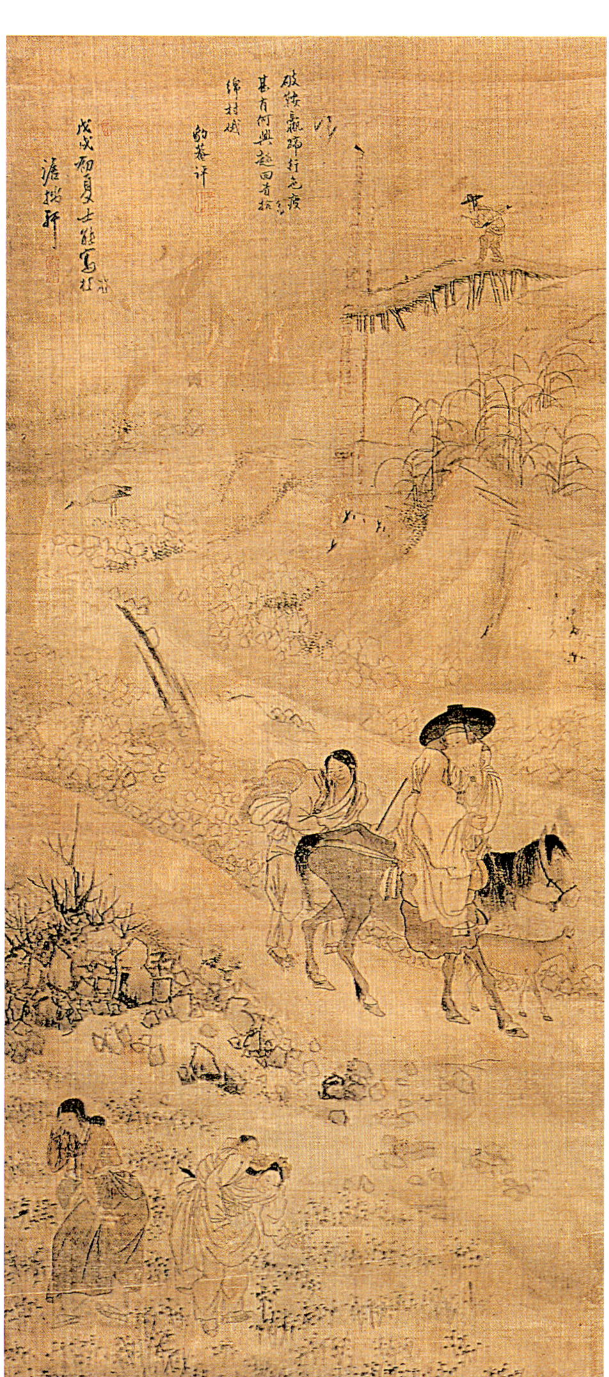

34 *Mirthful on the Worn Saddle* from *Haengryeop-ungsokdo*

1778. Ink and color on silk. 90.9×42.7cm. National Museum of Korea.

Although Kim Hong-do is most famous for his genre paintings, only a few such works still survive. This painting, containing the year it was painted, is in reasonably good condition except that the screen is rather dark. The inscription by Kang Se-hwang is interesting: Riding on a mangy horse with a worn saddle, the man looks very shabby. But, turning his attention to the woman picking cotton, how mirthful he is! As described, the rider is not even close to elegant: his thin horse is accompanied by a suckling foal. However, although he is shyly hiding his face with his fan, he keenly looks at the woman.

and genre paintings as Kim's best work. Although Ma states that he loves Kim Hong-do's work, a closer examination of the text suggests that he tacitly underestimated Kim's painting. In the traditional grading of painting ability–god-like, masterly and talented–Kim Hong-do was rated talented; the third grade. This is amplified in his work, *Written in the Back of Immocheop during my Illness for Hwasanja Gangjung Kim Deok-hyeong.*

> The landscape paintings of Gyeomjae Jeong Seon show dynamic dots and strokes at their best and are rare works of God. In addition, he was well versed in the *Book of Changes* and astronomy in addition to calligraphy. The brushstrokes of Sim Sa-jeong are elegant and mysterious and put him on an equal footing with artists of the Tang Dynasty. However, although his work is a masterpiece, it does not reach the virtuosity of Gyeomjae, the great artist. While there may be people whose techniques are good, I know of no painter who shows several talents at the same time....

Kim Deok-hyeong was a low-ranking officer in Gyujanggak and good at poetry, prose and paintings, especially of flowers. Ma Seong-rin highly praised his splendid *Immocheop* and his virtuosity in many kinds of art. Ma also comments again on the three grades of painting and praises Kim Hong-do by saying: "While there may be people whose techniques are good, I know of no painter who shows several talents at the same time." It is clear that Ma's high praise of Jeong Seon was because Jeong Seon was Ma's teacher. Although Ma noted, "Kim Saneung's Taoist, and Buddhist, and genre paintings are lifelike; his talent is sent from above," he ranked Kim as having the least of the three grades of painting ability. This requires further study.

In the 4th lunar month in 1778, at Damjol Kang Hui-eon's house, Kim Hong-do painted an eight-paneled folding screen entitled 'Haengryeopungsokdo,' which was representative of Kim's genre paintings (Plate 34). At the bottom of the painting, it reads, "In the 4th lunar month in 1778, Saneung painted at Damjolheon", another comment confirming Kim's close friendship with Kang Hui-eon.

On a rainy summer day the same year, Kim Hong-do painted 'The Gathering in the Western Garden' ('Seowon-ajipdo'; Plate 35), a folding fan painting for Lee Yong-nul. However, Kang Se-hwang's long inscription on the painting was written in the 7th lunar month of the previous year. Consequently, it seems that for some reason Kim must have painted the fan a year after the inscription was written. Although the name, "Yong-nul," in the inscription also appears on a folding screen painted the following year (1779), in 'Taoist Immortals' (Plate 38), the Yong-nul to whom it refers is unknown.

In the 12th lunar month of the same year, Kim Hong-do painted 'The Gathering in the Western Garden' on a six-paneled folding screen (Plate 36). Kang Se-hwang's inscription is again noteworthy.

35 *The Gathering in the Western Garden*
1778. Ink and color on paper. 26.9×81.2cm. National Museum of Korea.
The inscription was written in the 7th lunar month of 1777; the picture was painted on a rainy day in the summer of the following year. Kim probably received Kang Se-hwang s inscription first, but the completion of the work was delayed despite a longstanding promise. The figures are supposed to be Chinese gentlemen, but they look Korean.

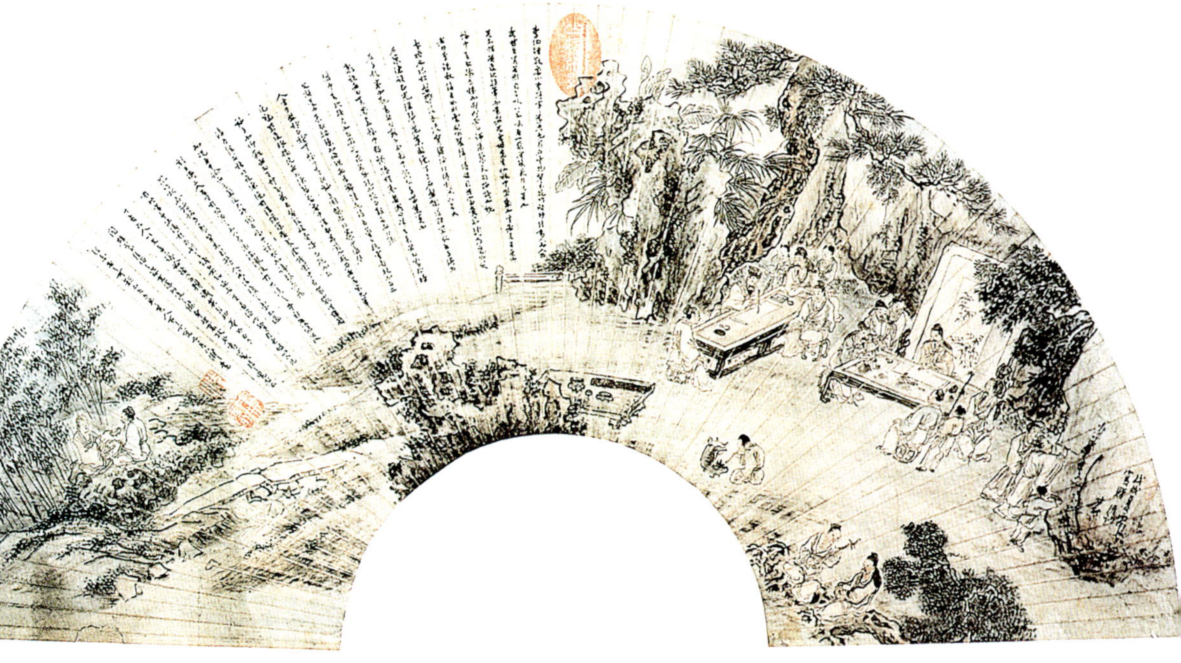

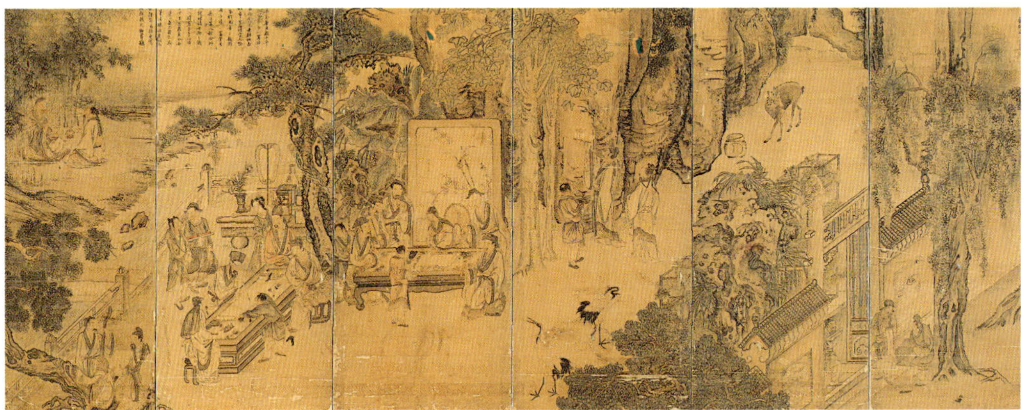

36 *The Gathering in the Western Garden*
1778. Ink and color on silk. 122.7×287.4cm. National Museum of Korea.
This is a graceful painting of figures from an old story, painted with a hair pencil on fine silk. Therefore, it is highly likely that it was painted for the royal court. The brushwork is strict and refined. Kim Hong-do s name is written in regular script. Kang Sehwang s inscription is dignified.

I have seen scores of different *ajipdo*, but the one by the renowned Chinese artist Chou Ying was the best. Since the rest were trivial, I did not bother to write about all of them. Now that I see this painting of Kim Hong-do, I find the brushstrokes exquisite and elegant and the composition appropriate. In addition, the characters are lifelike. The scene wherein Mi Fu is writing on the cliff, Li Gonglin is painting and Su Shi is writing poetry reveals that Kim Hong-do understood the true meaning of *ajipdo*. Each character in the painting is truly lifelike. He must have gained this talent through either a spiritual awakening or a gift from God. Kim Hong-do's painting is much better than Chou Ying's fragile work and is on a par with Li Gonglin's original. Joseon is lucky to have such a magnificent painter. My writing falls short of that of Mi Fu, and I only damn Kim with faint praise. I cannot escape the blame of others. Pyoam writes the inscription in the last month of the year.

'The Gathering in the Western Garden' was originally an old Chinese story, and was extant in Kim's day. However, as Kang Se-hwang noted, Kim did not copy the original but created a masterpiece in his own style. Note that Kang deemed Kim's work better than the Chinese original.

At the age of 35 in the early part of the 8th lunar month, 1779, Kim Hong-do asked Hong Sin-yu, a friend, for a poem. Hwiji Hong Sin-yu writes for Kim in *Bokheon and Baekhwa's Album* as follows:

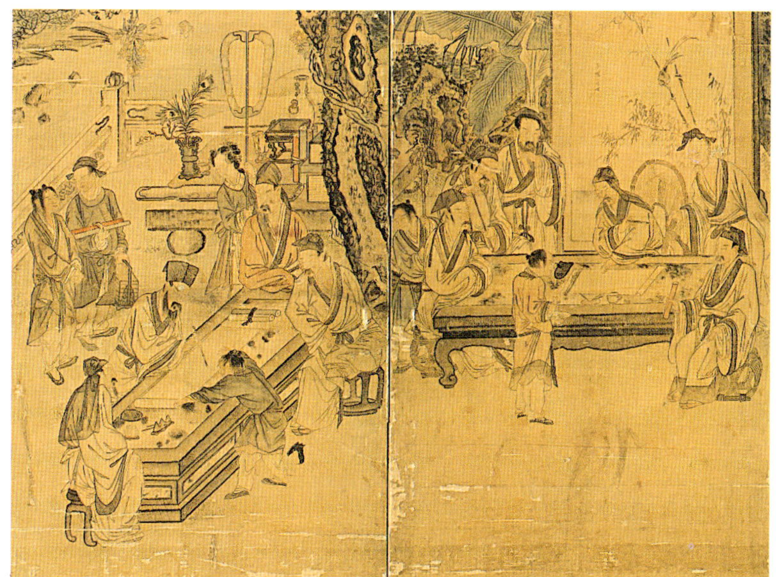

37 Detail of Plate 36
This depicts Wang Jinqing, the son-in-law of the king of Northern Sung, enjoying himself in his Western Garden with the most knowledgeable noblemen, Taoist Immortals and Buddhist monks of the time. Li Gonglin is painting on the right side, and Su Shi is writing calligraphy on the left side. Perhaps Kim Hong-do drew himself as Li.

> Kim Saneung gained fame for his art before he turned 30. One might say that his gift is a godsend. Furthermore, he was very tall and handsome. He did not look like a mortal; that is also true of his paintings. I was as fond of him and his paintings as he was of my poems and writing. However, although my affection for poetry and calligraphy began in my youth and has only increased as my hair grayed, my manual dexterity has not correspondingly increased. I assume that is because my talent and innate disposition are limited. Nevertheless, albeit crude, there are some works worth appreciating because I have studied diligently for a long time. Since Saneung asked me for inscriptions and poems for this album when I was about to return to the southern province forever, I am briefly writing for him before I depart. Written by Hong Hwiji in early 8th lunar month 1779.

Using the pen name Baekhwaja, Hong Sin-yu was a famous commoner poet. He was renowned as a calligrapher and is particularly highly esteemed as a poet even today. He usually painted the routine life of urban workers, in addition to the history, culture and customs of Joseon. His poetic style conforms to the so-called Poetry of Joseon or Joseon style of Park

Ji-won (1737–1805) and Jeong Yak-yong (1762–1836). His work defies imitation, seeking unique characteristics, the centers of which are spirited and realistic landscapes. These characteristics correspond to Kim Hong-do's genre paintings. One can assume from Hong's comment, "He was [fond] of my poems and writing," that Hong influenced Kim. This, again, requires further study.

Although Hong Sin-yu was a member of the bureaucracy, he was transfered from petty office to petty office because he was the son of an interpreter. After his patrons, the Won brothers (Inson and Gyeson) died, he abandoned hopes of advancing his career in the government, and in 1779, he left for Dongrae in Gyeongsang Province. Kim Hong-do made the aforementioned *Bokheon and Baekhwa's Album* as a memento for Hong Sin-yu by collecting Hong's poems. The 'Mount Geumgang' painting that Kim Eung-hwan painted for Kim Hong-do in 1772 and another landscape painting decorate the front and back of the book. Within the book lies *The Poem on Mount Geumgang,* written by Hong Sin-yu that reminisces about his, travel in the mountain the same year; nine *yulsi* with seven Chinese characters in each line; and a poem composed of numerous verses with five Chinese characters per line that Hong wrote, recollecting Won Gye-son. *The Poem on Mount Geumgang* is a long poem with 124 rhymes and 5 Chinese characters in each line. If Kim Hong-do were not able to appreciate this masterpiece, Hong Sin-yu would not have written it for him. Hong Sin-yu's remark that Kim Hong-do loved his poems and calligraphy supports this hypothesis and provides indirect evidence of Kim Hong-do's literary talent. Hong Sin-yu, the poet, met Kim Hong-do again and exchanged poems with him in 1784, when Kim was appointed *chalbang* in Angi.

In *Bokheon and Baekhwa's Album* Hong Sin-yu writes, "Kim Hong-do gained fame for his art before he turned 30." This is an important comment regarding Kim's youth because records are insufficient.

In the 10th lunar month of 1779, Kim painted 'Taoist Immortals' on an eight-paneled folding screen (Plate 38). The following is the inscription.

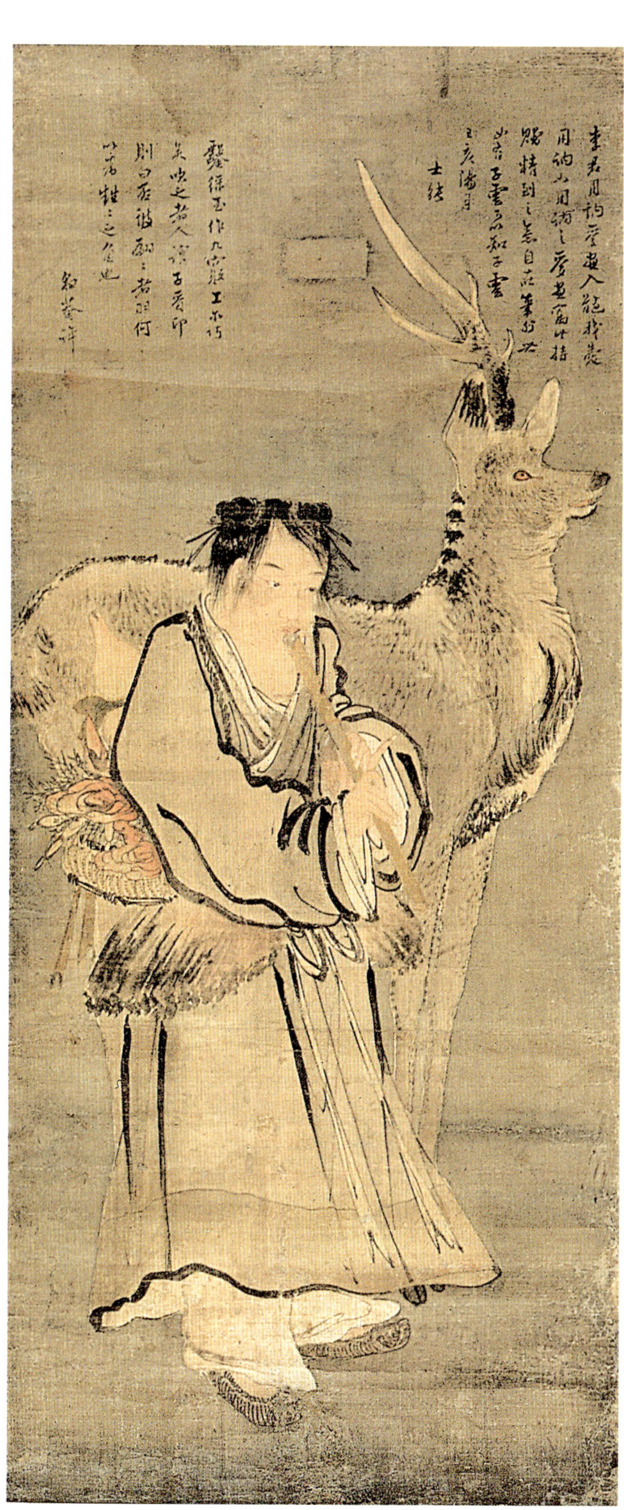

38 *A Taoist Immortal Plays the Flute* from *Taoist Immortals*

1779. Ink and color on silk. 130.7×57.6cm. National Museum of Korea.

Kang Se-hwang s inscription reads, Nine holes are made in blue jade with great deftness. They say that the man playing the flute is Wang Ziqiao, but I don t think so. The name of the Immortal is unknown today. However, the boy playing the flute is definitely a Joseon lad, with his wide face, broad forehead and bright eyes. In addition, the contour of the wrinkles in his clothes suggests the rhythms of old Joseon songs. In other words, the stress imposed on the brushwork in the beginning is comparable to the Hapjangdan (strong beat) of Korean music, and the rhythmically thicker and thinner lines match the traditional melodies of Korea.

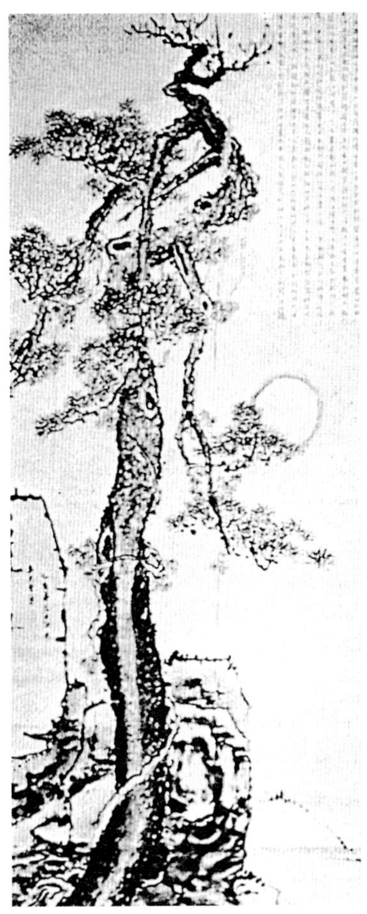

39 *A Pine Tree and the Moon*
1779. Material, size and collector unknown.
The painting, done when Kim was young, is based on Eo Yong-bin s dream. He said that the pine tree and the moon in his dream symbolized himself and that he had felt as though he were not in this world while he looked at the lonely landscape. As if the dream were a prophecy, he passed away soon after. Although the tall, exuberant tree in the bright moonlight exudes the grace typical of Kim s pines, the details are quite different. The bark is very detailed, and the twigs are meticulously expressed. It has long been noted that the flat lines and small dots on the rocks at the bottom are similar to those in Lee In-sang s paintings. The full moon conspicuously hangs in the center.

Lee-Gun's love for painting is bred in the bone. I admire Yong-nul as much as he loves paintings. I painted this for Yong-nul. The most exquisite meanings are beyond pen and ink. Only in the presence of Yang Xiong can people understand Yang Xiong. The 10th lunar month of 1779, Saneung.

Lee Yong-nul was given 'The Gathering in the Western Garden' (Plate 35), which was painted on a rainy summer day in 1778. Judging from Kim's calling him Lee-Gun,[42] Lee was probably younger than Kim, and Yong-nul was Lee's courtesy name. The warm feelings that can be read between the lines indicate that they were very close friends. Unfortunately, Lee's identity is unconfirmed.

In the same year, Kim Hong-do painted 'A Pine Tree and the Moon' (Plate 39). It is said of this masterpiece that one actually feels its subtle elegance. Although I have not personally seen it, I have carefully reviewed the background literature. In *Geumseokjip* by Park Jun-won (1739–1807; pen name Geumseok), who sired Subin Park (a royal concubine) and was the grandfather of King Sunjo on his mother's side, is *The Eulogy on 'A Pine Tree and the Moon' Owned by Eo Yong-bin* [1737–1781], which reads as follows:

Is that a pine tree, which is dark-green and straight? Is that the moon so calm and round? Pine needles like disheveled hair cover the brook in the ravine, while the moon is about to rise to brighten the sky. Why is it on the wall in Gyeongguk's [courtesy name of Eo Yong-bin] room? Since Gyeongguk sees this all the time, but never realizes that it is from his dream, how does he know that it is a painting? The dark green [pine tree] will become darker over the years, and the calm [moon] will shine brightly. The tree will rise from the ground to soar forcefully like the torso of a dragon, and the moon will hang about the empty sky to shine brightly. Can Gyeongguk do that? The dust of the mundane world cannot shroud the clouds and fog or the immense sky. Frost and snow cannot squelch thunder and lightning from on high. Grind and wipe it, so that it can shine on everything in this world. Grow it well, so that it can stay the same throughout the four seasons!

Park Jun-won explains the background to this eulogy, thereby revealing that the painting is by Kim Hong-do.

Since he was young, my friend Gyeongguk has been renowned for his refined taste and good-heartedness. However, in his old age he locked himself inside his house, which is in a deep alley, and read the words of sages. I lived next door to Gyeongguk and befriended him. One day, Gyeongguk pointed at 'A Pine Tree and the Moon' on the wall and told me, "This is my dream. I dreamt that I went deep into the mountain and found a pine tree rising high from a precipitous cliff as the moon shone on it. I caressed the tree with my hands, looked up at the moon and occasionally looked around, but it was quiet, and I was the only one on the mountain. I woke from the dream, and this was always at the back of my mind. When I came across Chwihwasa Kim Hong-do, I asked him to paint my dream, which I hung on the wall. Although I am standing right here, I may still be wandering in my dream. Pyeongsuk, [Park Jun-won's courtesy name] why don't you write something for me?" I said, "Why not? Your dream is quite extraordinary and deserves to be recorded." I came home to write a eulogy and had the inscription added to the painting. Upon reflection, I thought this was a strange dream because he said that the pine tree and the moon were the embodiment of himself from his former life. Since this implies that he wanted to get out of this dirty and muddy world and return to heaven where everything is clean and clear, I felt very sad and chilled. Gyeongguk died soon after that, and I have traveled around the country for the past 10 years. Since Gyeongguk's house has changed hands several times, I do not know whether the painting and eulogy are

42 Gun(君) is a Korean equivalent of mister used only for a younger addressee.

still there. Every moonlit night, I tarried outside and stroked old pine trees as if I were seeing Gyeongguk. Finally, I wrote this after the *Eulogy on "A Pine Tree and the Moon.'*

The mystic motif of this work is such that even a photograph of the painting projects the elegance of the Chinese Southern School of painting. Lee Dong-ju noted that this painting is similar to Lee In-sang's style. This is the earliest dated work of Kim Hong do's that followed the Chinese Southern School. The text also indicates that in 1779, Kim Hong-do was known as Chwihwasa.

We have no record of Kim Hong-do's activities for the following year, 1780, when he turned 36. However, it is possible that as a court painter, he accompanied the envoy to Ching to congratulate the emperor Qianlong on his 70th birthday. This speculation is based on the following poem by Jeong Yak-yong: *On 'A Taoist Immortal Riding on a Turtle that Makes Rain.'*

Never heard of a Taoist hermit riding on the back of a turtle,
There is no such comment in the Taoist book of Yuchu under the rule of Emperor Wu of the Han Dynasty.
Yeonam Park Ji-won wrote a strange account of his trip to China.
This story was painted by Danwon Kim Hong-do.
It is summer in the well-shaded mountain villa of the Emperor.
Blue palace, yellow curtain, glass-like tiles
With the sound of a whip, each one goes back from where they stood
The large garden is like a green, green field.
An old man with hair like flowers comes out riding on the back of a turtle
Green eyes, red cheeks, beautiful face
Yellow summer jacket with black lining, and red leather belt
A calabash fastened on and a peach held in one hand.
He carries a bamboo stick bound with five-color threads with his left hand
A fan in his right hand is as large as his hand.

The pace of the turtle is not so fast that the turtle moves like a comfortable carriage.

It makes a round around the garden holding up its head all the time,

Spouts water up into the sky, which makes a rainbow,

Calls out a fine rain in the broad daylight and makes the surroundings dim

Flying water drops splatter lightly to wet the stone.

A sudden rain pours and reaches the windows.

The pouring rain becomes stronger and the sound of it is clamorous.

The raindrops falling from the eaves are rapid like waterfalls, and ditch water runs fast.

The sunshine at dusk diffuses itself through half of the lattice window.

The hanging screen made of crystal beads shines dizzily

The eaves of the palace are soaked with rain so that my room becomes humid

The trees of the palace are clean as if bathed with water and shed their remaining water drops.

The stone steps and gardens are all washed so that they look flat as if ironed

He entered inside the embroidered curtains, riding on a turtle.

This scene was too charming to be described in detail

As the world goes the wrong way and public morals become corrupt, worries become stronger

Confucius did not talk about mysterious powers because it would not be instrumental to learning

While magical transformations occur in great numbers, who could stop them?

Spewing fire and swallowing the knife are so artless that I hate them

Calling out a rainstorm makes me deplore the reasons of everyday life

Men do not control ghosts, but ghosts control men

Stupid people surrounding the wall wonder at the trickery.

Jeong Yak-yong wrote, "The one who painted this interesting painting was Kim Hong-do." Furthermore, there is another text on the same subject matter entitled *A Taoist Immortal Riding on a Turtle that Makes Rain in Yeolhailgi*, comprising some travel sketches by Park Ji-won, who joined the envoy in 1780.

> We went into the summer mountain villa on the fourteenth. We saw the emperor behind yellow curtains in a deep corner of the royal palace. There were few people in the court, but there was one old man in the center of the court. He was wearing a Taoist garment, yellow summer jacket and black upper garment with wide sleeves. The hem and sleeves were lined with black cloth, the waist was tied with a red silk belt that flapped, and the shoes were red. He had a gray beard so long that it reached his chest. He held a stick decorated with a golden calabash and a silk cord and carried a fan in his right hand. He was touring the garden and standing on the back of a big turtle that lifted its head and spouted water like rainbow. The turtle was dark-blue and as large as a bathing tub. At first, it spouted fine rain to wet the eaves and hollows of the royal palace so that fine water drops were flying all over, and gathering like fog, or scattering towards the flowerpots, or spraying the artificial mountain in the court. After a while, the rain became stronger, and the water ran down the eaves like monsoon rain; the corner of the palace was shining with the diffused sunlight as if it were a screen made of crystal beads. The water on the yellow tiles began to run fast. The eastern leaves of the hill became brighter and more splendid. Water filled the garden as if it was pouring. Then they retreated inside the right side of the curtain. Scores of eunuchs swept away the water in the court with large bamboo brooms. Even if the turtle had a hundred *seom*[43] of water in the stomach, it would have been impossible to soak a court like this. Furthermore, as they did not let the rain soak the people, their ability to make rain is like that of a ghost. It would be wrong if the whole world needed that rain, but it fell only in this court.

Park Ji-won accompanied his third cousin, Geumseongwi Park Myeong-won (1725–1790) on the trip to China. The emperor held his birthday ban-

43 A unit of volume.

quet in his summer mountain villa in Yeolha [Rehe][44] on the 13th of the 8th lunar month. The above writing is included in *Sanjangjapgi*, which recorded miscellaneous events that Park experienced in the banquet. The above episode was witnessed on the 14th of the 8th lunar month in 1780.

Of course, it is possible that Kim Hong-do imagined his 'A Taoist Immortal Riding on a Turtle that Makes Rain' from the record. However, it would have been very difficult to paint the royal palace only from imagination. Since there were many things worth noting at the aforementioned congratulatory banquet, the king probably sent a painter so he could have an accurate record of the event. If so, Kim Hong-do, with his excellent reputation for genre paintings, would have been the right person for the job. The hypothesis that the painting was for royal inspection is supported by the probability that 'Full-view Painting of Geumreung,' about which Dasan Jeong Yak-yong wrote a long that following *On 'A Taoist Immortal Riding on a Turtle that Makes Rain,'* was a painting for royal inspection. These poems appear beside each other in Dasan's *Yeoyudangjeonseo* [Yeoyudang and Dasan are Jeong Yak-yong's pen names].

According to research, there are written records or dated art for Kim Hong-do from 1765, when he was 21, to 1806, when he died at the age of 62, for almost every year except 1780. Since Kim's trip to China is only hypothetical, it needs further study. Jeong Yak-yong, who wrote *On 'A Taoist Immortal Riding on a Turtle that Makes Rain,'* recorded several other interesting notes regarding Kim Hong-do.

44 Also known as Jehol, a defunct Chinese province that used to consist of part of today s Hebei Province, Shanxi Province and Inner Mongolia.

2. Elegant Lifestyle as Chalbang

On the 1st day of the 4th lunar month of 1781, at the age of 37, Kim Hong-do held a gathering called *jinsolhoe* together with Changhae Jeongran (1725–?) and Kang Hui-eon at Kim's house, which was named Danwon. Kim Hong-do's famous work, 'Danwon, the Garden of Birch Trees' (Plate 40), was painted in 1784 when Jeongran visited Angiyeok in Gyeongsang Province where Kim was working as *chalbang,* and confirms the existence of the gathering. Kim Hong-do painted it by recollecting the cozy springtime gathering of the group three years before at his house and gave it to Jeongran as a parting gift. The details are in Kim Hong-do's inscription, written in the upper portion of the painting.

> Changhae climbed Mount Baekdu in the north to reach the border and then went east to Mount Geumgang, whence he departed to visit me at my humble house, 'Danwon' on *cheonghwajeol* [the 1st of the 4th lunar month] in 1781. The sun was warm on the trees in the court, and everything was spring-bright. I played the geomungo, Damjol Kang Hui-eon supplied the alcohol, and Changhae was the senior of the gathering. Indeed, we had a genuinely simple get-together, but three years have passed unnoticed since then. Kang Hui-eon is no longer in this world, and a *thuja* has already borne its autumn fruit. As I was needy, I could not take care of the family, and stayed in Sannam. I ate and slept in the office where I was in charge of managing post horses, and one year has passed. Since I have met Changhae here, I found him with silver elegance gathered in his beard, eyebrows and hair like white clouds, and I thought that his strength had not weakened with age. When he said that he planned to climb Mount Halla in Jeju Island in the coming spring, I was very proud of him. After we drank and talked five days and five nights just as we had done at Danwon, I was saddened, so I painted 'Danwon, the Garden of Birch Trees' for Changhae. This painting is a scene at the time of our gathering, and Changhae cited the two lines of the above poem on the same day. Painted by Saneung Kim Hong-do, owner of Danwon, in the 12th lunar month of 1784.

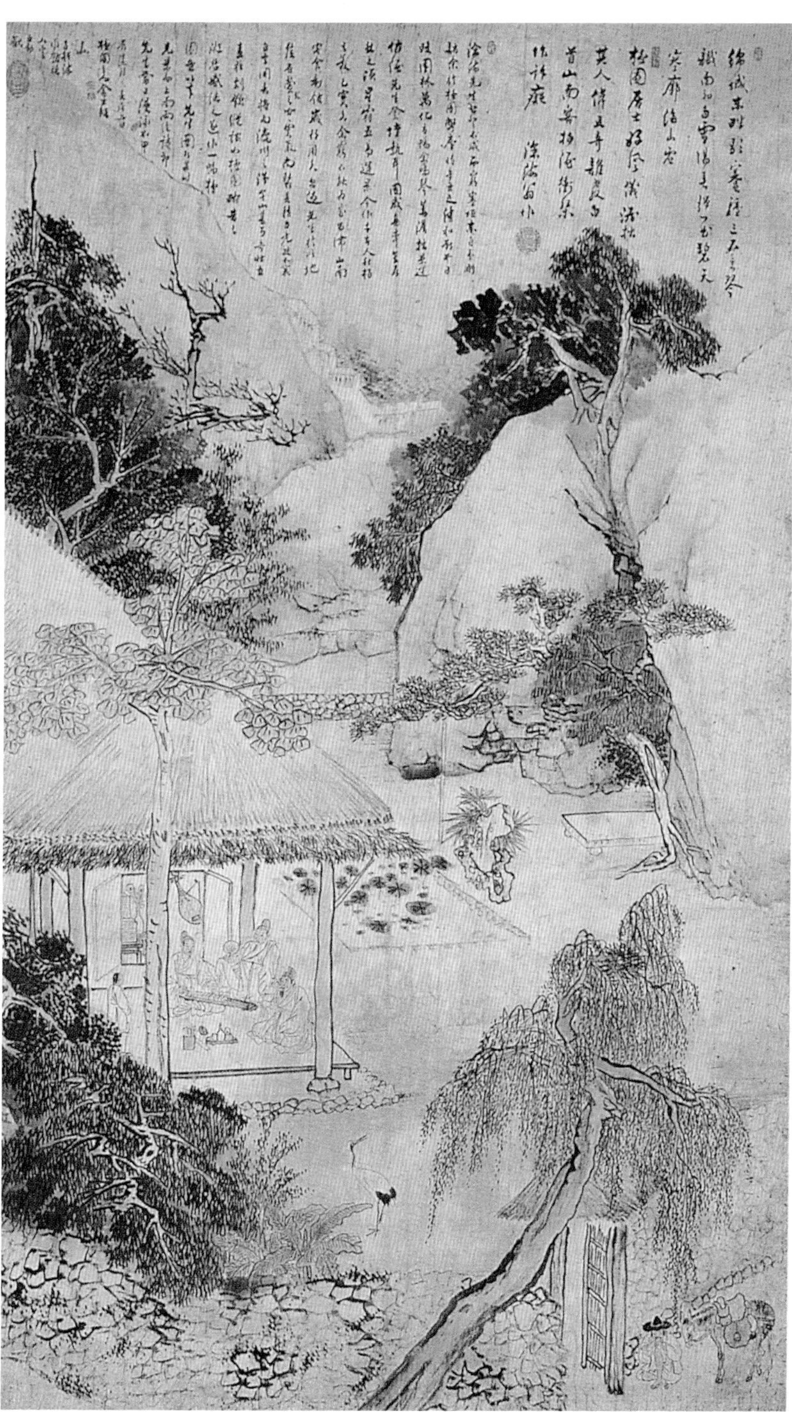

40 *Danwon, the Garden of Birch Trees*

1784. Ink and color on paper. 135×78.5cm. Collector unknown.

Incongruously, a straw-roofed house at the foot of the mountain has a large courtyard with a pond, a large rock and a stone bed. There are all sorts of trees, including *paulownia*, bamboo and pine. The garden seems to have been well managed, with the tilted branches propped up by wooden supports. The crane going back and forth in the garden is a pet.

Kang Hui-eon appeared with Kim Hong-do in the personnel appointment record of 1774. He was an *ungwan*,[45] and was a talented painter. He had the courtesy name Gyeongun and the pen name Damjol. His family was from Jinju, and after passing the *ungwa* (a government exam) in 1754, he was appointed Joji *byeolje*, then Uiyeong *jubu,* and finally Suncheon *gammokgwan*.[46] Although it is presumed that Kang Hui-eon's grandfather on his mother's side was Jeong Nae-gyo, a famous commoner poet, and that he was related to Kang Se-hwang, it seems that there is too great a social class distinction between them for this to be accurate. As mentioned earlier, Kim Hong-do painted with Kim Eung-hwan and Lee In-mun at Kang's house throughout 1777, and he painted 'Haengryeopungsokdobyeong' at Kang's house in 1778.

Kim Hong-do gave the painting to Jeongran, whose courtesy name was Yugwan and pen name was Changhae. His family was from Dongrae. He was an eccentric person, who traveled the country from Mount Baekdu to Mount Halla to see the beautiful scenery in each region. In the *Hyehwansicho* of Lee Yong-hyu [pen name Hyehwan], there are several records of Jeongran's travel, including those related to his journey to Mount Baeksan and Mount Halla. In the *Yeoamyugo* of Sin Gyeong-jun (1713–1781; pen name Yeoam), there is a letter entitled *To Changhae Going to Mount Baekdu*. Kang Se-hwang [pen name Pyoam] wrote in *Pyoamgo* that he painted a landscape (which he was unaccomplished at) in the *Bulhucheop* of Jeongran because Jeongran insisted that he do so. In addition, in *Changhae Had an Album of Beonamjip* by Chae Je-gong [pen name Beonam], written evidence indicates that Jeongran visited Chae with Kang Se-hwang's album. In the *Haejwa-Seonsaeng Collection* by Jeong Beom-jo, there is a *yulsi* with five Chinese characters in each line, entitled *Jeungjeongsaengran*. In *Taeeulamjip* by Sin Guk-bin (1724–1799), a work entitled *On 'Mount Baekdu' of Changhae* includes a comment that Jeongran made Choi Buk paint 'Mount Baekdu.' Seong Dae-jung (1732–1812; pen name Cheongseong) wrote in *Cheongseongjip* that Jeongran was such a famous traveler that many people took pride in owning "paintings depicting Jeongran looking out to sea and en-

45 An official working at the meteorological office.
46 An official in charge of managing horses at provincial stables.

tering mountains." Furthermore, he wrote that Jeongran's face resembled Matteo Ricci, the western priest much discussed at the time, and that he was like a Taoist Immortal because his eyebrows and cheekbones looked more elegant with age. The Jeongran depicted in 'Danwon, the Garden of Birch Trees' resembles that description; his servant and mule, which are both depicted in the painting, look as nimble as does their master. In *Bagongsicho* by Lee Myong-o (1750–1836), a poem entitled *On Changhae's Book on Pungak* [Pungak is the nickname of Mount Geumgang in autumn] indicates the existence of a collection of travel poems about Mount Geumgang. Furthermore, three poems in *Daedongsiseon* suggest that he was a member of the Songseokwon Literary Club and that he was from the *jungin* class. However, Jeong Yak-yong noted in *Yeoyudangjeonseo* that it is difficult to believe that Jeongran climbed Mount Baekdu. In any case, as a famous mountain climber, traveler and travel poet, Jeongran was extremely interested in painting. In addition, he was a close enough friend of Kim Hong-do and Kim Eung-hwan that he joined them at the Jangansa Temple when the two court painters were ordered by royal decree to paint Mount Geumgang in 1788.

Some, however, have misinterpreted 'Danwon, the Garden of Birch Trees' and thought that Kim Hong-do lived a wretched life and depended upon another government official who lived at the foot of Mount Namsan. However, the phrase, "As I was needy, I could not take care of the family and stayed in Sannam. I ate and slept in the office, where I was in charge of managing post horses, and one year has passed" was his modest way of saying that a year had passed since he had been appointed *chalbang* and gone alone to Angi. Sannam is an old name for Gyeongsang Province.

Jeongran's two poems on the upper right portion suggest the location of Kim Hong-do's house.

I let the tired mule get some rest close by the water east of Mount Geumseong,

Greeted with the tune of *geomungo* and
Played *Warm Spring with Remaining Snow*
The blue sky was wide and quiet, and the ocean and the sky look empty

Danwon was good-looking and showed good manners
Damjol was admirable and eccentric
Who made this old man with gray hair visit Yeongnam,
And act like a crazy man offering wine cups and playing *geomungo*?
Written by Changhaeong

The phrase, "I let the tired mule get some rest close by the water east of Mount Geumseong" refers to the servant who crouched down; and the mule outside the gate in 'Danwon, the Garden of Birch Trees.' Since "east of Mount Geumseong," seems to refer to the current Mount Geumseong in Seongsan-dong, if Kim Hong-do's house were at the foot of Mount Geumseong, it would have been beside the Han River. That coincides with the suggestion that Kim's early pen name, Seoho is connected with the former name of Mapo, Seoho. In addition, it seems that Jeongran and Kim Hong-do met there for the first time, and probably that is why three years later Kim remembered the gathering so well.

The poem depicts the three people at the gathering. It is noteworthy that Jeongran also remarked, "Danwon was good-looking and showed good manners." In addition, in the top left-hand corner, there is a sentence that reads, "Gosongyusugwandoin [Lee In-mun's pen name] Lee Munuk [Lee In-mun's courtesy name] saw this painting," which indicates that when Kim Hong-do was *chalbang*, his friend Lee In-mun, although far from Kim, saw this painting courtesy of Jeongran.

In the 4th lunar month, Kim Hong-do painted 'A Beauty' (Plate 41). An inscription on the painting reads, "In the 4th lunar month in 1781, Saneung painted this for the owner of Yeonpagwan"; however, the owner of Yeonpagwan is unknown. On *daeseo* [July 23, by the solar calendar], Seo Yu-gu wrote the inscription on Kim Hong-do's 'Segeomjeong Gathering' ('Segeomjeong-ajipdo'). The painting was a scene of distinguished families, including Nam Gong-cheol and Seo No-su, holding a literary gathering at Segeomjeong. The following inscription describes the painting in detail.

> Rummaging through an old box, I found a horizontal painting five *cheok* [about 150cm] wide and less than a third of that in length. A large stream whirls from right to left. The current splashes against scattered rocks and the current's white bubbles gather to become dark-blue. The thunderstruck sound of the current hitting the rocks is as if the current were spinning a cart and showing the strength of a hornless writhing dragon. Looking at this painting on the hottest day in midsummer, one feels clean and cool on the face. To the north, pines and Japanese cedars grow densely, and towards south is a precipitous cliff that is so high and steep that it looks like many layers of bamboo sprouts.
>
> Below, a small pavilion stands beside the water's edge against the cliff. Of the six people outside the pavilion, two young boys scoop up spring water to make tea, one person is asleep with his head bowed upon his knee, another is lying down with the reins in his right hand using his arms as a pillow, and the other two are sitting on a broad flat rock and washing their faces. One of the five people inside the pavilion is seated and playing with a brush on a piece of paper, one is standing and looking far off as he leans against the southern pillar, while the three remaining sit in a large circle below the eastern crossbeam as they laugh aloud and discuss poetry. As the sound of water increases, they cannot even hear the person sitting beside them. In the left portion of the painting, there are five poems by Geumreung Nam Gong-cheol, Holwon Seo No-su, Ucho and two Confucians named Han and Lee,

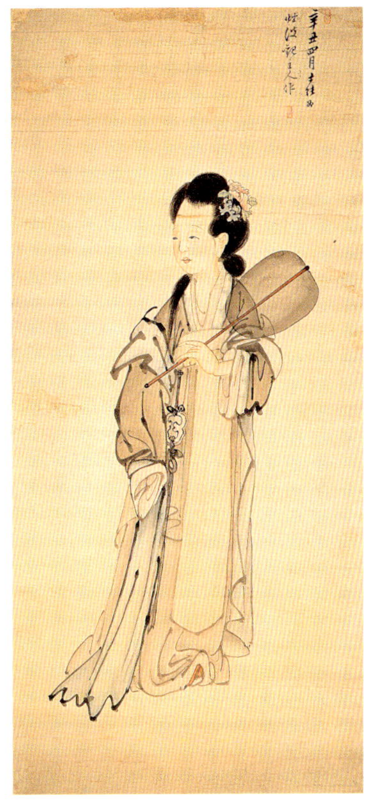

41 *A Beauty*
1781. Ink and color on paper. 121.8×55.7cm. National Museum of Korea.
This is probably Kim Hong-do s only painting of a court woman. Since the features of the beautiful young woman in the center, with no background, are quite similar to those of He Xiangu from Immortals, it is clearly a painting of a woman in the Chinese style. Although the face here is slightly blushed, and the hair and wrist are fairer, even the decorations in the hair are almost the same. The line of the wrinkle in the clothes looks animated, starts strong like a nail head and finishes sharp like a mouse s tail. However, overall, the brushstroke is reserved and elegant. The glossy black hair is painted so elaborately that the observer can even feel the strand of each hair. The light blue and brown shading provides a clean look.

and they are the five people who are inside the pavilion. Danwon Kim Hong-do painted the scene, and Daeyeon Lee Yu-ha composed the poem; neither Kim nor Lee is among the five people inside the pavilion. However, looking at the painting for a long time, people begin to feel like they are actually seated inside the pavilion and hearing the rush of the stream. This inscription was written on *daeseo* [July 23 by the solar calendar] 1781.

The painted scene reveals the virtuosity of the artist, and the covered area hints at hidden elegance.

This confirms that Kim Hong-do painted *ajipdo* at Segeomjeong, where prominent people such as Seo Yu-gu, Nam Gong-cheol, Seo No-su and Ucho gathered for literary readings. This inscription provides the earliest recorded use of the pen name, Danwon. Therefore, Kim probably used Danwon since the time of the *jinsolhoe* gathering, rather than beginning to use it three years later when 'Danwon, the Garden of Birch Trees' was actually painted.

In the autumn, Kim Hong-do painted a portrait of King Jeongjo and copied an original painting of King Yeongjo at the age of 80. The chief painter was Han Jong-yu, the associate painter was Kim Hong-do, and assistant painters included Kim Hu-sin, Kim Eung-hwan, Sin Han-pyeong, Jang Si-heung, Heo Gam, and others. On the 26th of the 8th lunar month, Han Jong-yu, Sin Han-pyeong and Kim Hong-do each drafted a painting of the king. The *Jeongjosillok*[47] dated the 26th of the 8th lunar month in 1781 confirms the draft paintings.

The king summoned the subjects working at Gyujanggak, the royal library, and said, "I would like to have my portrait painted … Although I commissioned one when I was 22 (1773), it has lost its true image, so I had it removed. I would like to have my portrait painted every ten years…I will not establish Dogam." Therefore, court painters Han Jong-yu, Sin Han-pyeong and Kim Hong-do were each ordered to copy the original painting.

47 The chronicle of King Jeong-jo s reign.

The Diaries of the Royal Secretariat of the same day provides additional details.

> ...His Majesty said, "... Have court painters, Han Jong-yu, Sin Han-pyeong and Kim Hong-do draft one painting each." His Majesty also said, "In Han Jong-yu's painting the chin is similar, but the rest [of the painting] is different from the real image." Jeong Min-si said, "When court painters enter upon the dignified presence of Your Majesty's face for the first time, they are so overwhelmed at the royal dignity that they have difficulty painting. As a result, they will only be able to capture your true image after painting several drafts."

On the 27th of the 8th lunar month, Kang Se-hwang, who had taught Kim Hong-do, was ordered to paint the king's portrait.

> Seungji Seo Jeong-su reported, "There was an instance of a nobleman who understood paintings participating in copying the original royal portrait. It would be desirable to have Buchongg-wan Kang Se-hwang and Sanguiwon[48] Jubu Jo Yunhyeong participate in painting." The king declared, "When copying the original portraits of King Sukjong and King Yeongjo, senior statesmen such as Kim Jin-gyu, Yun Deok-hui and Jo Yeong-seok participated in it from beginning to end. Therefore, have Kang Se-hwang and Jo Yun-hyeong prepare for the job."

However, Kang Se-hwang rejected the offer and asked to be appointed *gamdongyeok*,[49] and this was granted.

> The king went to Huiujeong and told Buchonggwan Kang Se-hwang, "Following the example of King Yeongjo, I am going to have my portrait painted. I understand that you are very familiar with paintings. So, just as Kim Jin-gyu participated in painting the royal portrait, paint a portrait of me." Kang Se-hwang responded, "Because I am old, I am afraid that I would make a mistake

48 The office in charge of managing the king s garments, gold and other valuable palace assets.

49 The same as *gamjogwan* or *gamyeokgwan*; a temporary post given to an officer responsible for the timely completion of national projects or public works.

painting the royal face. I believe it would be better if I just assisted in the process." The king replied, "Then help the court painters in areas where their thoughts cannot reach."

On the 3rd of the 9th lunar month, a draft portrait of the king in his royal crown and formal garments was painted.

The incumbent and previous officers, the subjects of Gyujanggak, Seungji Seo Jeong-su, Kang Se-hwang, the vice minister of *hojo*, and court painters all came up the stairs and looked at the portrait of King Yeongjo … The king summoned the *seungji* and the subjects of Gyujanggak and dressed in his royal crown and formal garments. Then he had Kim Hong-do, the court painter, draft a royal portrait.

On the same day, *The Diaries of the Royal Secretariat* confirms that associate painter Kim Hong-do painted the king's clothes.

… His Majesty said, "Let Kang Se-hwang, the vice minister of *hojo,* and court painters in"… The vice minister of *hojo* and the court painters came in and looked closely at the portrait of King Yeongjo … His Majesty said, "Since the *gyesanyeon* [1773] portrait shows the truest image of all portraits of King Yeongjo, I am going to have it copied …" His Majesty came to Seohyanggak dressed in his royal crown and formal garments, and ordered Kim Hong-do to come forward to draft a painting of His Majesty's garment.

On the 4th of the 9th lunar month, the royal portrait was reproduced on silk.

His Majesty came out at Yeonghwadang, where he summoned incumbent and former officers and the subjects of Gyujanggak to watch the royal portrait being reproduced on silk.

On the 16th of the 9th lunar month, the completed portrait was placed in

Juhapru. The king issued an ordinance to appoint Kim Hong-do to a *sanjik* in the *ijo*[50] or *byeongjo*[51] for his contribution to painting the royal portrait.

50 The Ministry of Personnel.
51 The Ministry of the Military.

Seo Yu-bang reported to His Majesty, "I am reporting on the rewards to the court painters, artisans and workers who participated in painting the royal portrait." The king replied, "I see ...Grant a foal to Kang Se-hwang, the vice minister of *hojo* and Sanguiwon Jubu Jo Yun-hyeong ... Appoint the chief painter Han Jong-yu, who used to be *sagwa*, as *byeonjang* in a good location. Associate painter Kim Hong-do, who used to be the *gammokgwan*, assistant painter Jeolchung Kim Hu-sin, former Manho Sin Han-pyeong, Heo Gam, and Sagwa Kim Eung-hwan all previously worked hard, as well as this time... Appoint them to miscellaneous positions among the *sanjik* of the *ijo* or *byeongjo*. Jang Si-heung has served his country for 20 years, but he has never been rewarded. Appoint him *byeonjang*."

Thus, Kim Hong-do first submitted a draft portrait of the king and then became an associate painter to paint royal clothes. Kang Se-hwang, Kim's teacher, was also involved as *gamdongyeok*, and at some point in time Kim Hong-do was appointed *gammokgwan*.

In the autumn of 1782, at age 38, Kim Hong-do painted 'Butterflies'

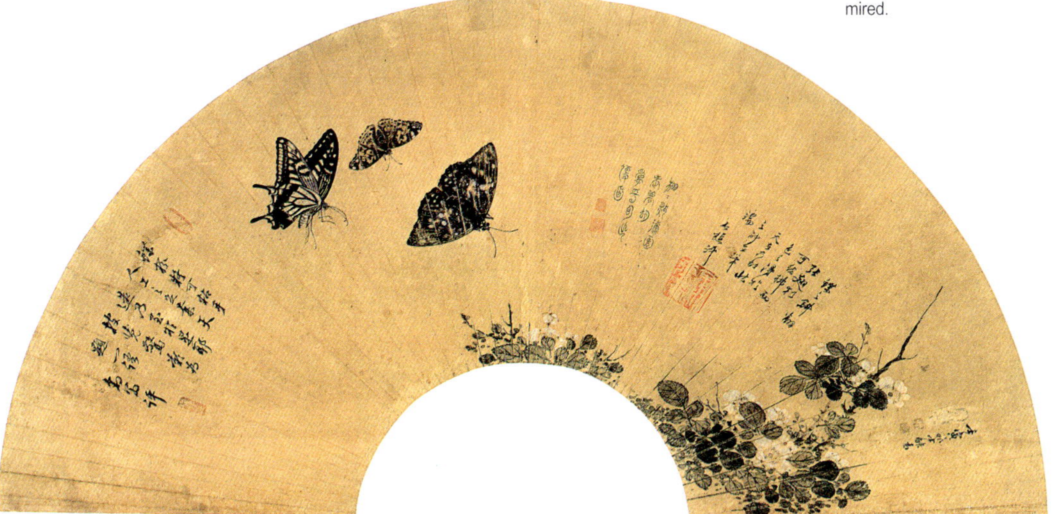

42 *Butterflies*
1782. Ink and color on paper. 29×74cm. National Museum of Korea.
A wide margin is in the background, making the three butterflies gathering around white wild roses look animated. Kang Se-hwang s inscription on the left side reads, As if the hands could be covered by butterfly powder, the deftness of a man stole the beauty of nature. Seokcho praised the painting in his inscription on the right side: Leaving aside that the spread wings of the butterflies are flying askew, how was he able to capture natural light in color? Outwitting the other two, the inscription in regular script in the center reads, How can the butterflies merrily flying in Zhuangzi s dream float on this fan painting? Before photography, such a painting was highly admired.

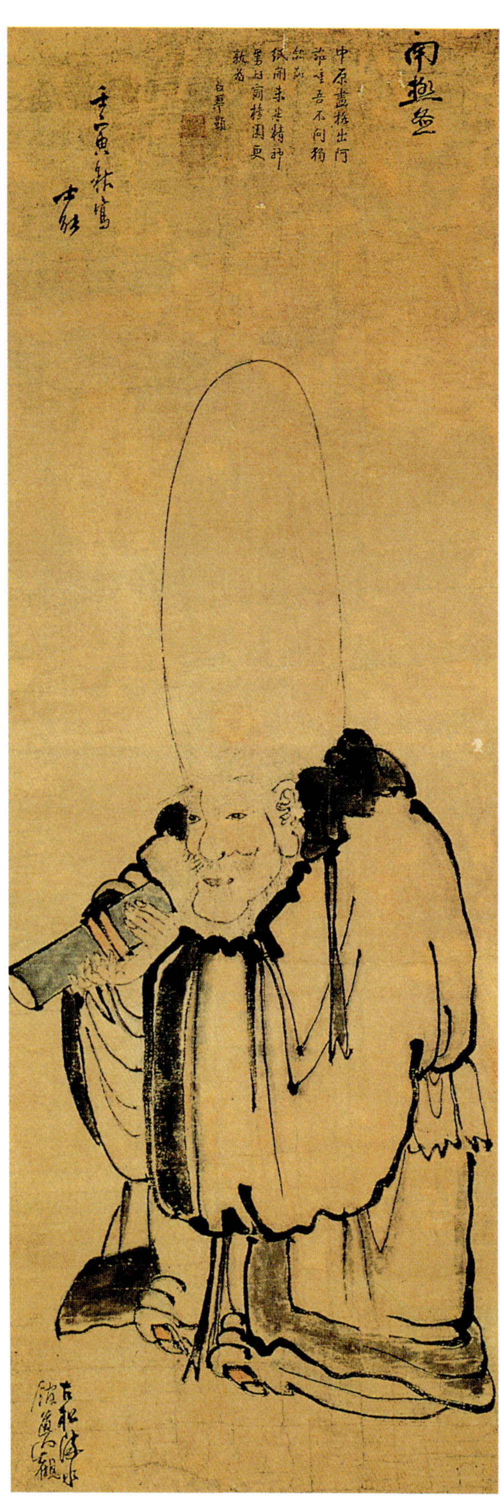

43 ***The Old Man of the South Pole Star***

1782. Ink and color on paper. 119.4×41.5cm. National Museum of Korea.

This bizarre-looking old man, who has a shiny, bald head that is half his height, is a Taoist Immortal. He is the personification of the south pole star, which is seen in the southern sky in spring. Since it was believed that people who look at the south pole star enjoy longevity, it was customary to paint this subject matter for old men s birthday banquets. The painting is in poor condition, and the surface is worn off in many places. In addition, there are some traces of repainting, which reduce the value of the work. However, the brushstrokes of Kim Hong-do s inscription, Hong Sin-yu s poem and the inscription of Lee In-mun (Kim s fellow court painter) clearly prove the work s authenticity. Kim must have painted this subject many times throughout his life, but unfortunately, none has survived in good condition.

(Plate 42) on a folding fan. The inscription reads, "In the autumn of 1782, Saneung painted for [...]," with the name of the recipient erased.

In autumn, Kim Hong-do painted 'The Old Man of the South Pole Star' (Plate 43). The inscription reads "Painted by Saneung in the autumn of 1782." The following poem by Hong Sin-yu in the upper portion of the painting is also included in Hong's *Baekhwajajipcho*.

On Danwon Kim Hong-do's Painting

Whose painting is remarkable in the country
I am the only one who knows the answer without being asked
Before unfolding the painting even halfway, one's spirit becomes full of life
If not you, Danwon, who else could do this again?

In the lower left corner of the painting is Lee In-mun's inscription "Gosongyusugwandoingwan," which means that Gosongyusugwandoin [Lee In-mun's pen name] saw this painting.

That year, severe famine struck Gyeonggi, Chung-cheong and Gyeongsang provinces. On the 7th of the 9th lunar month, there was a national festival to celebrate the birth of Crown Prince Munhyo.

On the 21st of the 11th lunar month in 1783, when Kim Hong-do turned 39, King Jeongjo initiated the innovative *jabidaeryeong* court-painter system in Gyujanggak. However, there is no record suggesting that Kim Hong-do participated in this system because the king already considered Kim to have a special talent and probably excluded him from the system. Therefore, regardless of its launch, Kim Hong-do was appointed *chalbang* of Angi in Gyeongsang Province on the 28th of the 12th lunar month for his contribution to the royal portrait. *The Diaries of the Royal Secretariat* record the appointment.

The *ijo* ratified a position as a performance-based appointment ... and appointed Kim Hong-do *chalbang* of Angi.

So, in the 1st lunar month of 1784, at age 40, Kim became *chalbang* of Angi in Andongbu. The following is from the *Angiyeokji*.

> ...Kim Hong-do is from Hanyang. (He was appointed in the 1st lunar month in 1784, and replaced after finishing his term in the 5th lunar month in 1786...)

The exact term of office as *chalbang* of Angi is recorded above. The only information that we have regarding Kim's days as *chalbang* is the aforementioned information indicating his term of office and location, and 'Damrakjae' (Plate 45), a tablet hung on Chehwajeong on which Kim Hong-do wrote calligraphy. Before examining Kim Hong-do's life as *chalbang*, it is worth noting that he had more than 1,300 people including *yeokri* and slaves under his command. According to building repairs recorded in the *Angiyeokji* of 1865, there were 10-*kan*[52] Soyanggwan, the main office, 8-*kan* private quarters, 1-*kan* assistant officers' office, 2-*kan nangcheongbang*,[53] 3-*kan gongsucheong*,[54] 6-*kan namhaengrang*,[55] 3-*kan* stable, 3-*kan* outer gate,[56] *inlicheong* inside the inner gate and *gwancheonggo*[57] outside the northern wall. Considering the Deokryugwan and Yuyeonjeong Pavilion inside the southern and western walls, Kim's *chalbang* office was quite large.

In Angiyeok on the 8th of the 4th lunar month, there was custom called *otoanmaje* (五土安馬祭) was observed, in the center of which a blue dragon, white tiger, red phoenix and the green turtle and snake, were worshiped. The *Seonghwangdang,* 10 steps east of the main office, was the center, *Gukwangsindang*, which enshrined the statuette of King Gongmin of Goryeo, was the blue dragon; *Sobaekdang,* below the *jusan* (主山) was the white tiger; the *josan* (造山) 100 steps south of the main building was the red phoenix; and the locust tree shrine, 200 steps north of the main building was the green turtle and snake. Each of these required sacrificial rites. In addition, there was a building 60 steps east of the main office that enshrined King Gongmin's *jeonja* (殿字). It was venerated on the 7th of the 4th lunar month, one day before *otoanmaje*. Since *chalbang* oversaw religious ser-

52 A unit of floor space.
53 Building where the military secrets are dealt with.
54 Building where the finances are handled.
55 Building where personnel and administrative affairs are handled.
56 Petty officials office.
57 A warehouse where office supplies are kept.

vices and *otoanmaje*, Kim Hong-do must have become conscious of his influence as a regional government officer. Although it is widely believed that Kim Hong-do's life and attitude reached a turning point when he became *hyeongam*, a magistrate of a small county, the process probably started seven years before when he was *chalbang*.

Chalbang Kim Hong-do was in charge of managing all individuals taking care of horses, as well as residents in Angido, and of supplying post horses. He was responsible for 11 posts located at 30 *li*[58] intervals, whose main function was the delivery of government orders or public documents. The details of Kim Hong-do's administration are unknown; however, since he completed his term in office, it seems that he served without making serious mistakes.

Kim Hong-do's life as *chalbang* included an encounter with Jeongran, which motivated him to paint 'Danwon, the Garden of Birch Trees,' around *ipchun* [the first of 24 seasonal divisions] in 1784, almost a year after he was appointed *chalbang*. On the 1st of the 7th lunar month in Hanyang, the king's eldest son Munhyo, who had been born to a royal concubine named Seong in 1782, was officially invested as the crown prince. However, he died of measles on the 11th of the 5th lunar month in 1786. That was about the time when Kim Hong-do completed his term of office and returned to Hanyang.

On the 17th of the 8th lunar month in 1784, Governor Lee Byeong-mo (1742–1806), Heunghae Gunsu[59] Seong Dae-jung, Bonghwa Hyeongam Sim Gong-jeo, Yeongyang Hyeongam Kim Myeong-jin, Hayang Hyeongam Im Hui-taek (1744–1799) and Angi Chalbang Kim Hong-do went to Mount Cheongryang and enjoyed poetry and music. This is recorded in Seong Dae-jung's *Cheongseongjip*.

> Mount Cheongryang is a celebrated mountain in Gyeongsangjwado. In the 8th lunar month of 1784, when Governor Lee Byeong-mo went to the mountain, I followed him as far as Cheongryangsa Temple. Bonghwa Hyeongam Sim Gong-jeo, Yeongyang Hyeongam Kim Myeong-jin, Hayang Hyeongam Im Hui-taek and Angi Chalbang Kim Hong-do accompanied us. Sim and I had

58 A unit of distance.
59 The chief magistrate of a county.

previously promised to go together, and Chalbang Kim Hong-do was renowned as 'the best painter in the country.' The mountain was quiet, and the moon was bright. We were seated on scattered rocks in the valley. Since Chalbang Kim played the bamboo flute well, we asked him to play a tune. The clear sound and beautiful melody resonated to the top of the forest. While all the other sounds of nature were muted, the sound of the flute lingered as if it were about to fly away, so much so that if one heard it at a distance, one would think that a Taoist Immortal playing a reed instrument was descending to earth mounted on a crane. In my opinion, when Kim Hong-do is seen from a distance, he is a Taoist Immortal; if he is seen close, he is a man. That is what the old stories say a Taoist Immortal is like. Deep into the night, the governor passed around a poem and told the *hyeongam* to add rhymes to it.

The aforementioned episode shows that Kim Hong-do's musical talent was so remarkable that the audience associated him with a Taoist Immortal.

Mount Cheongryang is a beautiful mountain located 30 *li* from Dosan-seowon, and 60 *li* from Andong. Historical remains such as Kimsaenggul, Chiwonam and Goundae show traces of Kim Saeng and Choi Chi-won of Silla. Ju Se-bung (1495–1554), who built Baekundong-seowon, the first established lecture/memorial service hall for Confucian scholars, named the 12 mountain peaks and they retain the same names today. Notably, Lee Hwang (1501–1570) loved this mountain so much that he gave himself the pen name Cheongryangsanin [Man of Mount Cheongryang] and composed several poems in Chinese praising the mountain's beautiful scenery, as well as the following famous verse in Korean.

The twelve peaks of Mount Cheongryang are only known to the white seagull and me

The white seagull would not deceive me, but it is the peach blossom that cannot be trusted

Peach blossom, don't leave, the fisherman might know.

The aforementioned gathering of the governor and his party is thought to be related to the poem by Toegye Lee Hwang. We will explore this possibility later. Furthermore, *On 'Bamboo flute played in Mount Cheongryang,'* the poemin Seong Dae-jung's *Cheongseongjip,* indicates that Kim Hong-do painted the assembled literary gathering.

On 'Bamboo flute played in Mount Cheongryang'

On the bridge outside Cheongryangsa Temple, the moon slants to one side
The color of the mountain and the sound of the stream are quiet tonight
Who sent the flute of a Taoist Immortal, beautifully played
Don't know that the Taoist Immortal playing a reed instrument riding on a crane left far away

'Bamboo flute played in Mount Cheongryang' is no longer extant. However, it is clear that when Governor Lee Byeong-mo and Kim Hong-do met, they composed poems, added rhymes and painted pictures deep into the night, and then created a large scroll. Although the scroll is lost, fortunately the *Cheongryang-yeonyeongcheop in Gyujanggak*, which is believed to be part of the scroll, still exists. According to this literature, Governor Lee Byeong-mo began his poem as follows.

Today is the 17th of the 8th lunar month, gapjinnyeon [1784]
It is the night of the governor, *gunsu*, *hyeongam* and *chalbang* in Mount Cheongryang
Lee Byeong-mo

Then, Seong Dae-jung, Sim Gong-jeo, Kim Myeong-jin and Im Hui-taek composed couplets as follows.

Pine trees and cinnamon trees are old now in the old mountain where Toegye used to make excursions

Still, it seems there are traces of his walking stick in the mossy stones.
Seong Dae-jung

Oksobong stands high, and the stars and moon shine brightly
In the old traces of the valley of Geumtapbong, fog gathers at night
Sim Gong-jeo

The fountain in the rocks flows quietly and Haksodae is empty
where can one find the traces of Choi Chi-won
Kim Myeong-jin

A monk serves the guests with seasoned vegetables, which are clean and simple
The mountain is half-green and half-red in autumn
Im Hui-taek

Finally, Kim Hong-do composed the following couplet.

The cloud screen and the fog curtain unfold themselves one by one
Whose talent is this, twelve panels of painting, distant and broad?
Kim Hong-do

Indeed, Kim Hong-do, "the best painter in the country," created a beautiful poem full of picturesque images; then Sa-in, whose family name is unknown, composed the couplet,

Seagull, will you not tell me if I can be here next year?
I will come back to see the blossoms in Utopia
Sa-in

The following appreciative words and poems by several *hyeongam* suggest how cheerful and natural this gathering was. Unfortunately, no other poem by Kim Hong-do is found here; perhaps since he was playing the bamboo flute and painting the scene, he could no longer participate in adding couplets.

Poetry does not have to be those by Li Bai and Du Fu
Calligraphy does not have to be that of Zhong You and Wang Xizhi
Paintings do not have to be those of Wu Daozi and Huang Gongwang
Who cares? Tonight's gathering is so peaceful and comfortable
that each one just enjoys what he likes
Lee Byeong-mo

Trustworthy, the *hyeongam* of Heunghae
He honored our promise to come to Cheongryang
The pine trees newly…
Who would know this kind of elegance?
Lee Byeong-mo

The day I went to Daegu to say hello
We already had a promise to come to this mountain
As we are about to go against the current with divine spirit
Mount Cheongryang notices it first
Im Hui-taek

Don't let the red flower flow away
Had a promise only with that seagull
This gusto below the twelve peaks
Only known to Toegye
Sim Gong-jeo

Thought he enjoyed the gusto of Mount Cheongryang alone,
But he came from far away to see the thick forest.

Toegye's love for mountains and rivers
was first given to the seagull
Seong Dae-jung

The seagull knows the twelve peaks of Mount Cheongryang
Please do not fly for fear the fisherman will come along riding the boat
The news was leaked out, if not by the peach blossom
Has the proud officer of Heunghae already entered the gate of Taoist Immortals?
Lee Byeong-mo

The above couplets and other poems were all written with Cheongryangsanin Toegye Lee Hwang's poem in mind. According to *Cheongryang-yeonyeongcheop*, it seems that the venue of the gathering was Eopungdae, which is the cliff to the right of Geumtapbong, and the best place to view Mount Cheongryang's twelve peaks. Notice also that Kim Hong-do composed poems extempore with dignitaries such as Governor Lee Byeong-mo, high-ranking Gyujanggak officials and Seong Dae-jung, a master of ancient classics. Academia has been reluctant to acknowledge Kim Hong-do's literary talent; however, there are numerous records indicating that Kim Hong-do was well versed in poetry and prose. In that regard, Kim Hong-do's teacher Kang Se-hwang left a significant record.

> Saneung [Kim Hong-do] was well versed in music and was remarkable with the *geomungo* and flute as well as poetry and prose.

Furthermore, the following poem, believed to have been composed when Hong Sin-yu met Kim Hong-do again while Kim was *chalbang* of Angi, attests to Kim's literary talent. As mentioned above, Hong is the one for whom Kim made *Bokheon and Baekhwa's Album* when Hong left Hanyang in the 8th lunar month of 1779.

Poetry Exchanged at Danheon

Wind closes and opens the book on the table
The sun shines on innumerable houses, and green shadows are piled up
The precious fan with the scent of the sky is from the royal palace
The golden cushion is from the ocean
It's the season of trees shedding flowers, making them all look alike
A swallow flies towards its favorite turret
Leaning against the window a moment to feel the great pleasure inside,
The blue sky after the rain is empty and spacious.

The "Danheon" here probably refers to either the main office or private quarters, which was part of the Angi government office that Danwon Kim Hong-do administered. In addition, "Poetry Exchanged" supports the contention that Kim Hong-do also composed poetry at times. Seong Dae-jung's *Letter Responding to Taehwa Hong Won-seop* confirms that Hong Sin-yu and Kim Hong-do again met at the Daegu government office.

> These days, few things please one's mind. Fortunately, Governor Jeong Su-jae was here to continue the *jinggakajip* (the Jinggak literary gathering). Taesang Hong Sin-yu's calligraphy and Chalbang Kim Hong-do's paintings are replete with elegance, so that they deserve to be called the great culture in the Yeongnam region [southeastern region of Korea]. The entertainment and appreciation we felt at Mount Cheongryang was painted on a beautiful scroll, but I am sorry that you are far away. Now that the governor has returned to Hanyang and Taesang Hong Sin-yu has gone south to the seashore in Dongrae, the graceful gatherings in Daegu seem to have ended. ...However, as I did not see your *Poem Appreciating the Fan from Jinggak*, I would appreciate it if you had someone deliver it to me together with *Haeseochuk*. ...Now that Governor Jeong Su-jae has gone to Hanyang, you can see him often, and see the *Jinggakagipchuk* and *Cheongryangcheop* in good condition.

The phrase, "the graceful gatherings in Daegu seem to have ended," relates to all the literary events that had taken place since *dalgujangun* in the 5th lunar month of 1783. *Dalgujangun* refers to Lee Deok-mu's going to Maejukheon, where Daegu Pangwan Hong Won-seop (1744–1807) lived, and his leaving behind a famous 22-rhyme a poem dedicated to Jeong Jigeom. At those events, dignitaries, including Hong Won-seop, Seong Daejung, Won Deuk-jeong, Lee Byeong-mo, Jeong Ji-sun, Kim Deuk-hu and Sim Nyeom-jo, composed poems with the aforementioned rhyme scheme. The gatherings later developed into a great literary event. That was seven months before Kim Hong-do became *chalbang*; Hong Won-seop left Daegu the next year. In the summer of 1784, Seong Dae-jung, Hong Sin-yu and Kim Hong-do gathered at *Jingcheonggak* in Daegu, where Governor Lee Byeong-mo lived, to hold the jinggakajip. There was also the aforementioned Mount Cheongryang gathering. The governor came to own both the *literati* paintings *Jinggakagipchuk* and *Cheongryangcheop*, the scrolls of poems from this assembly. In the 2nd lunar month of 1785, when Lee Byeong-mo finished his term of office and returned to Hanyang, all of these exciting events ended. This writing confirms that Kim Hong-do's paintings and Hong Sin-yu's calligraphy were considered "the great culture in the Yeongnam region," and that the artists met again, five years after they had parted in 1779, to enjoy poetry and paintings together. Hong Sin-yu recited the following poem at the end of this meeting.

Writing on the Fan of Kim Hong-do, Chalbang of Angi

Painted the sun and sky [referring to the king] and stopped stroking the color brush

Old traces of serving the king were high at a tall building

As we mount on the back of a swift horse, leaving Daegu,

The crane saw the cases of *geomungo* and *daegeum* and cried out for a long time.

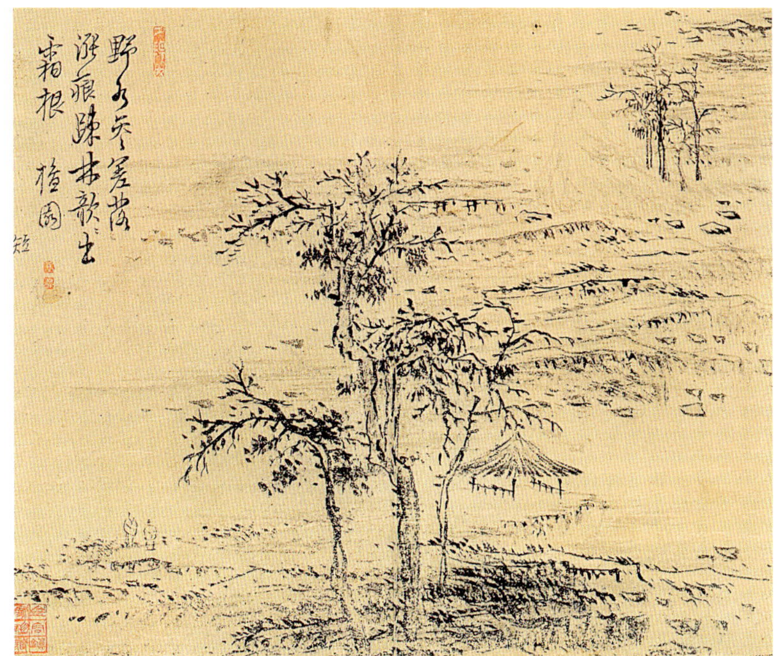

44 *The Sparse Wood and Water in the Field*
Ink and color on paper. 21.8×26cm. Kansong Art Museum.
As in the phrase of Su Dong-po s poem, the rough traces of water in the field are revealed, and the sparse branches and roots are exposed to sharp frost, this depicts a lonely, desolate landscape in autumn. The two small figures accentuate the wide space. The brushstroke, free from conformity, indicates that it is a work of Kim Hong-do s late years. It is an excellent example of his Chinese style painting of the Southern School.

It is interesting that the poem says that when Kim Hong-do mounted his horse to leave the governor's office with Hong Sin-yu, a crane in the yard cried out as it looked down on the *geomungo* and *daegeum* cases. It signifies the crane's sorrow at Kim Hong-do's departure because it would not be able to dance to Kim's beautiful tune, thus confirming that in Daegu, Kim Hong-do played the *geomungo* and *daegeum* as well as enjoyed poetry and painting.

The *Poem Appreciating the Fan from Jinggak* in Seong Dae-jung's letter confirmed Angi as the region where Kim was *chalbang*. Further evidence comes from Hong Won-seop's letter to Seong Dae-jung, which reads, "I expressed my gratitude for Jinggak's fan with a picture in a poem composed with the rhyme scheme we used in Daegu. This is an extension of *dalgujangun*." Against this background, let us look at the poem.

I composed this poem following the rhyme scheme used at Maejukheon in Daegu while a visitor in Byeokseong-gun to show my gratitude to Governor

Lee Byeong-mo for sending me Danwon's painting on a fan.

(Danwon is the pen name of Kim Hong-do, Chalbang of Angi)

When the sunshine at Buyongdang was the brightest in springtime
I told the governor in the banquet, I remember:
'As you have kept sending letters to me far away,
It is as if clean wind blows into the bamboo forest.'
Unfolding the fan that is as large as a wheel,
One finds the speckles of finely cut bamboo sticks like the tears of Ehuang and Nuing
Like the snow of Donghwasa Temple, the white paper is like white silk
Danwon stroked the brush dipped in colors
This is what I heard about, that Danwon learned the Chinese painting of the Southern School.
The mysterious technique in the painting is due to his talent at its best
He met with the governor as *chalbang*
But he could not help himself as if he were in his studio
He painted to his heart's content, freely stroking the brush
Both elegant motifs and secular scenes are remarkable
One of them shows true elegance
It is a lonely bamboo tree, rocks, forests and an island
A crying deer stands by the railing, and a *geomungo* is on the table
Tea is boiled under the shadow of a sparsely grown *paulownia* tree in the broad daylight
Did this painting satisfy the governor's intentions?
Did the governor think of the summer at Maejukheon?
I heard that when there was a big poetry composition event in Maejukheon last summer,
Couplets and scrolls of poems filled a box
Why wasn't I there?
I see the scene only today and can't stop admiring it

The governor told me that he deeply understood paintings
And sent me a painting on a fan despite the long distance
I held it in my hand a hundred times and held it to my chest
Although it is a small thing, the meaning is so lofty that we can feel each other
The fan was carefully inscribed, sealed and delivered to Hanyang from Yeongnam
Now I am facing the waterside imagining the painter painting the picture.

This poem indicates that the *jinggakajip* in the summer of 1784 was definitely a great literary gathering. Since Kim Hong-do spent time with nobles who recognized his talent, such as Governor Lee Byeong-mo and Seong Dae-jung, while he was chalbang, presumably Kim enjoyed a comfortable and pleasant life during the period. On the 12th of the 10th lunar month of 1784, Kang Se-hwang left for Yenching [Beijing] as a government envoy.

Two days before *ipchun* in the 12th lunar month, Changhae Jeongran visited Angi. He and Kim Hong-do drank for five days in a row and reminisced about the 1781 *jinsolhoe* gathering that they had enjoyed together with Kang Hui-eon, who had since died. Two days after *ipchun*, Kim Hong-do painted 'Danwon, the Garden of Birch Trees' (Plate 40) for Jeongran. There was also an earthquake that year.

On the 1st of the 7th lunar month of 1785, there was an eclipse. In 1786, when Kim was 42, there was another eclipse, this one on New Year's Day. Whenever natural phenomenon occurred at the beginning of a year, the king issued ordinances to government officials to report on the evils of the times and take relevant measures to correct them. King Jeongjo presided over a policy meeting on the 22nd of the 1st lunar month, and instructed his officials to submit their opinions in writing to "make the disaster an opportunity to seek peace." Examining the opinion of Han Jong-yu, a professor at Dohwaseo,[60] one catches a glimpse of the circumstances surrounding Kim Hong-do at this time, who was preparing to return to Dohwaseo after he completed his term as *chalbang* in the 5th lunar month.

60 The Office of Painting; also known as Dohwawon.

Opinions of Han Jong-yu, Professor at Dohwaseo

The duty of painting is indispensable for a nation, but because the relevant system was not properly established in the beginning, it functions poorly. Although the original quota of court painters was 30, there are only 11 positions on the payroll, so for half a year, they receive no salary. Therefore, allocating court painters to each military post was presented to His Majesty as a solution to this problem, and the plan was approved. However, the situation remains the same because the plan has not been implemented. Although His Majesty approved the plan again in 1773, so far nothing has been done. It is frustrating.

In addition, court painters are so frequently expelled that it has become increasingly difficult to nurture artistic talent. As a result, we have difficulty coping with major national affairs. To solve this problem, it would be a good idea to follow the example of how the *sajagwan*[61] are expelled; His Majesty should approve the expelling of those who commit misdemeanors. By doing so, newly recruited painters will do their best, talents will properly develop and national affairs will benefit from these measures. I dare to beg His Majesty that this request be implemented.

His Majesty responded, "It would be imprudent to uncritically fulfill your request to allocate court painters to positions on the payroll. There should also be rewards and penalties in education." Bibyeonsa reported, "That was the opinion of Han Jong-yu, a professor at Dohwaseo… His Majesty's response meant that although allocation of court painters on the payroll is not easily implemented, let the relevant *yejo*[62] handle the problem." The former *yejo* minister, Gu Yun-myeong said, "The court painters are correct in saying they only reach a certain level of competence after serving as court painter for a long time. If they are ousted for petty mistakes, that will be demoralizing in the long term and would not be the proper way to nurture great talent. From now on, based on the example of the *sajagwan*, if a court painter is judged guilty, there should first be royal approval to officially expel him. Clearly, appointing someone in the morning and ousting him in the evening causes him to lose the determina-

61 A documentation officer.
62 The Ministry of Rites.

tion to do his best and prevents him from dedicating himself to learning. Furthermore, as court painters and the sajagwan are the same rank and do the same sort of work, their appointment and expulsion should be the same, too." What the former *yejo* minister said makes a lot of sense. Since he was referring to following the example of the *sajagwan*, if guilty, court painters should be officially expelled after getting an approval. Why not implement the plan?"

His Majesty responded, "If an unofficial expulsion of court painters takes place without a royal ordinance to make it official, the officers responsible will be punished accordingly." Bibyeonsa reported, "If a court painter is ousted without cause, it is entirely because of the *yejo* officer's personal feelings. Those who do not meticulously follow Your Majesty's command will be subjected to strict punishment. Why don't we implement this according to the 'Clause on reprimand and discharge'? His Majesty responded, "It shall be thus implemented."

According to the above record, the court painters' salary problem remained unsolved. Secondly, the measures regarding rewards and penalties were to be implemented; however, there is no confirmation that the measures actually were implemented as the king ordered. Furthermore, the court painters' working environment was inferior to that of the *sajagwan*. Note also that some individuals were expelled due to the personal bias of the *yejo* officer in charge.

On the 1st of the 4th lunar month, Jo Su-sam (1762–1849) saw *Danwon's Album of Buddhist Paintings* at Dasangwan and wrote the following inscription, entitled *On 'Danwon's Album of Buddhist Paintings.'*

I received a painting of 12 Buddhist gods on a paper that was folded 12 times. The clean and splendid bottle and stick, and the mature and clean mat and garment mark it as Danwon's work. Pyoam Kang Se-hwang wrote the inscription with script following the style of Chen Jiru. On the 1st of the 4th lunar month of 1786, I went to Dasangwan to see some flowers, and spent the entire

> day appreciating this painting without noticing the red flower petals falling from the tree and piling up on the ground below. I enjoyed this with Yu Sin-eon and Lee Jae-sa. Written on the next day in a boat.

The painting is lost, but the above inscription confirms that Kim Hong-do painted Buddhist paintings when he was young. Around this time, there was an epidemic, and Crown Prince Munhyo succumbed to it on the 11th of the 5th lunar month. The Crown Prince's mother, a royal concubine named Seong, also died in pregnancy on the 14th of the 9th lunar month.

After completing his term as *chalbang*, Kim returned to Hanyang in the 5th lunar month and did two notable things. First, he painted a calligraphy that reads 'Damrakjae' (Plate 45) on a tablet in Chehwajeong, which was hung in the *sarangbang* (a room for the head of a family) of the Seonseong Lee family in Sangri-dong in the Pungsan-eup neighborhood. The inscription reads, "Written by Danwon in the summer of 1786," which suggests that it was written in the 4th or the 5th lunar month just before he left for Hanyang. *Damrak* is an abbreviation of *hwarakchadam* (和樂且湛), which means "peaceful pleasure is endless." The phrase appears both in *Nokmyeong* (鹿鳴) and *Sangche* (常棣), both of which are from *The Book of Songs* (*Shijing*). Danwon seems to have quoted from *Sangche* because Chehwajeong, the *sarangbang* of the house, was named after the first phrase of this poem, sangchejihwa (常棣之華, hawthorn flower). Kim's calligraphy 'Damrakjae' and his seal, which reads *Gomyeongeosa,* suggest that Chalbang Kim Hong-do was living free of worldly cares at the time.

Second, Kim engraved a monument to Governor Kim Sang-cheol and Governor Lee Byeong-mo. The original engraving was on a large rock wall located in San 154, Icheon-dong in Andong. Because this site became a waste dump, the rock surface was moved to a garden in the Andong Folklore Museum. The stone is severely eroded, so it is difficult to read some characters, but the substance of it is as follows.

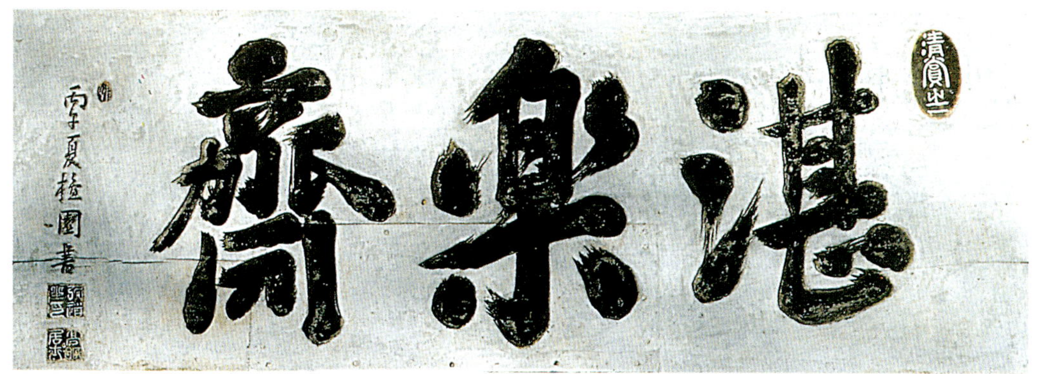

45 ***Damrakjae*****, the tablet of Chehwajeong**
1786. 35×90cm. Private collection.
Chehwajeong was built by Jinsa Manpo Lee Min-jeok during the reign of King Hyojong. Lee lived there with his elder brother, Lee Min-jeong. It is thought that when Kim Hong-do was *chalbang*, the owner of the house was Yongnuljae Lee Han-o (1719-1793), Manpo s son, for whom a memorial gate was established by King Sunjo commemorating Lee Han-o s filial devotion to his old mother.

The Monument to Governor Kim Sang-cheol and Governor Lee Byeong-mo

If you bestow favors impartially, it moves people; if your good deeds are hidden, so much the more. Angi is an impoverished area in the Yeongnam region. During King Yeongjo's rule in 1762, Sanggong Kim Sang-cheol was appointed governor of Gyeongsang Province. He distributed a great amount of money to 11 posts, so that each post would benefit from the interest accrual. In 1784, Governor Lee Byeong-mo granted a large tract of land to the posts so they could use the grains from the land for public funds. The two men granted great favors to the posts. Although what they did was for the public good, we feel their favors were partial, especially because Angi was such an impoverished area. We would like to record what was given to us [...] however, engraving it on a stone is merely a token; we should also engrave it in our hearts. The people of Angi wrote this in the 5th lunar month of 1786 in the tenth year of King Jeongjo's reign.

The monument is composed of eight lines, and is 145×100 centimeters. The first two lines are the title of the text. According to the monument, "the people of Angi wrote this," and there is no acknowledgement of Kim Hong-do. However, Kim is believed to be the author because it concerns funding for Angi and was erected in the 5th lunar month of 1786 at about the time when Kim Hong-do returned to Hanyang after completing his term. Of course, while it is possible that Kim's successor Jang Se-gyeong, inscribed it, it is unlikely that one of his first jobs as *chalbang* would be to erect a monument. Furthermore, the aforementioned *jinggakajip* and the gathering at Mount Cheongryang already confirmed Kim's close friendship with Governor Lee Byeong-mo. Despite the eroded calligraphy, Kim Hong-do probably composed and inscribed the text himself.

King Jeongjo had a profound trust in Lee Byeong-mo from the time he ascended the throne. Lee was well versed in composition and calligraphy, so much so that he served as *wonimjikjehak* of Gyujanggak and governor of Gyeongsang Province. Most significantly, in 1797 he presided over the writing of *The Five Moral Rules with Illustrations* by royal ordinance. Although it is unconfirmed, the late Dr. Kim Won-yong believed that the illustrations in the book were painted by Kim Hong-do. Since we now know that Lee Byeong-mo was the principal figure behind the writing of *The Five Moral Rules with Illustrations* and that he was close to Kim Hong-do when Kim was *chalbang*, the aforementioned possibility is greater.

Kim Hong-do returned to duty as a court painter back in Hanyang.

Kang Se-hwang wrote in *Danwongiuilbon*:

> After completing his term of office, Kim came back to Dohwawon. Occasionally, he painted court banquets. Unknown to those outside the court, every night, Kim wept tears of gratitude for His Majesty's kindness in not having abandoned his humble self.

Soon after returning to Hanyang, Kim met with his teacher, Kang Sehwang, and asked him for *Danwongi*.

> He was appointed to a post supervising post horses. After completing his term of office and returning to Hanyang, he bought a house with a garden. He cleaned it and planted good flowering trees so that no dust rose in the house. Near his writing table lay an old inkstone, high-quality brushes, a good ink stick and silk as white as autumn frost. So, he gave himself the pen name, Dan-

won and asked me to write *Danwongi* for him. I think 'Danwon' is the pen name of Li Liufang of Ming whose courtesy name was Changheng. Why did he take Danwon as his own pen name? It is only because Kim admired Li's elegance as a man of letters and the refinement of his paintings.

However, Kang's account that Kim took Danwon as his pen name after he returned to Hanyang is inaccurate, because Seo Yu-gu had already dubbed Kim as Danwon in the summer of 1781 in his inscription on 'Segeomjeong Gathering,' which depicts a literary gathering of dignitaries that included Seo Yu-gu, Nam Gong-cheol and Seo No-su.

In the 6th lunar month, the Songseokwon Literary Club, a literary club of the *jungin* class, was established. It seems that Kim painted 'Anreungsinyeongdo' in the autumn, but is difficult to believe that the extant painting is the original. There is no record of Kim for 1787 when he was 43. On the 11th of the 2nd lunar month, King Jeongjo took a daughter of Park Jun-won as a royal concubine.

3. Sketch Travels to Mount Geumgang and to Other Scenic Places

Kim Hong-do drew the 'Eunam Gathering' on the 7th of the 3rd lunar month of 1788 at the age of 44, which is indicated in "*Eulogy to 'Eunam Gathering*'" (1788) by Kwon Sang-sin (1759–1824).

It is not that we should avoid merrymaking on a certain day of the year or with anyone in this world. Most of the time, however, we try to find the right time and the right person with whom to connect. After the date and the com-pany are set, we decide on the appropriate venue. We could have picked no better time than the warm spring day of the Day of the Snake in the 3rd lunar month [The first Day of the Snake in the 3rd lunar month fell on the 7th that year], no better company than *the sincere and frank poets* and writers, and no better venue than the quiet open lot in the woods where clear spring water flowed. When the three elements are appropriately set, the rest of the world learns about the party. This is all mentioned in The Lanting Collection of Poems, but no one has managed to continue this beautiful tradition in these godforsaken times. It seems that if it is easy to find the right time and the place, it's difficult to find the appropriate companions; or given the appropriate companions, the time can't be found. For the millennium since the Jin Dynasty, only Han Yu's *Taehakgeumseo* and Bai Juyi's *Nakbingyesi* served the purpose, but unfortunately none can please the eyes and ears of the people like Lanting's story.

We are now in the 12th year of King Jeongjo's rule (1788). The government is fair. The country is peaceful. Crops are good every year. Farmers and merchants are happy. I told my friends, "We fought a war many springs ago. The people of Hanyang have forgotten what war was like and are enjoying themselves, and dancing to the beat of a drum in time of blessing. The villages, in blossom, and the creeks lined with willows resound with folk music. The people are indebted to the king for his kindness. If we were to set the date for inviting noble friends to play at Chundangdae inside the Changgyeong Palace to sing praise for the king, today must be it." On the first Day of the Snake in the

3rd lunar month, fourteen of us gathered at the Great Eunam with Gyeongsan Lee Han-jin present. Wine jars and glasses were scattered about, and dozens of poems and stories were recited. Half-drunk, Gyeongsan wrote in seal script, Yu Hwan-gyeong played the *geomungo*, and Kim Hong-do painted birds, flowers and bamboo. Appreciation of the scenic beauty and the pleasure of enjoying ourselves were not easily abandoned.

Only when the moonlight shone on our backs did we return home. Everyone was satisfied and agreed that there would never be another gathering quite like this one. I took the ink stone and said, "Today we all enjoyed Nanjeong's writing, Taehak's *geomungo*, and the poetry recited by the river frothing with water drops. But we never made a painting to tell the tale. What an immense loss it would be not to capture the beautiful moment in a painting so that our descendants can appreciate the same kind of elegance and serenity." Danwon Kim Hong-do was commissioned to paint the Eunam gathering, and the eulogy was written after the painting was complete.

Looking at the haze far away, I wonder whether it is the bottom of Mount Bukak. Water springs from beneath the rocks and flows into the deep valleys. Is that part of the rapids some 10,000 *li* away? Amidst the stream, a house and a fence stand by a tree. Is that the villa of the Great Eunam? Wine glasses are passed around, the sound of the *geomungo* is heard, and brushes and paper are lying about. Does this mean that it is a lovely season? The spring clothes are done and a group of people are making merry. Is this to follow the footsteps of Confucius? The day's beauty was captured in a painting. Is it to bring back the memories every time people set their eyes on it?

There were fourteen people at the event: Gyeongsan Lee Han-jin's brothers, Jayong Yu Sa-mo, Sukdo Kim Sang-im, Myeongyeo Kim Yi-yeong, Gyeyong Kim Sang-hyu, Taecho Kim Hui-sun, Wonryang Lee Myeong-yeon, Munyeon Kwon Jeon [Kwon Sang-sin's childhood name], Eondo Im Yi-ju, Sijung Lee Do-jung, Iha Sim Sang-gyu, Hoemun Yu Hwan-gyeong and Danwon Kim Hong-do. Jugye Na Yeol was supposed to come but had other urgent matters.

All the participants at the gathering were born to great families of the time. Lee Han-jin was especially important because of his relationship with Kim Hong-do. As a member of the *bukhak* school along with Yeonam Park Ji-won, Park Je-ga, Seong Dae-jung, Hong Won-seop, Lee Deok-mu and Seo Sang-su (1735–1793), Lee wrote for the *yeonam* club and was a leading academic of the late 18th century. He was especially talented at writing in seal script, and his calligraphy occasionally appears on Kim Hong-do's paintings. Lee was also close to Seong Dae-jung, so naturally Seong's book of poems, *Cheongseongjip*, frequently mentions him. The book also briefly mentions his wish to have his portrait and Lee Han-jin's painted by Kim.

Lee Han-jin was also well versed in music and played the bamboo flute so well that he was supposedly the match for Hong Dae-yong's *geomungo*. He was fond of *shijo* and edited *Cheongguyeongeon*, the Korean book of odes, which as previously noted, contains two of Kim Hong-do's *shijo*.

On the 3rd of the 4th lunar month, a little less than a month after Lee Han-jin attended the Eunam Gathering, Lee went to a birthday celebration for Lee Deok-mu's father and sat with Kim Hong-do. In the 9th lunar month of 1792 when Kim Hong-do was *hyeongam* of Yeonpung, the two again met at the Seowon Gathering, which was hosted by Lee Gwang-seop, the newly appointed *byeongsa* of Chungcheong Province. Further details are provided later. Lee Han-jin is also mentioned in one of Kim Hong-do's letters.

> I say these words with my head bowed since I am in my three-year mourning period. Are you well in this cold weather? A wretched person sends his condolences and his respect. Having lost my parents, I feel anew the pains and sadness as the year ends. While I was in mourning, my disease became worse and I almost died. I only just got better. What more can I say? Gyeongsan Lee Han-jin said he had been to your house this morning, and so I asked after your health. I am sending a bottle of wine and some fish with the letter. Please accept my wish to seek your guidance in this time of trouble. Forgive me for dispensing with formalities.

Written by candlelight on the 14th by one who is ashamed to write his name since he is so wretched a son after losing his parents.

As was witnessed in Seong Dae-jung's poem, which mentioned the desire for Kim Hong-do's portrait, Lee Han-jin and Seong were close friends and were the same age. Seong was also close to Kim Hong-do from his days as *chalbang*. The above letter was probably addressed to Seong.

At the 71st birthday celebration for Lee Deok-mu's father, held on the 3rd of the 4th lunar month, Kim painted pictures of a plantain, chrysanthemum, plum, bamboo and the god of longevity. Seong Dae-jung, Lee Han-jin, Lee Gwang-seop, Seo Sang-su, Kim Hong-un and Seong Hae-eung also attended, and Lee Deok-mu's son Gwang-gyu recorded the event in *Cheongjanggwanjeonseo*.[Cheongjanggwan is Lee Deok-mu's pen name.]

On the 3rd of the 4th lunar month of 1788, a party was held and drinks were served. People gathered to celebrate the 71st birthday of Lee Deok-mu's father. Guests enjoyed themselves by sipping wine, and relatives and old friends wrote many poems. Many guests also played with the ink in the evening, and Neunggye Kim Hong-un wrote on the scroll of the painting, "When Sajip Seong Dae-jung grabs the brush the letters look ready to fly off the paper. When Jungun Lee Han-jin writes in seal script, it seems to create haze and gathering clouds. Hwajung Lee Gwang-seop was good at inscribing official script, and Deokjae Gu Hyang-won was good at cursive script. Gigong Seo Sang-su painted lotus flowers and leaves. Seokyeo (Neunggye himself) got drunk and then sobered up. Yeongsuk (Lee Deok-mu's brother-in-law) fell asleep. Cheongjanggwan Lee Deok-mu was tired from drinking too much, Chicheon Park Jong-san was too sleepy to write, and Musang (Lee Deok-mu's younger brother), Yongyeo Seong Hae-eung (Seong Dae-jung's son), Bonggo Lee Gwang-gyu (Lee Deok-mu's son) and Sahwang (Neunggye's son, Lee Deok-mu's son-in-law) wrote something at the end of the scroll. Jungrae, Lee Deok-mu's six-year-old nephew, wrote the Chinese character for sky while two *gisaeng*[63] watched. If

63 A female entertainer.

Danwon (Chwihwasa Kim Hong-do) had not drawn his plantain, chrysanthemum, plum, bamboo and god of longevity we could not have captured the joyous moment. After three rounds of drinks, someone spread the scroll and wrote something, and somebody else drank too much and got really drunk. Someone else screamed at the top of his lungs, and someone else staggered as he danced, while luxurious strings and the rapid blaring of brass instruments added to the excitement. Lee Deok-mu was very pleased to see that every guest wished his father a long life."

The detailed record allows us to envision the day. The guests invited to the party were all romantics and well versed in poetry, writing and calligraphy. Lee Han-jin and Kim Hong-do were very close friends, as was previously mentioned. Although having a different academic background, Seong Dae-jung was close to Lee Deok-mu and three other Gyujanggak officials. Seong himself was also an accomplished painter and writer, close to Lee Gyu-sang (who had left an observation of Kim Hong-do), and wrote *Yuyudanggi* for him. Park Ji-won complimented Seo Sang-su by saying he had mastered the art of appreciating painting and literature. Along with Lee Deok-mu, Seo was a core member of the *bukhak* study, and was skilled in painting landscapes by using a special technique in which the ink spread like small powders of rice. Lee Gwang-seop was appointed *byeongsa* of Chungcheong Province, and he hosted the Seowon Gathering in the 9th lunar month of 1792, when Kim Hong-do was *hyeongam* in Yeonpung. This will be discussed in detail later. Lee Deok-mu was an excellent writer and painter, especially of birds, animals and spiders. His collection of writings includes two inscriptions attached to Kim Hong-do's paintings.

In the fall of the same year, King Jeongjo ordered Kim Hong-do to paint his famous 'Mount Geumgang,' which contains the beautiful scenery of the twelve thousand mountain peaks. Seo Yu-gu's writing gives us a hint about the masterpiece.

Danwon's 'Mount Geumgang'

Kim Hong-do went by the pen name Danwon, and he was such an excellent painter that he served as *gongbong* of the Office of Interior during King Jeongjo's reign. Having received the orders from the king, Kim spent 50 days on Mount Geumgang and painted the 12,000 peaks and Guryong Waterfall. The beautiful scenery filled several silk scrolls. The colors had class, and the brush strokes were elaborate and skillful. The importance of this painting should not be overlooked simply because it follows the typical court painting style and uses bright colors.

'Mount Geumgang' is painted on a very long scroll and must have been a masterpiece of deep-colored pigments. Other than the scroll format for the king, the painting also came in the form of an album entitled *The Ocean and the Mountain*, which is mentioned by Hong Gil-ju (1786–1841).

On the Ocean and the Mountain by Danwon

The area around Mount Geumgang boasts of the most beautiful scenery on earth. The deceased king ordered Kim Hong-do to paint the mountain, and the king kept the 70-page, five-volume album in the palace. Hong-do, whose pen name was Danwon, was an excellent painter. In 1809, the present king ordered that this album be given to the late king's son-in-law, who is my younger brother. Three years later, in 1812, Yeoncheon, my elder brother, wrote the preface to the album. Nine years later, in 1821, Yeoncheon wrote poems for the album, one quatrain for each page, totaling 70 in all. Not all the writings and poems were included in the album. Eight years later, in 1829, the late king's son-in-law asked me to write the calligraphy. Praise the king! I cannot thank him enough for this honor; I cannot forget a great painter's hard work; I can only look at and admire the scenery; and I must express in words the joy my brothers got from the painting. After finishing this writing, I briefly summarized what had happened so far. Today is the 12th of the 3rd lunar month of 1829.

The above record tells us that Kim Hong-do's *The Ocean and the Mountain* was a 70-page five-volume album, a supplement to the scroll format of 'Mount Geumgang,' and that King Sunjo presented it to his brother-in-law Hong Hyeon-ju (1793–1865) in 1809. Hong Gil-ju copied what his elder brother Seok-ju (1774–1842) had written in *On the Ocean and the Mountain, which is owned by my youngest brother, the late king's son-in-law,* which is as follows.

> My youngest brother Hyeonju became King Jeongjo's son-in-law when he was very young, so he was unable to pursue a career as a government official although he was academically inclined. Instead, he developed the habit of collecting scrolls of paintings and writings he was fond of, and collected several hundred volumes. I thought it was better for him to follow those interests than be worried about the things that concern a king's son-in-law. I also enjoyed examining his collections. My brother once showed me Kim Hong-do's 'The Ocean and the Mountain'; Kim was a very famous painter. The album was done under the direct order of the previous king, so I am writing an inscription, and I am urging my brother to continue his interest in artistic matters.

This was written in 1812. Nine years later, Hong Seok-ju wrote a quatrain for every picture, and 23 of the 70 were included in his collection. Seok-ju wrote, "*On the Ocean and the Mountain by Danwon*; I selected 23 out of 70 quatrains. Danwon is the pen name of painter Kim Hong-do," which was copied in *The Ocean and the Mountain* in Hong Gil-ju's handwriting.

Cheongheo Tower

Fate extends over two generations in this beautiful land
Looking at the painting I am overcome with grief
I could never take the road to the east in my lifetime
It is almost eleven years ago since my heart was broken
(The tower is in Wonju. My deceased grandfather and uncle had written a travel log, based on which I wrote the poem.)

Cheongsimdae

The cliff is so high it takes the breath away from on-lookers
A horse is resting by the waterside against the sunset
I only knew the high places were rugged
Little did I know they were as complicated as the inside of a sheep.

Archive

The fire that burned the archive of the Han Dynasty
Never rose again with the help of Buddha and the Mountain God
Twenty years ago what I had done with paper
The ink stain flew into the air and fell into the pond.

Upper House

Amidst the dark tone of the mountain, in the highest tower
The blue door to the temple is left open, I wonder for whom
Never say that men underneath the woods are invisible
When sometimes a bridled horse neighs, [...] comes.

Daegwanryeong

The roads on the hills are treacherous and very remote
At the end of the road is the giant ocean
I never repaid the king his grace but am retired now
I lost heart and am deploring over his kind but stern words.

Cheonyeon Pavilion

Under the shade of ten thousand trees stands a straw cottage
The cool winds of the 7th lunar month blow in through the doors
A gentleman standing in a remote spot knows not the fidelity of bamboo
Peaks reflected in the water look lonely and blue.

Gusan Seowon

Thin bamboos and cold *paulownia* trees keep the phoenix away
The lecture hall is empty, waiting for people to come up the green mountain
The meaning of time is melted in the spring water and green trees
We can hear the sound of the walking cane and the footsteps of the scholar.

(Gusan Seowon is where Lee Yul-gok was born. His birth house Ojukheon is there.)

Jukseo Tower

The tower of Three God Mountains hovers over the distant water
Revealed is the protruding railing of the west corner of the military office
The songs from the boat sound farther and farther away at night
Under the moonlight a fishing rod is cast into the river from a hilltop.

Mureung Brook

The stone gate is deeply immersed in water, never meeting people
Only the brook is flowing by, it is spring inside the valley
Around the bend of the valley are pretty peach blossoms
Who should I ask the way to Mureung ferry?

Waseondae

The springtime is an idle season on the platform
The white stone and green moss each serve as pillow and blanket
There is no way of knowing where the Taoist hermit lay
Only the sound of the water and shadow of the pine trees fill the mountain.

Cheonggan Pavilion

The blue ocean is vast enough to support the sky above
The sun and the moon appear in front of the eaves
From far away flower of a wave rises
That must be the yellow dragon's boat carrying its heavy load.

Gahak Pavilion

On Yeongrang Lake Hill where the wild roses are red and the sand white
The water close by meanders and the distant island looks vague
Pray tell me where the traveler on a donkey from Huaying went
Did he not stay at Hwanghak Tower and write an inscription?

Hyeonjongam Rock

The Yellow River god's drum stopped beating and the pretty girl fell asleep
The sound from the ancient times had died down
The ripples are soaked with the bright moonlight
Who dares stop the boat of Su Dongpo?

Yeongrang Lake

Gentle breeze blowing by, barely stirring the water in the rice paddies
Boat bobbing up and down in the moonlight with no one on board
All the Taoist gods from the sea must have stayed here
By chance the lake earned its name Yeongrang.

Daeho Pavilion

The Namgang River in spring is greener than the moss
The aura of the stone comes spiraling down the ladder against the blue cliff
The door to the sea is too deep to see
The lazy oars in the sunset are bringing the fishing boat back home.

Samil River Bank

Taoist gods of Lake Dongjeong descend from the cloud carriage
With subtle and beautiful makeup on, there is no need to draw again
Peaks out of the fog number thirty-six in all
The loneliest island in the water stands out the clearest.

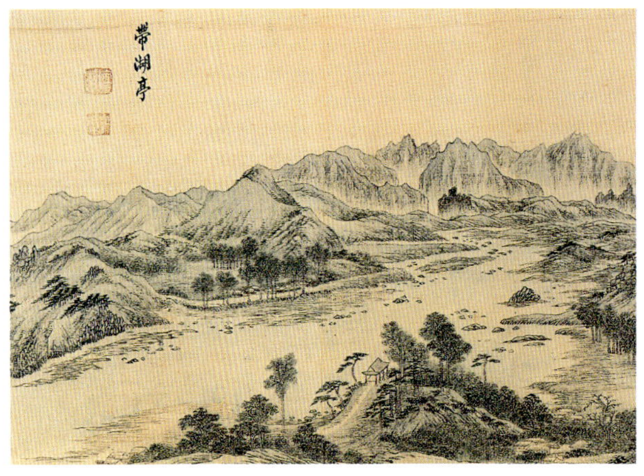

46 ***Daeho Pavilion***

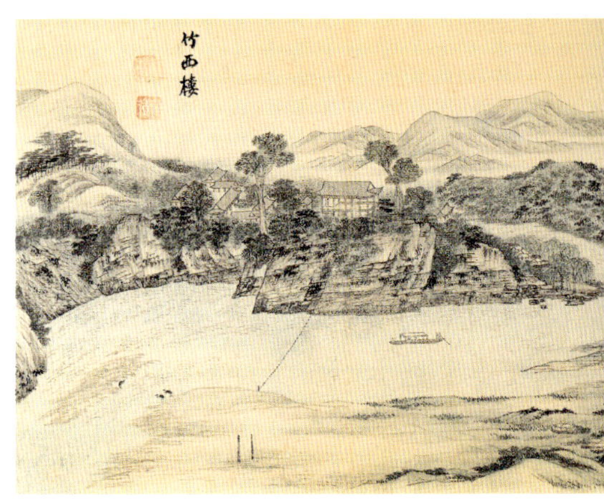

47 ***Jukseo***

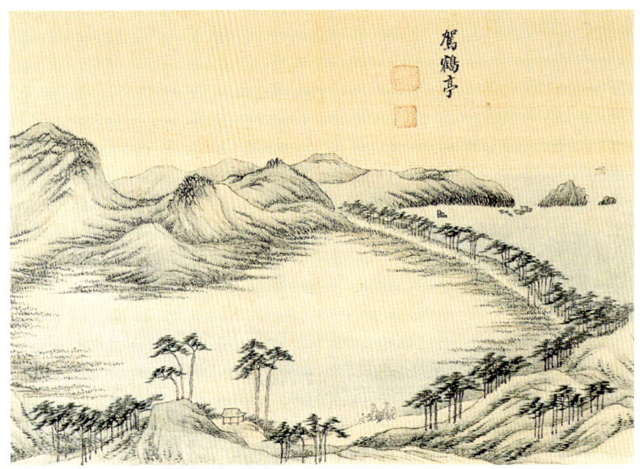

48 ***Gahak Pavilion***

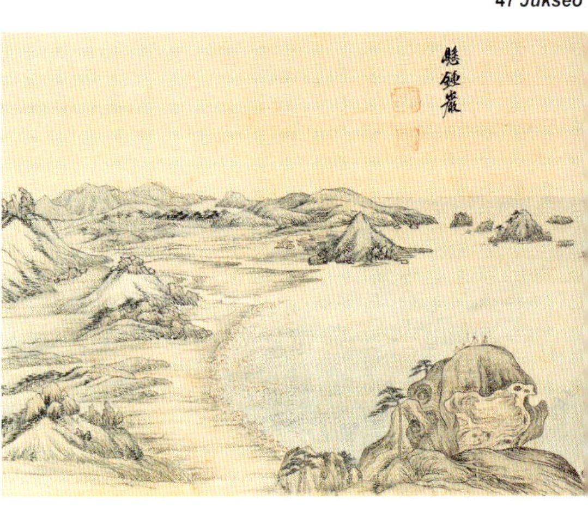

49 **Hyeonjongan**

46-64 From *The Ocean and the Mountain*

1788. Ink and color on silk. 30.4×43.7cm each. Private collection.

The Ocean and the Mountain made its first public appearance in 1995. Until then, it was known only through photographs. The sparse imitation seals and incomprehensible ink writings raised doubts as to the paintings authenticity, but these traces make them more realistic. It was customary for paintings that were to be viewed by the king not to have the painter s seal stamped on them, but to have labels separately attached to indicate the name of the place being depicted. As the album disintegrated and each picture was sold separately, numerous seals and explanations were added to each individual work. The writings of the family who had originally owned the album do not appear for the same reason. Most important, however, are the characteristics of each painting. King Jeongjo dearly wanted to see the true landscape of Mou Geumgang, so paintings contained in *The Ocean and the Mountain* were pain very realistically, resembling photographs, and had considerable effort in each stroke-so much so that the details undermine the paintings elegance. Such fo art was typical of paintings for the king. The first draft of the underlying ink sketc *The Ocean and the Mountain* was recently discovered. The two works share t same form, but the first draft is more lively and dynamic, while the finished pair shows more formality and rigidity. The quality of *The Ocean and the Mountain* high.

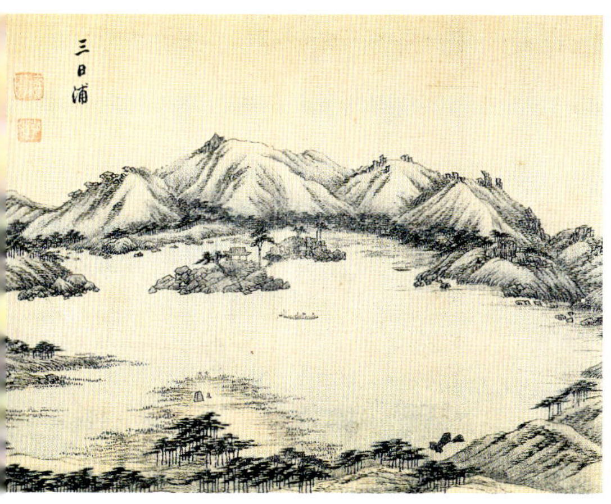

50 *Samil River Bank*

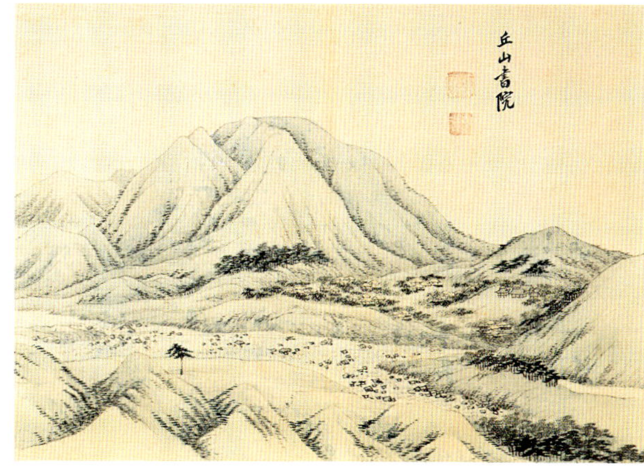

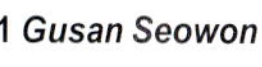

51 *Gusan Seowon*

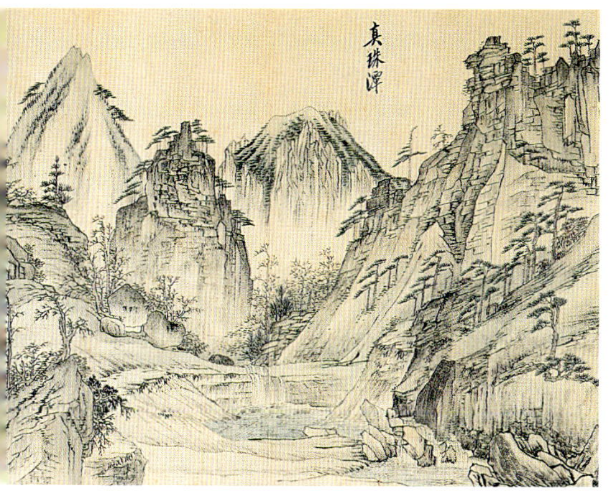

52 *Jinju Lake*

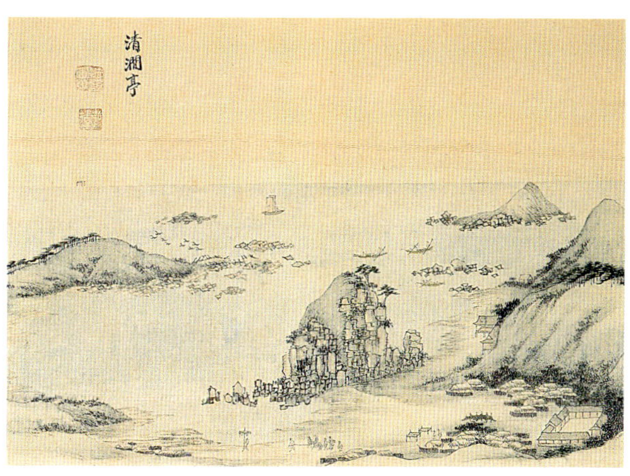

53 *Cheonggan Pavilion*

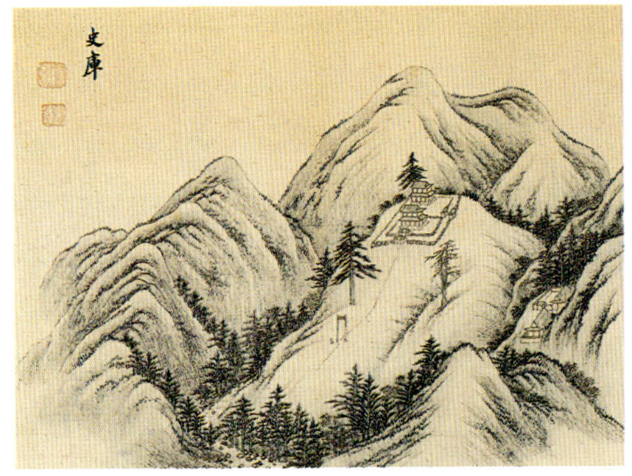

54 *Archive*

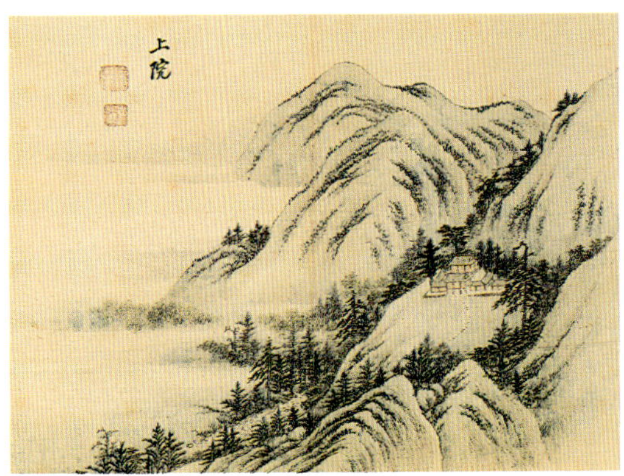

55 *Upper House*

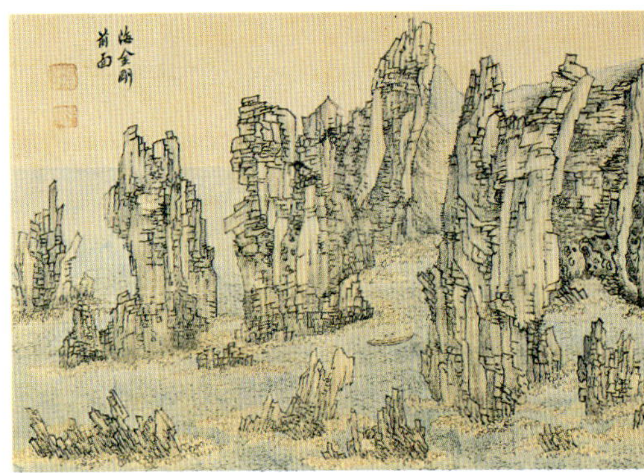

56 *Haegeumgang*

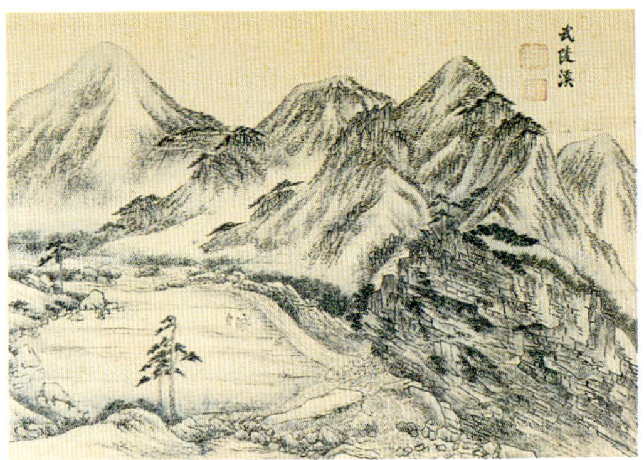

57 *Mureung Brook*

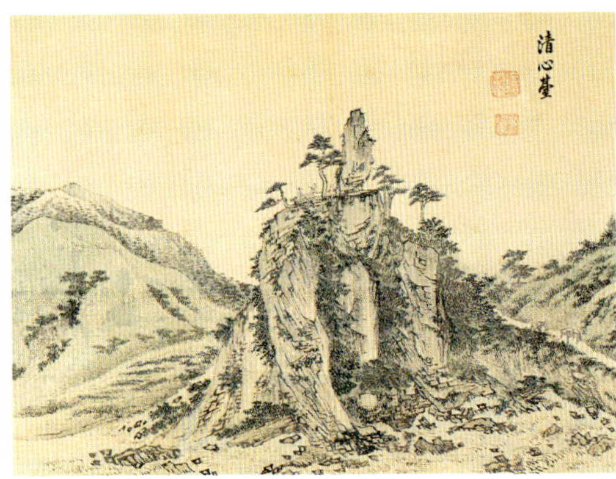

58 *Cheongsimdae*

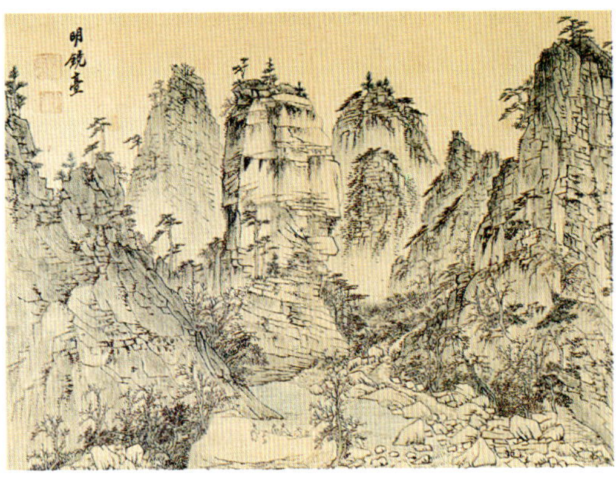

59 *Myeonggyeongdae*

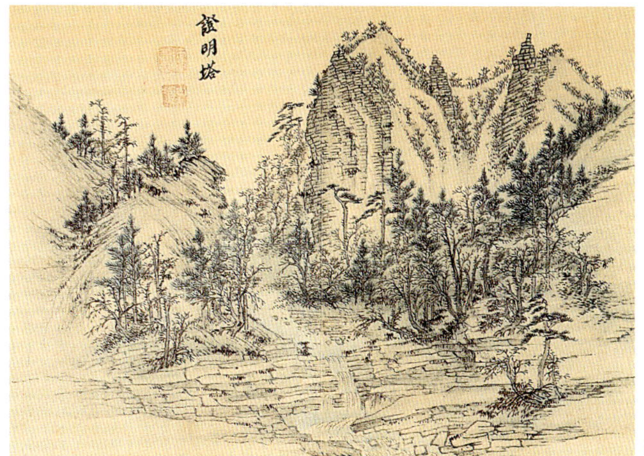

60 *Jeungmyeongtap*

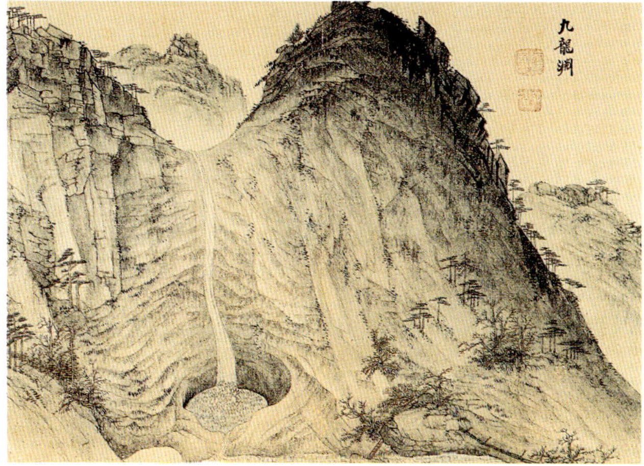

61 *Guryong Pond*

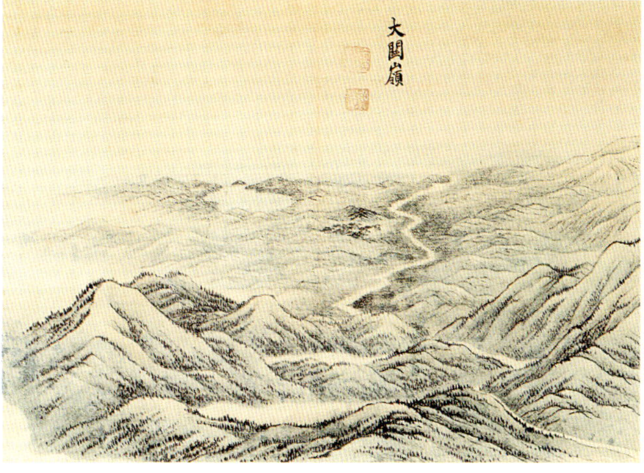

62 *Daegwanryeong*

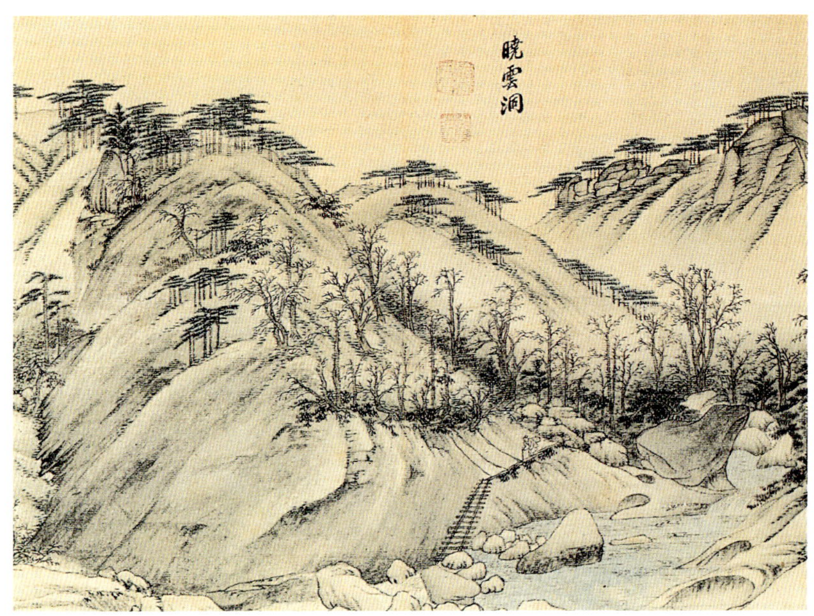

63 *Hyoun-dong*

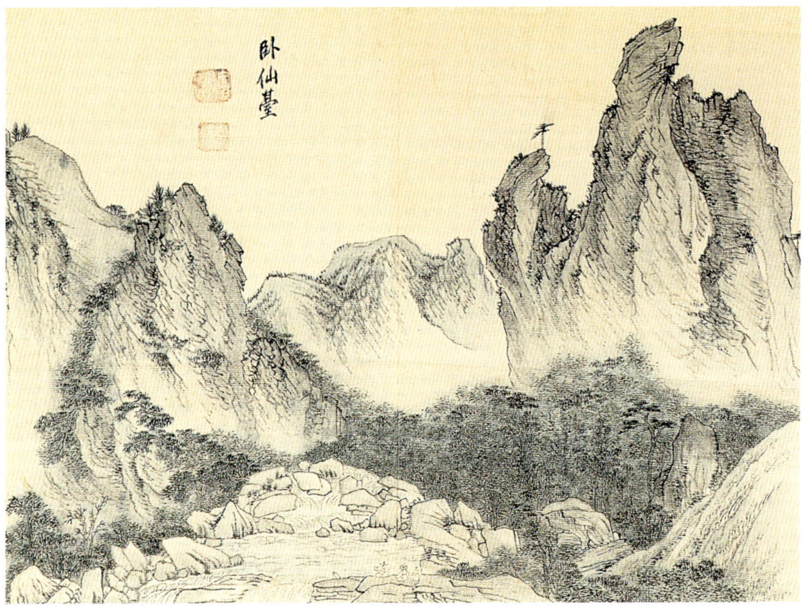

64 *Waseondae*

Haegeumgang

Did the Taoist god produce a lotus from his palm?
Did he scatter among the blue waves and find the jade dragon?
Are the clouds and birds above the water real or imaginary?
I ask these questions to the 10,000 peaks of Mount Bongrae.[64]

Jeongyangsa Temple

It was in spring when I was nineteen that I climbed Mount Bongrae
Even to this day I wonder if I had really been up there
When the moon rose near Heolseong Tower at night
Everyone and everything on this earth felt unreal.

Jinju Lake

The Taoist god gave me a bottle to catch the breeze
I spilled out the contents on a tray and beads of moonlight came out
The tray was too slippery for the beads to stay still
Better place them under the chin of an old dragon as the cintamani.[65]

Myeonggyeongdae

Rising high and wearing a beautiful crown of yellow sunset
The shadow cast on the pond; the jade mirror is ice cold
The face gained twenty more years and white hair
It is still embarrassing to stand in front of it and stare at my reflection.

Jeungmyeongtap

The roof tiles and stone fences all add up to Buddha's body
Even a cold-looking stone displays naiveté
The monk who was paying worship to the Buddha just now is nowhere to be found
Water flows and flower blossoms but no man in sight.

64 Bongrae is the nickname of Mount Geumgang in summer.

65 A magical jewel believed to possess the power to grant every wish. It is an attribute of the Buddhas and bodhisattvas, hence a symbol of a mind that has attained its proper desire.

Hyoun-dong

The high tower on top of the stone hides the bridge that was cut off
Is that passer-by the woodcutter who appeared in the dream where time goes quickly?
Away from the valley and into the early morning under the mountain clouds
In my dreams the Taoist hermit from Huayang is playing the bamboo flute.

Guryong Pond

Thunder and winds roar in the dark valley during daytime
The waters rise up and water drops scatter everywhere
It has been a while since the dragon lay down in the pond; when will it get up?
Right close by is the East Sea and great waves.

The existence of these nineteen poems with the exception of "*Cheongheo Tower*," "*Cheonyeon Pavilion*," "*Yeongrang Lake* and *Jeongyangsa Temple,"* was proven in the *Full-view Painting of Mount Geumgang*, a private collection that has only recently been opened to the public.

Hong In-mo (1755–1812), the father of the three Hong brothers, wrote his own book of poetry, *Joksudangjip*, which includes a poem entitled *"First Draft Landscape."*

Great rivers and mountains are in front of my eyes
Something blue and something white wind and unwind, filling up the space
High is the Kunlun, and low is the small hill
Great is the vast blue sea, and small is the stream
Waves stretch far outward adjoining the sky and the land
The mountains are blue and remote, forming a shield of fog
Difficult to fathom the depth of the rough waters
Unable to count how many peaks there are
I have a boat and a set of oars as well as a walking stick and moccasins

I can travel far without any discomfort
Mystical trace of a hundred years lives within
A person close by would not be able to get a glimpse
Go back in time to find good friends
And they are Zong Ping, Luyan, and old Du Fu.

The format of the collection indicates that it was probably written in 1810. This is one year after his son Hong Hyeon-ju received the album from the king. From the content we immediately know it refers to the *The Ocean and the Mountain.* Hong In-mo's wife, Lady Seo (1753–1823), also added a poem entitled "*On 'Landscape'*" to the same work.

Surprised was I when there was a storm in the house
Suspicious was I to see a house on a piece of paper
Ocean of silver and mountain of jade are exquisite to the eye
Wondrous is the brush stroke; a ghost must have been swinging his ax
A deer is hopping gracefully among green bamboos and purple herbs of eternal youth
Phoenix and crane are dancing in the red laurels and green pines
Fish are swimming in the sunset, which resembles scattered beads
Waterfall hurries to the stones, sounding like angry thunder and lightning
The sun and the moon in the valley sometimes lose their brilliance
Heat waves in the valley keep shimmering and disappearing again
Errand boy of the Taoist hermit went to the mountain in the west to find herbs
Fairy went to the stream in the south to pick up beads
Never say it is impossible to stay in the Taoist hermit's lands for too long
I plan to let my hair down and live the rest of my life here
I had a quick tour of the outskirts of the fairyland
But how could I have not set the walking stick outside the home again?

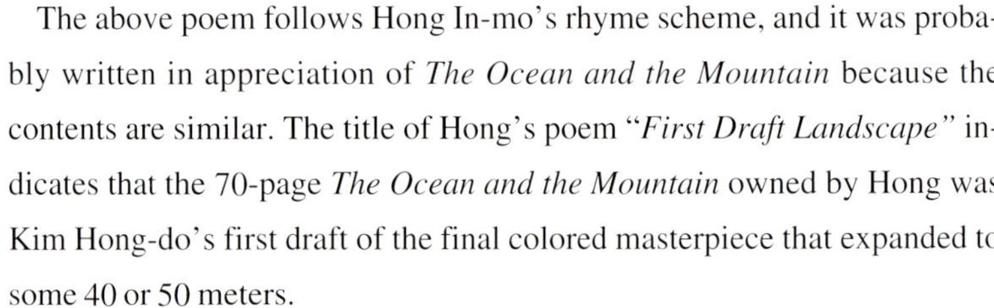

The above poem follows Hong In-mo's rhyme scheme, and it was probably written in appreciation of *The Ocean and the Mountain* because the contents are similar. The title of Hong's poem "*First Draft Landscape*" indicates that the 70-page *The Ocean and the Mountain* owned by Hong was Kim Hong-do's first draft of the final colored masterpiece that expanded to some 40 or 50 meters.

Kang Se-hwang's *Record of Mount Geumgang Travel* provides glimpses of Kim Hong-do's travels during the sketching period.

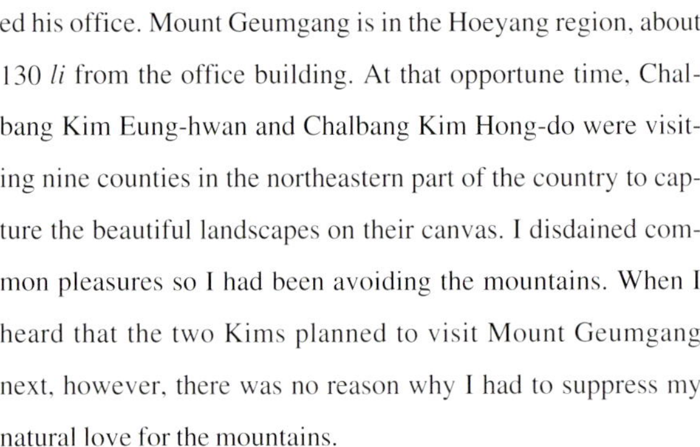

In the fall of 1788, my eldest son was appointed *busa* in Hoeyang, and I visited his office. Mount Geumgang is in the Hoeyang region, about 130 *li* from the office building. At that opportune time, Chalbang Kim Eung-hwan and Chalbang Kim Hong-do were visiting nine counties in the northeastern part of the country to capture the beautiful landscapes on their canvas. I disdained common pleasures so I had been avoiding the mountains. When I heard that the two Kims planned to visit Mount Geumgang next, however, there was no reason why I had to suppress my natural love for the mountains.

On the 13th of the 9th lunar month, I left the regional office for Sinchang with the two Kims, my third son Bin, my concubine's son Sin, and my friends Im Hui-yang (1737–1813) and Hwang Gyu-eon. The next day, I noticed the leaves in the mountains had turned beautiful colors. Suddenly a gust of wind blew and snowflakes brushed against our sleeves. Sin and Saneung Kim Hong-do each played the flute and exchanged tunes as we rode. There is an old saying, "On a very cold day, although you are shivering inside, you scream very loudly complaining few people recognize you." Playing the flute in this cold weather seemed like a desperate act to make ourselves heard, so everyone laughed at the joke. We didn't arrive at Jangansa Temple until

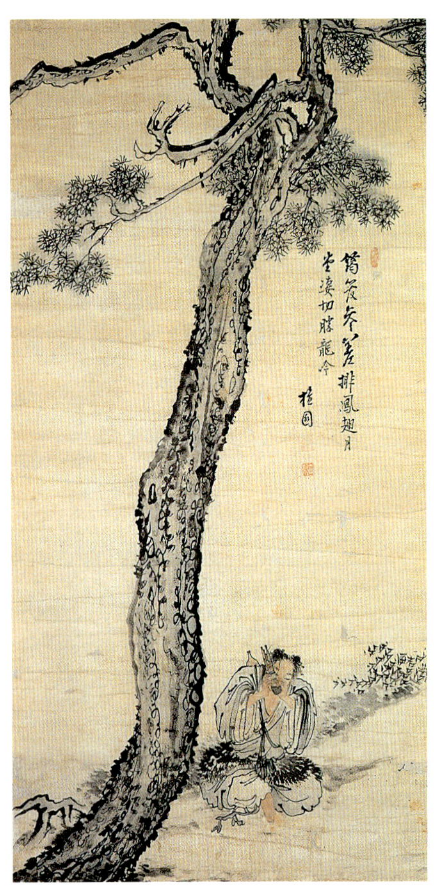

65 *Playing a Reed Instrument under the Pine Tree*
Ink and color on paper. 109 × 55cm. Korea University Museum.
The tall pine tree boldly divides the screen in two. The painter has removed the roots on the bottom and the branches on the top thereby drawing the observer directly into the scene. The bark is expressed with bouncy spiral movements to give a sense of unconventionality.

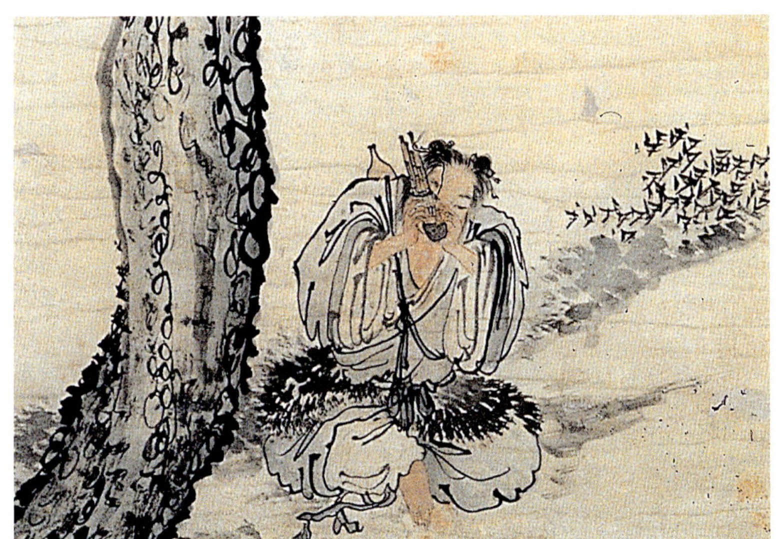

66 Detail of Plate 65
The inscription reads, The bamboo reeds resemble the wings of a phoenix. The sound coming from a moonlit house is more miserable than the cry of a dragon. Clad in a feather robe, a Taoist hermit plays a reed instrument. The painter drew the instrument sideways so the hermit s intelligent eyes are visible. The creases in the robe are very fast and rhythmic, as though the viewer can see the sound. The wave-like fold on the left shoulder is highly impressive.

after sunset. The temple used to be very famous, but now it was very old; both the bridge and the house were in need of repair. The monks had deserted the place. It looked like a grand villa with no master and only a few slaves to take care of it. It made a great impression on me. We all slept in the dormitory to the right of the sanctuary, and a relative, Park Hwang, and Changhae Jeongran joined us.

The following day was the fifteenth. The temple was a gate to Mount Geumgang, and we were already overwhelmed by the grandeur of the mountain, its spirit and the sound of the waters even before we had entered it. The two Kims had already drawn the general outline of the mountain. I sat in the temple yard and painted what I saw. After the two Kims returned from Baektapdong on the night of the 16th, we all slept at Pyohunsa Temple. The rest of us returned to the office building on the 17th while the two Kims went to Yujeomsa Temple. They promised to look around at more sights and come back to the Hoeyang Office.

Thus, Kim Hong-do and Kim Eung-hwan returned to the Hoeyang office to see Kang Se-hwang after touring and painting the famous sights of nine counties in northeastern Korea. Kim Hong-do left from the office building on the 13th of the 9th lunar month and was accompanied by Kang Se-hwang,

Kim Eung-hwan, Kang Bin, Kang Sin, Im Hui-yang and Hwang Gyu-eon. The road to Mount Geumgang was pleasant with its beautiful foliage, and despite the cold weather Kim Hong-do and Kang Sin played musical instruments. Kang Sin (1767–1821) was Kang Se-hwang's illegitimate son and a talented musician and painter, undoubtedly, the reason he got along so well with Kim Hong-do. Kang Se-hwang may have outwardly laughed at their unseasonable merrymaking, but inside he must have been proud. In the evening of the 14th, Park Hwang and Jeongran joined them at Jangansa Temple. The previous chapter discussed the famous traveler and poet Jeongran who appeared in 'Danwon, the Garden of Birch Trees.' Kim sketched the surroundings of Jangansa Temple the next day, and on the 16th sketched some more in the area around Baektapdong, sleeping at Pyohunsa Temple. The following day, he left for Yujeomsa Temple, which is probably where he parted from the Kang Se-hwang party. Kang specifically asked Kim to stop by the Hoeyang Office and show him what he had drawn. Kim Eung-hwan and Kim Hong-do complied with the request, and after seeing their paintings, Kang Se-hwang wrote "*Seeing off Chalbang Kim Hong-do and Chalbang Kim Eung-hwan*," which was previously examined.

Kim Hong-do's 'Mount Geumgang' still exists in the form of an album, but the 40 to 50 meter colored scroll does not. We can only imagine that in contrast with the stark, realistic paintings in the five-volume *The Ocean and the Mountain*, the 'Mount Geumgang' scroll must have been an artistic reconstruction of the beautiful scenes that freely flowed, transcending the limitations of life-like pictures. King Jeongjo apparently adored this work, but unfortunately it was lost in a palace fire in King Sunjo's time.

After returning from the mountains, Kim Hong-do went to Chungryeolsa Temple in Chungju on the 20th of the 11th lunar month. From the 21st of the 11th lunar month to the 14th of the 12th lunar month, he copied the portrait of General Im Gyeong-eop, which when completed was moved to the temple on the fifteenth. The primary source for this information is *The True Record of General Im Chung-min*, but the artist is not mentioned by name.

This evidence, when taken with Jo Hui-ryong's record, indicates that Kim Hong-do probably painted the aforementioned portrait of General Im.

> I passed by the town of Dalgye and came across the portrait of Chung-min General Im Gyeong-eop. He looked very handsome, and the portrait had a certain air that made it difficult to approach him. This is the work of Danwon Kim Hong-do. His reputation as a good portrait painter had not preceded him, but even while I was still unaware that Kim had painted the portrait, I could sense the artist's skill. An analogy to literature would be that even Sima Qian's brush could not have written about the great sagas of the time if he had not met great heroes of Western Han. As Danwon painted one of the greatest heroes of the time, his nascent skills and the righteousness of the general were synergetic, and without much effort, the brush expressed what it needed to. There is no arguing with that logic.

A Chinese painter painted the original portrait of General Im that Kim Hong-do had copied. Because it was an exact replica, it is difficult to distinguish Kim Hong-do's unique style from the existing portrait. A closer inspection of the three surviving portraits of the general that are in the National Museum of Korea, the family shrine and Chungryeolsa Temple may identify which one was painted by Kim Hong-do.

Toward year-end, in the 12th lunar month, Gosongyusugwan Lee In-mun, Seomukjae Park Yu-seong, Gojol Kim Gwang-guk, Uiwon Kim Ga-il, Oncheon Bang Yu-neung and Yu Gye-yeon gathered at Sibudang in Noguiwon. They appreciated 'Landscape,' which was copied and painted by Kim Eung-hwan in 1779. The epilogue mentions that the plums were in blossom.

> In early 12th lunar month of 1788, Yu Gye-yeon, Danwon Kim Saneung, Gosongyusugwandoin Lee In-mun, Gojol Kim Gwang-guk, Uiwon Kim Ga-il, Seomukjae Park Yu-seong and Oncheon Bang Yu-neung looked at it at Sibudang in Noguiwon. At the time, the plum trees were in blossom.

Perhaps Kim Hong-do painted the great mountains of the southeastern part of the country in 1789, and then continued to Gangjin County in Jeolla Province, and then to Tsushima Island, but the record is not certain. The evidence for speculation is the following record from which O Se-chang quoted, *Genealogy of the Kims*.

> Kim Eung-hwan was famous for his paintings. In 1788, the 12th year of King Jeongjo's rule, he obeyed a royal order to travel across Mount Geumgang and return with a painting of the mountain. The following year, he received another royal order to go to Japan and secretly draw a map, but he died in Busan at the age of 48. The young Kim Hong-do, who was accompanying him during the travel, handled the funeral, went to Tsushima Island alone, drew the map and returned to present it to the king.

The king supposedly ordered Kim Hong-do and Kim Eung-hwan to secretly go to Tsushima Island to draw a map, but Kim Eung-hwan suddenly died in Busan. Kim Hong-do arranged his funeral and went alone to the island to complete the mission. We already examined the erroneous phrase "the young Kim Hong-do." The following piece by Yu Jae-geon (1793–1880) raises the likelihood that the two Kims had been to Busan.

> Kim Eung-hwan was famous for his painting as was Danwon Kim Hong-do, and he was especially talented in painting landscapes. During King Jeongjo's reign in 1788, he went to Mount Geumgang with Danwon, painted the beautiful scenery and submitted his paintings to the king. In 1789, he was dispatched to southeastern Joseon to paint the great mountains in the region. The paintings are contained in an album, which is stored in the palace. People said Bokheon Kim Eung-hwan was a better painter than Danwon.

Harmonizing the two records indicates that in 1789 the two Kims were together in the southeastern part of the country, completing their assignment. Yu Jae-geon lived 70 years before O Se-chang, and Yu was about the same age as Kim Hong-do's son. Since he had worked as an official at Gyujanggak, he was well informed of palace affairs; thus his account cannot be lightly dismissed. The problematic area in *Genealogy of the Kims* is Kim Hong-do's age, but since we know Kim Hong-do's age now, the best guess is that the record was mistaken about Kim Eung-hwan's age. If Kim Eung-hwan had been 8 or 9 nine years older than what we know now to be true, O Se-chang's hypothesis of his being Hong-do's mentor might have been true. At any rate, if indeed the two painters went to the southeastern part of Joseon in 1789 and Kim Hong-do went to Tsushima Island to paint the map, then the following poem "*Full-view Painting of Geumreung*" in Jeong Yak-yong's *Jinjuseon* becomes all the more relevant.

> To the north of the Geumsabong Peak is Geumreung
> On top of Geumreung is the Udubong Peak, which resembles a bull's head
> The sky is blue above the Gusip Port
> The water in the Twin Well is always clear
> An old village called Tamjin is nearby
> It has a good name, Geoneop
> A pond is connected to a waterway and is as round as a mirror
> The square fortress stands in a straight line
> The spring season is sliced on a golden platter like the snow
> Wind blows in the colored tower, cool enough to freeze the summer fly
> A thousand houses outside the fortress are lined up like wild geese
> From a distance away, they look like fishnets
> Sailboats are docked with their black and red flags flying in the air
> Yellow crops are dancing in the wind, the rice sea sending out waves
> Mount Mandeok is green because of the *torreya* nut and old pine trees
> Guryeong Fortress is bluish because lotuses and water chestnuts are plentyiful
> When the moon shines in the remote village, a moss-covered gravestone stands out

The tower is leaning against the bamboo railing as if to quiet down the sound of waves

The thunderous morning drum chases away the wild geese and ducks

The water level dropped in autumn on the stepping-stones, attracting a fish hawk

In the western fortress the provocative *gisaeng* play ball

In the northern temple a bell tolls; there must be plump monks

I ask the name on a red sleeve, and the answer is in some form of flower or moon

Politics are done with the royal seal on yellow chain but the experience is none too pleasant

Jillin Sea is so vast a python lies underneath

Mount Iyeong has deep valleys which elks and deer enjoy

Baekdobong Peak is pointy, delivering the smoke signal from the port

Chilyangcha is bent, showing the lights on fishing boats

Mount Suin altogether defends the nation

The barrack gate of the *byeongsa* office openeds brandishing its power

White battlement and red towers look like they are part of a painting

Cold frost and bright light look dignified

The colors of a famous fortress are pleasing to look at

But it takes a master painter to capture them on a canvas

As every nook and cranny of this quaint town are described in a history book

Danwon used a ruler in the painting; he must be a learned man

Over the heat haze, there are houses with dual eaves

The landscape is all there on a roll of silk

Do not say there is a degree to luxury

The beauty of Malleung is concentrated all in here.

The above "*Full-view Painting of Geumreung*" mentions numerous geographical points such as Gusip Port and Geumsabong Peak, which stands on the opposite side of Gangjin. It is probable that the painting is of the

Gangjin County in South Jeolla Province. The nickname of the place is Geumreung because it has a rich history and resources, and is located on the delta of Tamjin River. Its geographic characteristics are similar to those of Nanjing. Geoneop and Malleung, which appear in the text, and are all old names of Nanjing, which was the capital city of the Southern Dynasties.

'Full-view Painting of Geumreung' is a type of colored *gyehwa*[66] painted on silk. The painting is an overview of the entire village, and its essential theme is "eight scenic spots in Geumreung." For Kim Hong-do to have completed the full-view painting in colored *gyehwa*, which would consume a considerable amount of time and effort, he had to have spent several days in the town. Consequently, the 'Full-view Painting of Geumreung' must have been for royal inspection. Jeong Yak-yong, who wrote the above poem, was the king's servant and had access to pictures to be examined by the king; this makes the scenario more likely. If Kim Hong-do did tarry in Gangjin to finish this painting, then we cannot overlook Gangjin's being the conduit to Jeju Island, and thus Tsushima Island. Consequently, perhaps the assignment Kim had to finish led him and Kim Eung-hwan to Gangjin on their way to Tsushima Island, but this cannot be confirmed.

66 A painting that uses a ruler or other implements to make the painting more precise.

67 *Three Tathagatas*
1790. Color on silk. 440×350cm. The main worship hall of Yongjusa Temple.
Sakyamuni is in the center, Amitabha is on the left, and Bhaisajyaguru, Buddha of medicine, is on the right. The three Tathagatas are gathered in the middle, and circling them are the Eight Great Bodhisattvas including attendants. The Four Devas (heavenly kings) are in the four corners. There is no empty space in the painting; it is entirely covered by bodhisattvas and family to express Buddhism, which indicates that all existence is governed by law and wisdom.

4. Difficulties Encountered as *Hyeongam*

In the 7th lunar month of 1789, King Jeongjo decided to move Yeongu-won, the grave of his father Royal Crown Prince Sado, to Suwon and rename it Hyeonryungwon. The reconstruction of the Yongjusa Temple began a year later, and the temple was to serve as a memorial temple for Hyeonryungwon.

On the 14th of the 8th lunar month of the same year, there is an entry in *The Record of Daily Reflections* where Minister Lee Seong-won (1725–1790), soon to be appointed government envoy, requested that Kim Hong-do and Lee Myeong-gi accompany him on his trip to China.

> As government envoy to China, Lee Seong-won asked, "I need to take Kim Hong-do and Lee Myeong-gi this time, but it is impossible with their current titles. I shall take Kim as my military officer and Lee as an additional member of painters," and his request was granted.

From this, we can surmise that as the plans for building Hyeonryungwon and reconstructing Yongjusa Temple were confirmed the previous month, Lee Seong-won tentatively decided on Kim and Lee as the painters to paint the Buddhist paintings. He wanted them on the entourage so that they could examine Ching Dynasty temples and Catholic Church murals in Yenching. Kim Hong-do and Lee Myeong-gi probably left near the time of the winter solstice and hurried home in the 2nd lunar month the following year. Kim Hong-do reached 46 in 1790, and in the spring famine struck the northern part of the country and the sufferers fled to Hanyang.

The 19th of the 2nd lunar month was the groundbreaking day for the reconstruction of Yongjusa Temple. For the next 216 days until the 29th of the 9th lunar month when the eyes were finally painted on the Buddha's statue, Kim Hong-do supervised and completed the works 'Three Tathagatas' (Plate 67) in the main worship hall and 'Chilseong' (The Big Dipper, Plate 69) in Chilseonggak.[67] Kim Deuk-sin and Lee Myeong-gi assist-

67 A Taoist shrine consecrated to the Big Dipper.

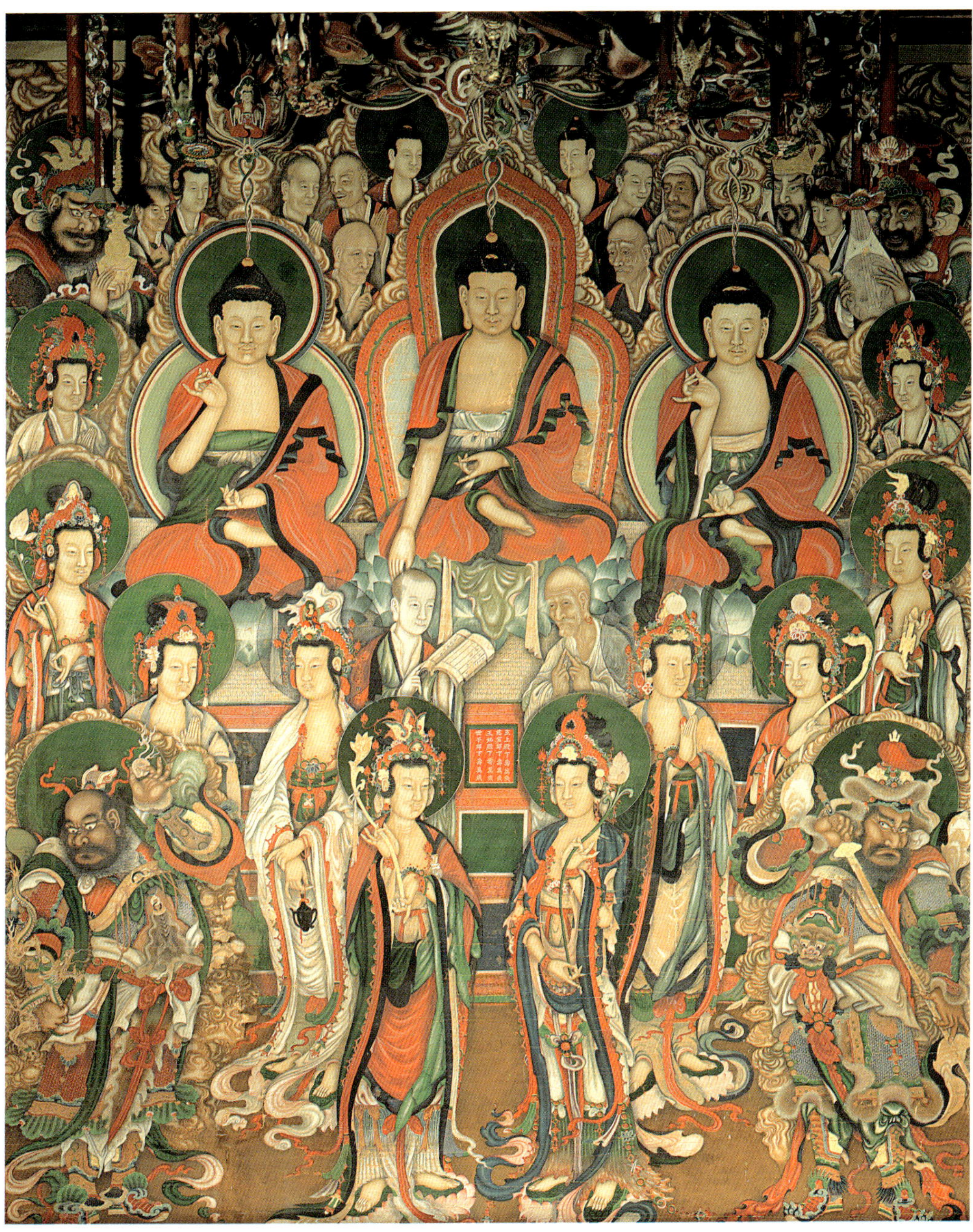
主上殿下壽萬歲
慈宮邸下壽萬歲
王妃殿下壽萬歲
世子邸下壽萬歲

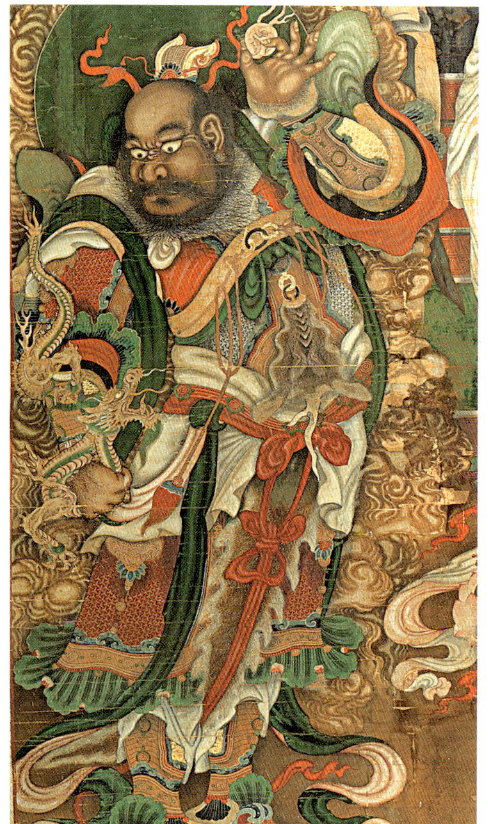

ed Kim as *gamdongyeok*. As can be seen later, Lee Myeong-gi was the chief painter of King Jeongjo's portrait the following year, and he was the best portrait painter in Joseon. Kim Deuk-sin was a *jabidaeryeong* court painter as famous as Kim Hong-do. The detailed schedule of platform painting production is as follows.

The 19th of the 2nd lunar month in 1790 between 11AM and 1PM was the groundbreaking ceremony at the temple. Construction of the Buddha's statue began on the 16th of the 8th lunar month, and the eyes were painted on the 29th of the 9th lunar month.

The names of the painters who participated in the works of the temple list the following.

The stone plate and steel plate of *Eunjunggyeong*[68] were handed down from the royal palace on the 22nd of the 6th lunar month in 1802. 'Three Tathagatas,' the platform painting in the main Buddha hall, was painted by Yeonpung Hyeongam Kim Hong-do; 'Tri-pitaka'[69] by Min Gwan; 'Memorial Platform Painting' by Sanggyeom; and 'Chilseong' in Chilseonggak by Gyeongok, Yeonhong and Seol Sun.

68 Detail of plate 67
Of the Four Devas, Virudhaka (the Guardian of the South) on the bottom left is covered in luxurious armor. The right hand is twisting the neck of a yellow dragon, and the left hand is holding a cintamani. The heavenly king looks ferocious. He is standing askew with his eyebrows raised and throwing a piercing glance sideways. He is shorter than the bodhisattvas are, but has a bulkier body. The halo is bigger, which makes him look braver, as he defends the Buddhist paradise.

The above quote mentions "Yeonpung Hyeongam Kim Hong-do," but Kim was not appointed hyeongam until the 12th lunar month of 1791. Furthermore, according to the quote, 'Chilseong' was painted by three painter-monks, not Kim Hong-do. The author explained these inconsistencies in an earlier paper, but the critical evidence that proves Kim Hong-do's participation in the painting of Buddhist paintings in Yongjusa Temple is the na-

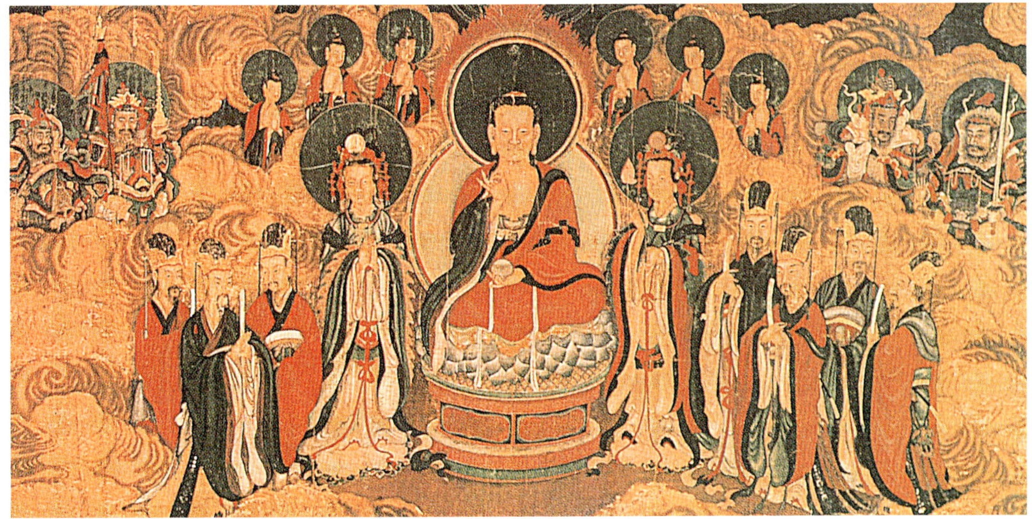

69 *Chilseong* (The Big Dipper)
1790. Color on silk. Location unknown.
This was a very important Buddhist painting in Yongjusa Temple, along with Three Tathagatas, but was stolen. The Big Dipper is thought to be responsible for extending a person s life, and thus this painting was done to wish for the health and longevity of the king and his family. Standing in the center are the Buddhist Triad - Chilseong holding a medicine cup in his palm, flanked by Ilgwang and Wolgwang, whose crown has at its center the red sun and the white moon respectively. Seven Buddhas, one for each star, are dressed in civil officers garb and lined up on each side.

tional document called the *Suwon Construction Records*. The entry dated 6th of the 10th lunar month of 1790 reads as follows:

> Former Chalbang Kim Hong-do, Jeolchung Kim Deuk-sin and former Jubu Lee Myeong-gi, who inspected the platform painting, along with Hwang Deok-sun and Yun Heung-sin, who supervised the construction of the Buddhist statue, spent 216 days from the 19th of the 2nd lunar month to the 29th of the 9th lunar month working at the site. Painter-Monk Sanggyeom and Painter-Monk Mingwan worked 45 days from the 12th of the 8th lunar month to the 29th of the 9th lunar month.

The work log is very detailed and provides the following entry for the 7th of the 10th lunar month of 1790, which notes the following rewards:

68 Sutra on the importance of parental love.
69 The Three Baskets of sacred Buddhist writings.

Former Chalbang Kim Hong-do who inspected the platform painting work shall be appointed to a *jeong 6 pum sagwa* position according to the king's special orders. Jeolchung Kim Deuk-sin and Sagwa Lee Myeong-gi shall receive ample rice and cloth for their supervisory work. Gwansok Hwang Deok-sun and Yun Heung-sin, who inspected the Buddhist statue construction, shall be rewarded appropriately. Painter-Monk Sanggyeom and Painter-Monk Mingwan will also be rewarded accordingly.

In return for his service, Kim Hong-do received a long-term appointment to *jeong 6 pum sagwa*. The Buddhist painting in Yongjusa Temple that Kim Hong-do produced is significant because it used shading, perspective and other Western art techniques as seen in the Catholic churches in Yenching. At the same time, Lee Myeong-gi applied traditional portrait techniques in drawing the details of the Buddha's face and hands in the platform painting. Because of the various artistic techniques that were used in combination, people did not believe the painting could have been done in 1790. Many factors, however, contributed to the production of such a work using many heterogeneous techniques. Most importantly, King Jeongjo, who ordered this painting had a very progressive attitude toward painting, and it was relevant to the influence of *bukhak*, the philosophy in vogue at the time. The unique characteristics of the Buddhist painting in Yongjusa Temple were in line with the construction of Hwaseong (augmented from Suwon Fortress) from 1794 to 1796, which embraced the theories of the *bukhak* school.

The following two episodes shed light on King Jeongjo's ardent response towards Western art technique. Lee Yu-won (1814–1888) delivers the following interesting tale in his anthology, *Imhapilgi*.

Folding screen with the Painting of a Golden Rooster

A very talented Japanese painter painted this. Yellow chrysanthemums are in full bloom under a maple tree, and in between there are traces of orchids and bamboo. A golden rooster cries morning on a rock, and the sea is lightly col-

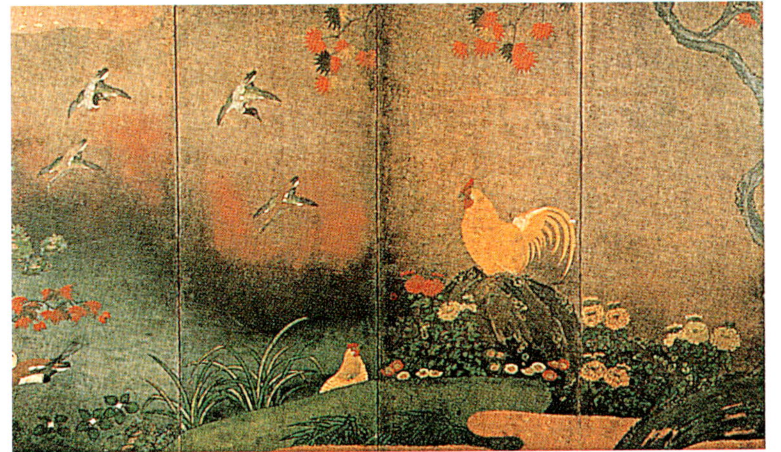

70 Anonymous. Folding screen with the painting of a *Golden Rooster* (partial)
Color on paper. 112×327cm. Hoam Art Museum.
Lee Yu-won s description of the Golden Rooster folding screen matches this work perfectly. The work was famous as a folk painting, but was controversial because the brush strokes are very accurate and the painting contains many Japanese elements. The decorative coloring on the bottom and the gradation in the middle are Japanese in style. Kim Hong-do copied this type of painting as well.

> ored. This is an excellent painting that King Jeongjo had Kim Hong-do copy. The painting was kept in the secondary palace of Hwaseong. The motif of the painting came from the song *Golden Rooster*, whose style follows the *yuefu* song of the old Han Music Bureau.

Hoam Art Museum houses a piece that is very similar to the 'Folding screen with the Painting of a Golden Rooster' (Plate 70). The folding screen in the museum used a very distinct shading technique. It used excessive Japanese painting style, however, so the author has presumed for a long time that it was Japanese and not Korean. There is no affixed seal, which makes it very difficult to confirm whether Kim Hong-do was the painter.

King Jeongjo was fond of *chaekgeori*[70] paintings done in the Western style, and this is mentioned in Nam Gong-cheol's anthology, *Geumreungjip*. [Geumreung is Nam Gong-cheol's pen name.]

> King Jeongjo had the painter paint a *chaekgeori*, and when it was done, he placed it behind his throne. He told his subjects, "According to the words of the wise men before our time, even though we may not have the time to regularly read and study, it is just as good to step into a study and run our hand over the

70 *Chaekgeori* screens are essentially still-life paintings that depict scholarly items, such as books, paper, an inkstone, ink, a pencil holder, etc. Displayed in men s quarters, the *chaekgeori* screen conveys an air of dignity, luxury and reverence for scholarship.

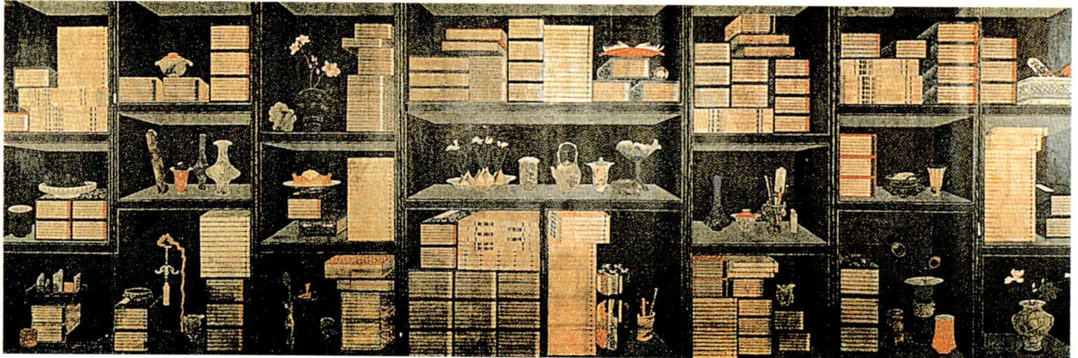

71 Lee Hyeong-rok. *Bookshelf and Various Utensils*
Color on paper. 140.2× 468cm. Hoam Art Museum.
The perspective is in its own style, and the dark brown tone is classic, which leads the observer to believe it was painted for the royal palace. The seal case in the lower-left corner contains a seal bearing Lee s name. Such hidden seals help identify the artist. Kim Hong-do produced many such *chaekgeori* paintings.

> desk. I usually have the time to read, but some urgent situation may arise which prevents me from my leisurely reading and memorizing. When that happens, I will take the wise men's words to heart and look at the *chaekgeori* painting. Isn't it a wise deed?" [Written in 1798]

This is a tale about the theme of the *chaekgeori* painting. In general, the *chaekgeori* is special because it is the most typical genre of painting that uses Western shading and perspective. The following record, Lee Gyu-sang's *Ilmonggo*, did not specifically state that it was a royal painting, but it does mention a luxurious *chaekgeori* done by Kim Hong-do.

> For the first time, Dohwaseo's painting copied the Western painting style of perspective. If you look at the finished painting with one eye closed, everything in the painting seems to be in perfect order. People called this type of painting a *chaekgeori*. The painting was always in color, and at one time, people of noble birth all decorated their walls with it. Hong-do was very good at this genre.

Kim Hong-do was great at *chaekgeori* paintings using deep colored pigment and applying the Western painting techniques. It was about this time that Joseon artists attempted the Western-style three-dimensional paintings applying shading and perspective. In fact, the method had previously been introduced in Joseon. The aforementioned record indicates much less resistance and greater acceptance by the painters. This background suggests that Kim Hong-do was the painter of King Jeongjo's *chaekgeori* mentioned in Nam Gong-cheol's record. Famous painters of the genre include the father and son Lee Yun-min (1774–?) and Lee Hyeong-rok (1808–?). The history traces back to Yun-min's father Lee Jong-hyeon (1748–1803), then to Kim Hong-do.

In the latter half of the Joseon Dynasty, bright-colored *minhwa* folk paintings included *chaekgeori* paintings as well as paintings of the golden rooster and flowers, which are all exemplary pieces of work applying the Western painting method. The truth of the matter is, however, most were not *minhwa*, but were either royal paintings or trendy works that wealthy Hanyang families appreciated. Kim Hong-do was talented at painting such pictures. King Jeongjo himself was an enthusiastic supporter.

The illustrations in the *Military Training Manual* (Plate 72) published in the 4th lunar month show traces of Kim Hong-do's style. He may have been the principal illustrator, but there is no way to confirm it.

Before the 4th lunar month, Kim Hong-do painted a fan painting, 'Riding a Donkey' (Plate 73). Kim Hong-do's and Kang Se-hwang's inscriptions read as follows:

72 Illustration in *Military Training Manual*
King Jeongjo had Lee Deok-mu and Park Je-ga publish a 4-volume, 4-book martial arts manual, which was more practical than theoretical, so it includes numerous illustrations of specific stances and gestures. Considering his affection for Kim and the friendship between the painter and Lee Deok-mu, King Jeongjo probably appointed Kim Hong-do to draw the pictures. Danwon s style is pervasive in the illustrations.

> Dust from the battleground on my coat, mixed with wine dregs
> I have traveled from afar and my heart was broken
> Must I be a poet?
> I ride into Mount Geommun on a donkey in the rain
> The 4th lunar month in 1790, by Danwon

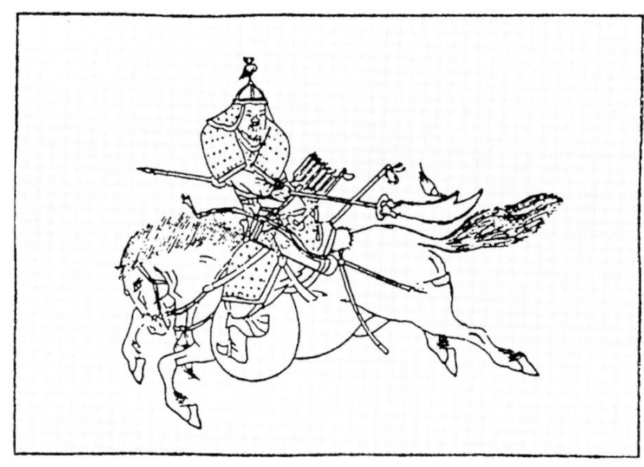

> I knew that Saneung had completely recovered from his grave illness; other-

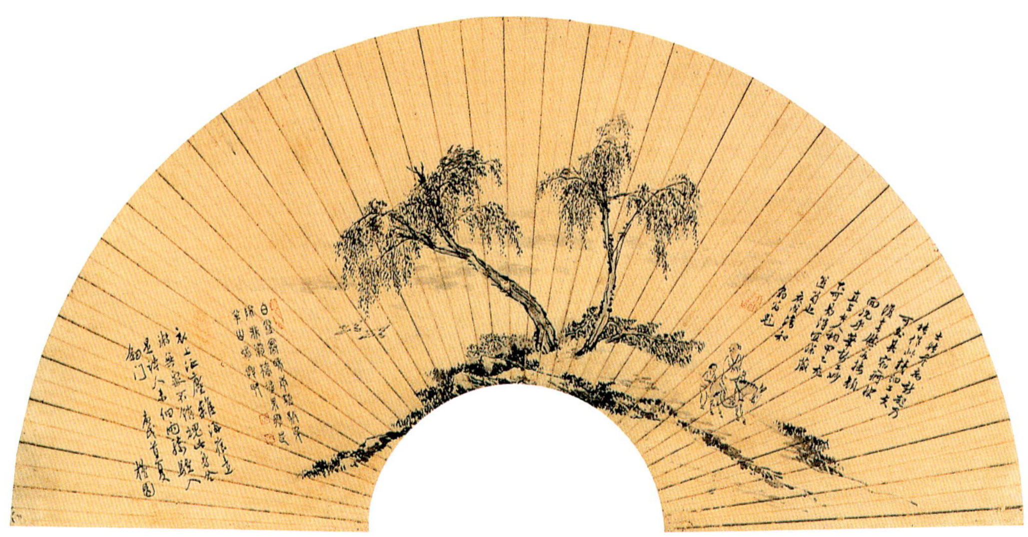

73 *Riding a Donkey*
1790. Ink and color on paper. 28×78cm. Kansong Art Museum.
An old man accompanied by a servant boy is riding a donkey along a quiet riverside road. Two old willow trees on the hill are imbued with the sense of early summer. Two white waterfowls fly off in the other direction as if they are surprised by a sound, and the old man nonchalantly looks in their direction. It is a very peaceful scene.

wise, he could not have painted such an elaborate painting. I was very relieved; it felt like I was seeing him in person. His brushstrokes are clean and exquisite and they compete shoulder to shoulder with those of his ancestors. Such treasure is hard to come by and must be cherished. On *cheonghwajeol* of 1790, by Pyo-ong [Kang Se-hwang's pen name]

Kang's inscription tells us that Kim Hong-do became seriously ill before the 4th lunar month at 1790. The 18th of the 6th lunar month was the birthday of King Jeongjo's mother, Lady Hong, and on that day, the king's eldest son (later crowned King Sunjo) was born.

On the 29th of the 9th lunar month, Kim Hong-do participated in the ceremonial painting of the Buddha statue's eyes at Yongjusa Temple. This concluded his 216-day *gamdongyeok* role in the painting of the platform painting in Yongjusa Temple. On the 6th of the 10th lunar month, a record of the painting assignments in Yongjusa Temple was made, and the following day, the king granted Kim Hong-do a long-term appointment as *jeong 6 pum sagwa* in return for his service. The crops were very good that year.

On the 23rd of the 1st lunar month of 1791, Kim's mentor and sponsor

Pyoam Kang Se-hwang passed away at the age of 79. Later in the year, 47-year-old Kim Hong-do painted 'Nightly Gathering of the Songseokwon Literary Club' (Plate 74), which depicts scenes from the gathering held on the 15th of the 6th lunar month. In 1797, Ma Seong-rin added the following inscription to the painting:

> On a very hot summer night in the 6th lunar month, the clouds and the moon were hazy. The harmony of the brush tip takes the person by surprise and makes him dizzy.

On the 19th of the 6th lunar month, Sim No-sung (1762–1837) wrote a prologue to the poem that he had written during his travels in Pyeongan Province. "*The Prologue to the Poem about the Trip to the West*" mentions Kim Hong-do's genre paintings. It was a justification after receiving criticism from his brother, Sim No-am, that his works were "as secular as Danwon's genre paintings."

> Four days after yudu (the 15th of the 6th lunar month) of 1791, Taedeung (Sim No-sung's courtesy name) wrote at the Mongsandang.
>
> Contemporary painter Kim Hong-do was good at painting the secular world and objects in our everyday life. He was meticulous in choosing what shape and colors to use to make the painting more realistic. His landscape paintings, however, were not lively enough and not impressive. The stark difference in the quality of the genre paintings and landscapes made it hard to believe they were painted by the same person. Genre paintings are not as esteemed as other types of paintings. That is why people despise a genre painter even though he may have excellent skills. However, if reality is expressed exquisitely, is there a need to differentiate between landscape and secular objects?
>
> Genre painters cannot paint landscapes, and landscape painters cannot paint secular objects. Both have skills that are geared to a specific area. Making the robes more beautiful, painting the flags in brilliant colors, carving pictures on

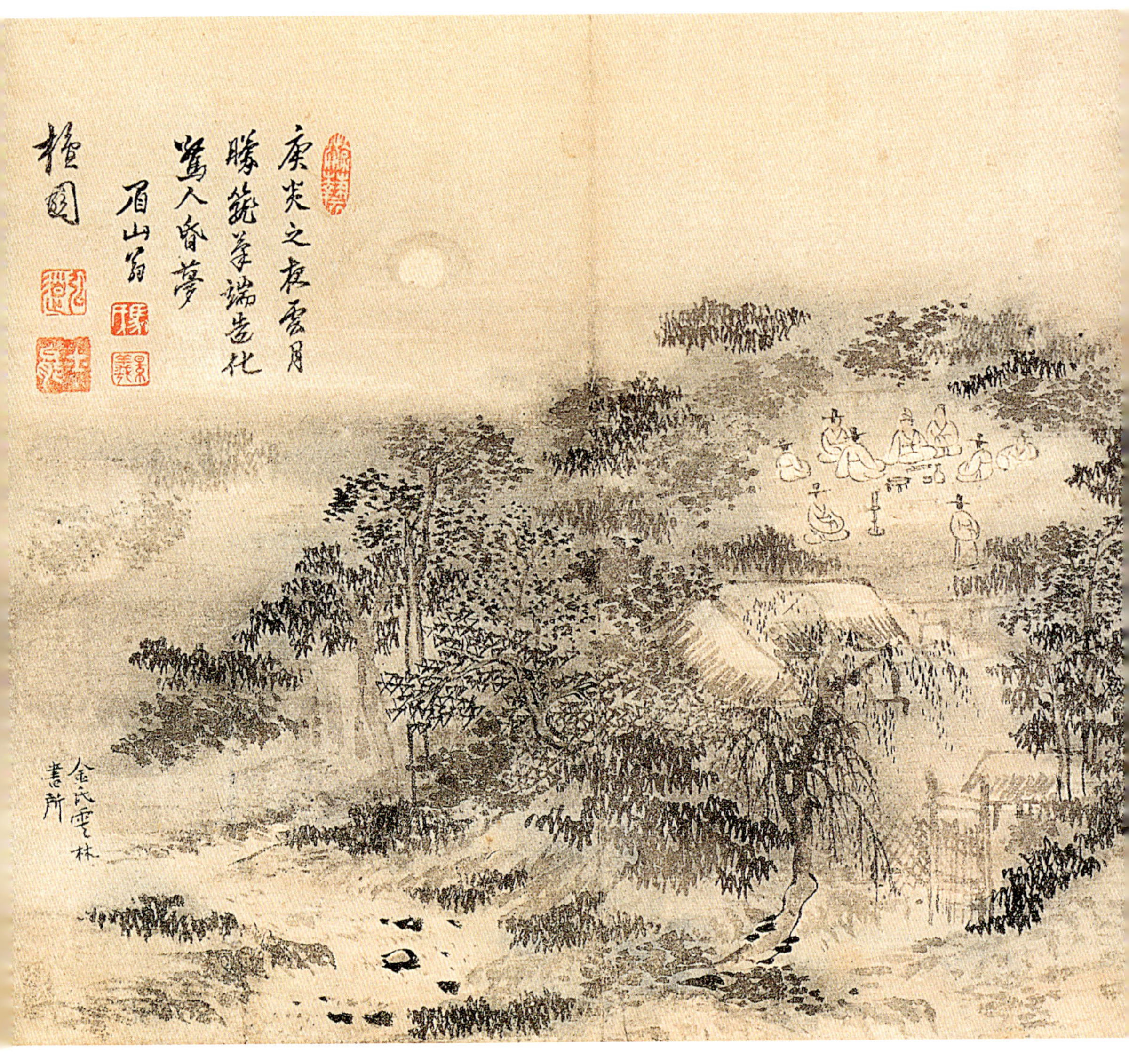

74 *Nightly Gathering of the Songseokwon Literary Club*

1791. Ink and color on paper. 25.6×31.8cm. Korea-Germany Medical Museum.

The Songseokwon Literary Club leading the jungin s literary movement met at night. Songseokwon was the name of the house that belonged to an active member, Cheon Su-gyeong. The observer can almost see the elegant meeting of poets under the moonlight on a hot summer night, and almost hear them reciting their poetry. The painter used a lighter shade of ink to convey a night atmosphere.

utensils used in religious services and attaching eaves to buildings are all part of the secular painter's job. They are recruited to work for the government, ancestral shrines of the royal family and the military, and through their work, they indirectly rule the nation, carry out sacrificial services and give orders to soldiers.

Landscape painters take as long as ten days to draw a stream and five days to draw a rock. The paintings may be "profound and not at all vulgar," but they are only appreciated in a mountain tower or a river pavilion and all too soon put away in a box. They become dusty, never see the light of day, and then they disappear. What good are they?

My brother Taeseom said my poems are "like Kim Hong-do's genre paintings," and I think he was being critical. I reply, however, and try to have the last laugh.

Sim No-sung admitted that Kim Hong-do was good at genre paintings and that genre paintings were regarded as the least sophisticated of paintings. He expressed the very progressive viewpoint that it did not matter whether the painter drew scenes of everyday life or landscapes; as long as the paintings reached a certain level of artistry, they were excellent. It is rather awkward, however, to accept the subsequent sentences at face value. First, it is not precisely true that genre painters and landscape painters are skilled only in their respective areas. The Kim Hong-do we know was very good at all types of paintings and made his name that way. Second, Sim put genre paintings at one end of the spectrum and described how they were secular but served a greater purpose in life. Landscape paintings, however, were at the other end of the scale, and he dismissed them as sophisticated but useless. This reflects his black-or-white mentality and pragmatic perspective. Sim seems to have used rather simplistic reasoning to defend his literary perspective.

The portrait of King Jeongjo was painted in the fall of the same year. The chief painter was Lee Myeong-gi, the associate painter was Kim Hong-do, and assistant painters were Kim Deuk-sin, Byeon Gwang-bok, Sin Han-pyeong, Lee Jong-hyeon, Han Jong-il and Heo Gam. The three painters who were responsible for the Yongjusa Temple painting assignment–Kim Hong-do, Lee Myeong-gi and Kim Deuk-sin–were again assigned to paint the king's portrait.

On the 22nd of the 9th lunar month, the king named Lee Myeong-gi the chief painter of the portrait and Kim Hong-do the associate painter. The day's record mentioned the title *byeolje* of Jangwonseo. The following is the corresponding entry in *The Diaries of the Royal Secretariat.*

> Regarding the Gyujanggak affairs Seo Yong-bo said to the king, "I plan to assign former Sagwa Lee Myeong-gi as the chief painter and Jangwonseo Byeolje Kim Hong-do as the associate painter in painting the king's portrait. How does this sound to you, Your Majesty?" The king said, "I give you my permission. Assign Heo Gam, Han Jong-il, Sin Han-pyeong, Kim Deuk-sin and Lee Jong-hyeon as the assistant painters. Byeon Gwang-bok is the son of Byeon Sang-byeok who was the chief painter of the king's portrait in 1763 and 1773. Let him be part of the team. Former Cheomji Jo Yun-hyeong served as *gamjog-wan* for he understood painting. Assign him to the team as well."

The entry dated 28th of the 9th lunar month of 1791 reads:

> The king gave his orders through Lee Man-su. "The painting of the king's portrait has begun. Announce Kim Hong-do's appointment today and switch his title with someone else's." Jangwonseo Byeolje Kim Hong-do and Binggo Byeolje Kim Jae-geom exchanged their titles.

This indicates that there was an organizational shift in time for the painting of the king's portrait. On the 7th of the 10th lunar month, Kim Hong-do was appointed to a new post in return for his service as the associate painter in the painting of the king's portrait.

> The king gave a special order to appoint Chief Painter Sagwa Lee Myeong-gi and Associate Painter Binggo Byeolgeom Kim Hong-do to new positions. Assistant painters Gaseon Heo Gam, Jeolchung Han Jong-il, Kim Deuk-sin, Lee Jong-hyeon, former Cheomsa Sin Han-pyeong, and Sagwa Byeon Gwang-bok were to follow the precedent of 1781.

As seen from the above, Kim Hong-do participated in the painting of the king's portraits in 1773, 1781 and 1791. Before examining another phase of his career, it is worth examining an episode related to Songhaong Jo Yun-hyeong (1725–1799), who twice assisted in the painting of King Jeong-jo's portrait as *gamjogwan*. King Jeongjo favored Jo Yun-hyeong because he was one of the most renowned calligraphers of the time. Jo was the son-in-law of Yun Sun (1680–1741) who was good at *Donggukjinche* calligraphy. Jo married his daughter to Sin Wi (1769–1847), who was a famous poet and calligrapher. Yun Sun, Jo Yun-hyeong and Sin Wi were famous calligraphers and were in-laws over three generations. They were also well versed in painting, and Jo and Sin in particular made their names painting bamboo in black ink. Sin Wi wrote that he had spent time in the art community with Kim Hong-do, and a Chinese poem included in O Yeon-sang's *Yakwonyugo* confirms that Jo Yun-hyeong enjoyed the same elegant hobbies as Kim. First, let us examine the following footnote at the end of the seven-character *yulsi*.

> Park Yun-muk was enjoying the foliage in the pavilion on Pilundae with Danwon Kim Hong-do, Songha Jo Yun-hyeong and Giwon Yu Han-ji. King Jeongjo suddenly summoned them. The king praised them for having partied at such an elegant place and sent them back with plenty of food and drinks from the palace. He asked to see the scrolls of poetry written during the gathering. It is an honor to have received such favors from the king, and the people talk of this episode even to this day. Thus, it is mentioned at the end of the poem.

Sin Gwang-ha (1729–1796) sang in his poem how Kim Hong-do had spent more time in the palace than at home because King Jeongjo frequently summoned him on short notice. The above quote provides an actual example. Park Yun-muk, who received the poem as a gift, was a famous commoner poet who closely observed Kim when he painted, and wrote poems about it. Yu Han-ji (1760–1834) was a famous calligrapher who wrote the titles for the *Danwon-jeolsebo Album* in 1796 and 'Giroseryeongyedo' (Plate 93) in 1804 in official script. Kim's relationship with the renowned Jo Yun-hyeong, who was many years older, is most important. Jo knew enough about paintings to have served twice as *gamjogwan* in the painting of the king's portrait, and he and Kim shared the same refined taste. The seven-character *yulsi* to which the above footnote was attached goes as follows.

To Jonjae Park Yun-muk

Pleasantly surprised we were at the chrysanthemum field
Upon entering the palace gate, he smiled first before he spoke
Du Fu could not even afford a bottle of wine, and his poem was always thin
Whereas Zhang Chang lived to be 100. Toothless, he drank milk from a young woman; he was born a lucky man
How can we envy the leisurely play at the Eastern Fortress?
Look far away with expectant heart from the southern window
Surprise to the poet and calligrapher, having received food packages from the king
This old tale is much talked about among poets to this day

The above poem confirms that when the leaves were turning color, Kim Hong-do, Jo Yun-hyeong, Yu Han-ji and Park Yun-muk went on a picnic with food and drink they had received from the palace. We do not know the year exactly, but it must have been a great honor for public servants. Songseokwon poets handed this tale down from generation to generation. The episode adds further evidence of King Jeongjo's affection for these artists and proves once again how groundless the rumors are about Kim Hong-do having painted pornography and infiltrated Japan as a spy.

On the 22nd of the 12th lunar month in 1791, King Jeongjo rewarded Kim for his service in painting the king's portrait by appointing him *hyeongam* of Yeonpung in Chungcheong Province.

> The ijo ratified a position in performance-based appointment ... appointed Kim Hong-do *hyeongam* of Yeonpung.

> The Yeonpung Records note, "Kim Hong-do served as *hyeongam* from 1791 to 1795."

His appointment as of the 22nd of the 12th lunar month of 1791 lasted until he was dismissed on the 7th of the 1st lunar month of 1795, meaning that he was in office for three years. Before examining his life as *hyeongam*, we have to verify if Kim was really the only court painter in 500 years of Joseon history to have served as *hyeongam*. This assumption proves to be far from the truth. Kim Hui-gyeom (1710–?) and Byeon Sang-byeok (1730–?), who participated in the painting of the king's portrait, were *hyeongam* of Sacheon and Gokseong, respectively. A clause in the law allowed technical officers to become officials in either central or local governments without taking the civil/military exam, although the clause was rarely enacted. During King Seongjong's reign, the court painter Choi Gyeong rose as high as *jeong 3 pum*. Since local intellectuals had taken over politics in the mid-sixteenth century, however, technical officers had begun to be looked upon with disdain. This explains why people thought Kim was an exception. Kim was a participant in painting the king's portrait three times, but in every instance, he was the associate painter who drew the body, and was never the chief painter. Even so, he was appointed *hyeongam*, and that is worthy of our attention.

Yeonpung-hyeon is the current Yeonpung-myeon Goesan-gun in North

Chungcheong Province. It is a small village surrounded by high mountains. To get to Yeonpung, Kim had to go through Goesan. The Samgwan Gate on Joryeong Hill takes one from Yeonpung to Mungyeongsaejae in Gyeongsang Province. Quite a few students who lived in the southeastern part of the country took this road to go to Hanyang to take the national exam. Today, we can reach Yeonpung by traveling from Chungju via the Suanbo Hot Springs to Mungyeongsaejae, then taking the road down the hill to the new Route 3 toward Ihwaryeong Hill. The cozy town of Yeonpung is about one-third of the way up the hill. Yeonpung-hyeon was a strategic logistics hub to Gyeongsang Province, yet at the same time, it was such a small and remote village that there was talk of shutting it down. Village records from the 19th century say that there were 1,500 households and less than 5,000 inhabitants. The people lived simple lives and were diligent farmers. We can refer to the following myth about the village to learn a little about the town of Yeonpung, and how Kim Hong-do lived his life there as *hyeongam*.

The Village Head who Comes in Tears and Leaves in Tears

Yeonpung-myeon of Goesan-gun was the old village of Yeonpung and known as a remote village surrounded by mountains. The newly appointed village head silently cried inside his *palanquin* as servants, secretaries and petty officials flanked him.

He was from a well-to-do family and spent his childhood and adolescence poring over books. He had no spare time to enjoy the flowers in the spring or the foliage in the fall as did everyone else. He did not score that well on the second-level government examination, but he did manage to get his career started as a government official. After a few years, he reached the level of 6 *pum*, which landed him a post of *hyeongam*. So far so good. It seemed ages ago that he had bowed respectfully to the king at Hanyang in appreciation of the king's kindness, and he had sobered up from the drinks his friends had poured into him at his celebration party. He had traveled long enough to forget the lovely *gisaeng* who had sung at the party, but still there were only mountains and brooks around him. The village was not supposed to be far off, but to get there one had to go into mountain after mountain. The rice paddies and fields were nowhere in sight. In these mountainous regions, it was doubtful that they had a proper guesthouse and a main office building. The petty officials and footmen will be rough in their manners and the *gisaeng* will probably be a fat woman in a skirt. What has he done wrong to deserve such a punishment as to be appointed *hyeongam* in this wretched town? Only sighs came out of his mouth, and the more he thought about it, the bitterer he felt. He tried to be a man about it, but he could not help the tears. This was the day the newly appointed *hyeongam* arrived in Yeonpung.

On the day he left the town when his term of office ended, he could not fight back the tears, either. How peaceful and happy these days had been! Yeonpung may be a small remote village, but contrary to one's first impression, there was plenty to eat and wear. People were thrifty and warm-hearted, and they followed the village head as if he were their father. No one brought gold and silver by the bushel and tried to make a quick profit from it. The villagers instead brought seasonal merchandise like uncooked pheasant and pig's gall bladder. He vividly remembered the pine nut porridge with an aroma that filled the room. He had sat across the *hyeongam* of Mungyeong and looked down at the flaming leaves of Mungyeongsaejae boasting of his town, as they drank chrysanthemum wine and ate wild boar and mushrooms. Servants and duty officers did not merely pay lip service, but they were sincere and attentive. Where could he find such a happy life if he left this village? Perhaps he should forget about promotion and personal glory, settle down in this dear village, get old and die here. His legs were reluctant to carry him off, and silent tears wet his cheeks.

This was the day when the incumbent hyeongam left his post.

This is the origin of the old saying, "the Yeonpung village head comes in tears and leaves in tears."

Kim Hong-do succeeded Jeong Sok in the post of *hyeongam*; it is easy to believe that since Yeonpung is a small town in Chungcheong Province with the least amount of acreage of rice paddies in the country, it was only good enough to be governed by a court painter. But according to Han Jin-ho's *Sainam Rock of Dodam Travel Log*, Kim was probably appointed to the post because he had an assignment to carry out.

> There are supposed to be five rocks that are the attractions of Danyang: Sangseonam, Jungseonam, Haseonam, Unam and Sainam. Looking at Sainam, I cannot help but think it is exquisite. The way I heard it, King Jeongjo appointed Kim Hong-do as *hyeongam* of Yeonpung and had him paint the landscapes of the four counties–Yeongchun, Danyang, Cheongpung and Jecheon. Hong-do arrived at Sainam and tried to paint it, but he could not fully grasp the meaning of the rock. He stayed for a dozen days, observed the rock carefully and paid a great deal of attention to it, but he could not get a proper reading of it.

The record focuses on Sainam's being so magnificent that even Kim failed to capture its beauty. It seems that King Jeongjo sent Kim to Yeonpung for a specific reason; the Danyang area is so beautiful that it is known as the second Mount Geumgang, and King Jeongjo wanted Kim to paint these beautiful scenes. This job was probably a continuation of his 1788 assignment to paint Mount Geumgang and the eastern part of the country. This time, Kim was able to remain near the site because he was posted in the area, so he could paint more leisurely and freely. Even though 'Sainam Rock' (Plate 14), 'Dodam Sambong' (Plate 15) and 'Oksunbong Peak' (Plate 75) are included in the *Danwon-jeolsebo Album* of 1796 as paintings of the Danyang area, the paintings he made while in office and presented to the king are lost.

At any rate, Kim Hong-do became *de facto* governor of the area. He presided over an office that was newly constructed in 1764 as follows:

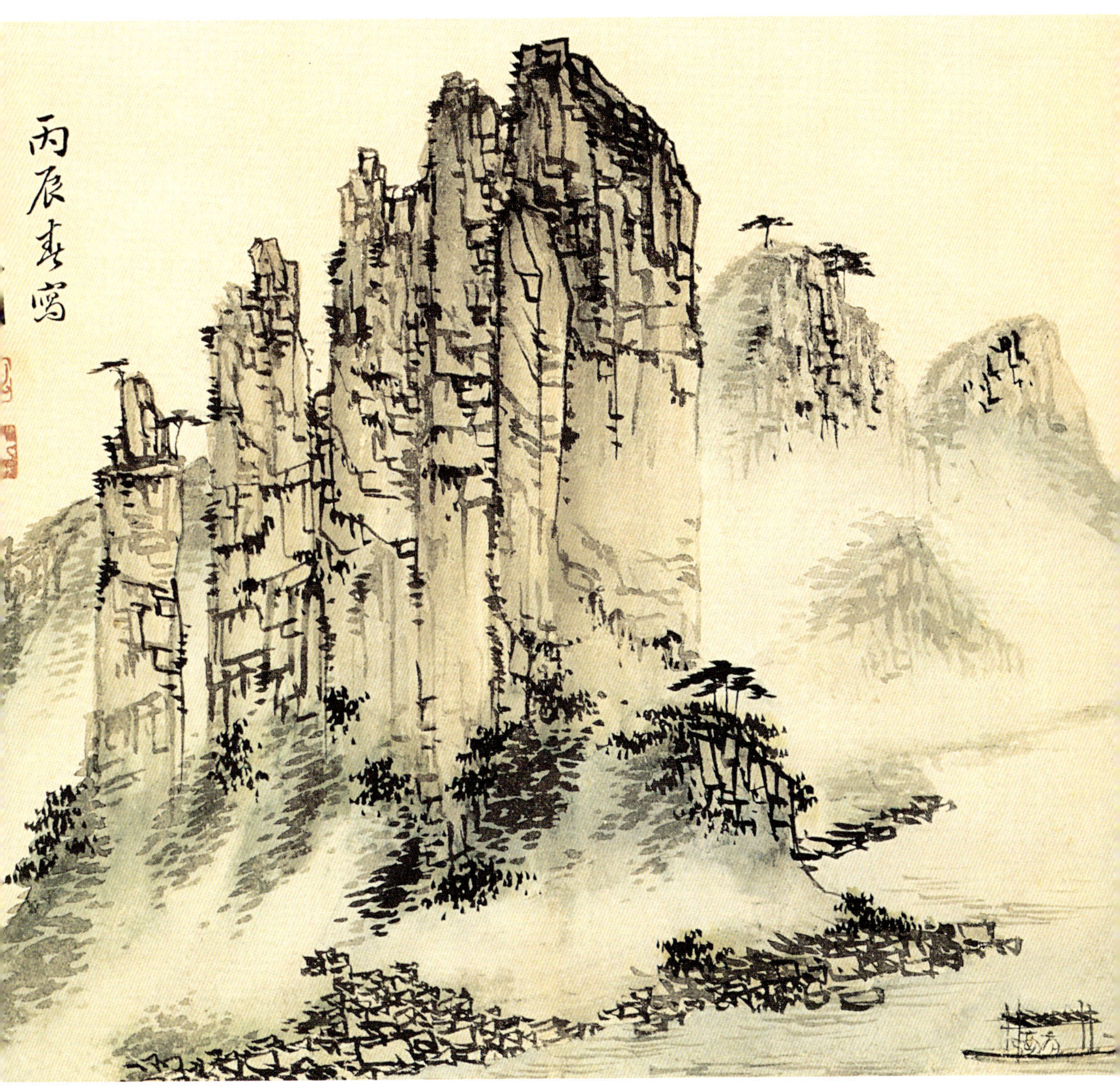

75 *Oksunbong Peak* from *Danwon-jeolsebo Album*
1796. Ink and color on paper. 26.7×31.6cm. Hoam Art Museum.
The tall peaks on the riverside look like bamboo sprouts after a rain, which is how the mountain got its name. The tallest peak is in the center, and the others slope down to the left. The right side trails off into the far distance. The rocks look overbearing, and the space looks open and wide. A small boat with a canopy is floating by, and two travelers appear very much at their leisure.

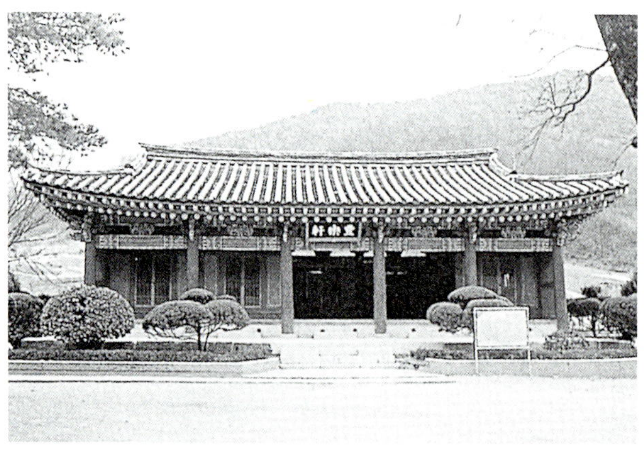

76 Pungnakheon
This is the small main building of the Yeonpung government office. It has been moved 30 meters from its original position and is now in the playground of Yeonpung Elementary School. However, the building is the same as it was when Kim Hong-do was in office; few government office buildings from that time have survived in good condition. The greatest painter of the time, Kim Hong-do served as *hyeongam* for three years, but there is no indication of this at the site.

Pungnakheon[71] (Plate 76) was 15 *kan*, the middle gate was 8 *kan*, Iuiru[72] was 12 *kan*, the *chwisubang* was 15 *kan* and the arsenal was 10 *kan*. Twelve *kan* of the *sachang*[73] was built later, and the *hyangcheong*,[74] *jangcheong*,[75] *isa*[76] and the slaves' quarters were restored or successively added to the complex. According to the surviving map of the building, the slaves' quarters were next to the main office building, behind which the *hyeongam's* private quarters were located. The archives were adjacent to his quarters. The *saryeongbang*[77] was inside the main entrance Iuiru, and to the *saryeongbang's* right were the *jangcheong*, *sachang* and a lotus pond. A fence divided the office building on the right from the guesthouse on the left. The guesthouse had a main entrance as well as a middle gate. The arsenal, *jakcheong* and *hyangcheong* were in front of the guesthouse. Other peripherals included the *hyanggyo*,[78] *sajikdan*,[79] *yeodan* and the grain bank.

When Kim was appointed in 1792, Yeonpung was suffering from a serious drought. Searching for a holy place to perform a ritual for rain, he went to Sangamsa Temple in Mount Joryeong. Kim was 48 years old at the time but still without a son and he deemed the place holy enough to pray for a son as well. He offered a monetary sacrifice that was sufficient to pay for the gilding of a Buddhist statue and restoration of Buddhist paintings. This is mentioned in the record, *Restoration of Sangamsa Temple located on Mount Gongjeong in Yeonpung County*.

> There is always a Buddhist temple to protect a famous mountain by Buddha's power and the devotion of the people. Only Buddha can prompt people to do certain things. If it were not for the people, who would worship Buddha? Sometimes, Buddha's power is not exercised, and the people's devotion

71 The name of the main office building in Yeonpung.
72 The name of the main entrance.
73 A storehouse for tax in kind.
74 A building that housed an advisory board of local residents who assisted the *hyeongam*.
75 Petty officials office.
76 Petty officials quarters.
77 Duty officers quarters.
78 A Confucian temple with an attached school.
79 An altar to the state deities.

erodes. That is why temples once built sometimes fall into ruin. This is in line with the circulation of luck and energy. I witnessed it in Baekunam on Mount Gongjeong.

There were many fires after the construction of the small temple, so no record remains. We do not know when the temple was built; it was probably built in either the Silla or Goryeo Dynasties. Mount Joryeong is in Chungcheong Province and the temple was high up in rough terrain. People had to hang onto vines and climb over dangerous, rocky steep hills to reach the temple. People who climbed mountains at their leisure time rarely visited the temple. The head monk did not stay there long. The temple was eroded by wind and burnt down; we do not know how many times it was rebuilt and destroyed again.

In 1789, Monk Gyesun of the temple prayed and collected money to fix the broken roof and walls. The strong foundation of the temple looked better than before. Three years passed and Kim Hong-do was appointed *hyeongam* of a nearby village. He came up to pray for rain and observed, "The temple is the cleanest and neatest in the village, and it deserves to be the place for prayers." He offered a sacrifice from his own salary. With that money, the faded Buddhist statue was newly gilded and torn portraits and paintings were restored and recolored. Chungcheong Governor Lee Hyeong-won and Goesan Gunsu Lee Yeong-gyo heard the news and helped as well. Visitors to the temple and the monks were very happy. They said, "Hyeongam Kim Hong-do's devotion is so complete as to have affected both his people and the temple." This shows that the combination of Buddha's power and people's devotion was strong enough to resurrect the ruinous temple.

Hyeongam Kim did not have a son until he was very old, and after praying to the spirits in the mountain, he had a son. His goodwill was repaid in the most delightful way, and the monks said Buddha provided what he deserved in return for his good deeds. According to Su Shi, "Everything continues its cycle of birth and death as a cause and effect." The temple was so old that its time was up, but it was salvaged by a good monk's prayer and a kind officer's sacrifice.

> Monk Gyesun was worried that this beautiful tale would be forgotten by the outside world, so he asked me to put it in writing. I lived quite close to Hyeongam Kim and we were very close friends. I was honored to have my name written in this record and so I agreed.
>
> Written by Punggyegeosa at the end of the 2nd lunar month of 1795
>
> Engraved by Kim Cheon-taek in the 6th lunar leap-month of 1797

Sangamsa Temple was located in the middle of Mount Gongjeong in the eastern part of Yeonpung in the town of Wonpung-li, Yeonpung-myeon, Goesan-gun. It stood until the Korean War when South Korean soldiers fired mortars at North Korean soldiers who were in hiding there. Now only the temple grounds remain. It is a momentous tragedy, particularly if we think about the loss of Kim's paintings and writings.

The above record confirms several things. First, in 1792 when Kim Hong-do was appointed *hyeongam*, there was a severe drought in the town, and Kim went to Sangamsa Temple to pray for rain. Second, Kim considered the temple clean and neat enough to pay sacrificial services. He offered his own salary and had the Buddhist statue gilded and Buddhist portraits and paintings restored. Third, Chungcheong Governor Lee Hyeong-won (1739–1798) and Goesan Gunsu Lee Yeong-gyo helped Kim. Fourth, the villagers and monks thought Kim's devotion was so complete as to have affected both the people and the temple as well. Fifth, Kim Hong-do, at the age of 48, was still without a son, but after praying to the spirits in this temple, he had a son. Sixth, Kim Hong-do was on friendly terms with Chief Monk Gyesun, Chungcheong Governor Lee Hyeong-won, Goesan Gunsu Lee Yeong-gyo and a person who went by the name of Punggyegeosa. Punggyegeosa, who wrote the record, which was later engraved on a stone, lived close to Kim, and they were good friends. Seventh, the record was written immediately after Kim left his post. Surprised by Kim's sudden dismissal, Monk Gyesun, who had been touched by Kim's sacrifice, wasted no time in requesting that there be a written record of the event so that Kim's deed would be remembered. Two years later he had the engraver Kim Cheon-taek engrave the writing and erected the stone.

The son that the forty-eight-year-old Kim Hong-do sired after praying to the spirits at Sangamsa Temple must be Kim Yeon-rok, whose name appears in *Danwon's Posthumous Works*. It was Kim Yang-gi, however, who put the book together. Other people mentioned the name Kim Yang-gi in the foreword and epilogue, but in the main text, Kim Hong-do never addressed his letters to a Kim Yang-gi. Supposedly, Kim Yang-gi edited his father's writings while he was still very young, and he must have kept the letters his father had sent him. Yeon-rok is probably Kim Yang-gi; Yeon-rok was his childhood name. Presumably, the name means, "the son that was sired when Kim Hong-do was *hyeongam* of Yeonpung"; the 'yeon' derives from Yeonpung, and the 'rok'(祿) means salary.

The monument in Sangamsa Temple recognizes the benefactors' donations, and it is only natural that it praised how Kim Hong-do's devotion was so complete as to have affected both the people and the temple as well. This is quite a contrast to the assessment of the Kim Hong-do dismissed from his office on grounds of misgovernment. In all likelihood, Kim had very close ties with senior officials, because Chungcheong Governor Lee Hyeong-won and Goesan Gunsu Lee Yeong-gyo helped him restore the dilapidated temple. Governor Lee had served in the post of king's advisor, and he came as governor in the 5th lunar month of 1792, at about the time Kim prayed for rain. He came into conflict with Chungcheong Byeongsa[80] Lee Gwang-seop, who was appointed later in the fall. This incident is examined below. In the 9th lunar month, when Lee Gwang-seop was appointed Chungcheong Byeongsa, he hosted the Seowon Gathering in Cheongju and invited Kim Hong-do, Lee Han-jin and Hwang Un-jo. The gathering is described in detail in Lee Gyu-sang's *Records of Contemporary Celebrities.*

80 Short for *byeongmajeoldosa:* general of the provincial army.

Hwang Un-jo's courtesy name is Sayong, and pen name is Dogok. His current position is the village head of Yeongi. Un-jo had a very good handle on the regular script. The strokes were sharp and the form was strict. He copied the two Wangs' writings very well and was especially talented in copying *beopcheop*[81] and relics. His copies of the inscription on Cao E's tombstone and of the Chinese Emperor's foreword in the translated Sutras were exact reproductions of the original. His skills were that good. He had studied with Baewa Kim Sang-suk since he was young, so they share a similar form. The difference is Hwang writes in swift strokes but Kim has more style.

When Sayong ruled the village of Yeongi, Lee Gwang-seop was appointed Chungcheong Byeongsa. Lee was good at writing in seal script and official script, and at playing the bamboo flute and zither. Lee Han-jin was also good at seal script and the bamboo flute. Kim Hong-do, who was a talented painter, was *hyeongam* at Yeonpung. When Lee came to the *byeongsa* office from Hanyang, Kim left his quarters to greet him. Byeongsa Lee wanted to meet the Yeongi *hyeongam*, but Sayong did not respond to Lee's invitation. Lee issued a stronger appeal; only then did Sayong come. Byeongsa reassured the guests that they could dispense with the formalities. He had them dress more casually to better show off their talents. Seal script and paintings were difficult and elaborate; consequently, there were only a dozen or so sheets of paper. Writing was faster, and the Yeongi village head produced hundreds of pages in the blink of an eye. Byeongsa Lee planned to knock Hwang down a peg, so he told everyone to offer Hwang a large glass of wine. The Yeongi village head, however, was an experienced drinker and remained sober throughout the evening. When night fell, he made his way back to Yeongi by lighting the way with a torch. The gathering was named the Seowon Gathering. A certain officer had maintained his dignity during the Massacre of Scholars between 1721 and 1722, and Byeongsa Lee is his descendant. At the time, Lee was in his thirties.

81 A book made from rubbings of old scholars writings that had been engraved on stone or wood.

The Seowon in Seowon Gathering comes from the Seowongyeong, which is what Cheongju was called during the Silla Dynasty. Cheongju is where the *byeongsa* office is. The name may have also come from the Seowon Gathering (Gathering in the Western Garden) of the North Sung Dynasty. Lee's Seowon Gathering was held at the *byeongsa* office, which is inside the present-day Cheongju Central Park. The episodes mentioned earlier affirmed the friendship between Lee Han-jin and Kim Hong-do. On the 3rd of the 4th lunar month of 1788, they both attended a birthday party for Lee Deok-mu's father; Byeongsa Lee Gwang-seop was also there. So, Kim and Lee Gwang-seop were already acquainted. Kim voluntarily went to Cheongju to see the *byeongsa* because of the hierarchical relationship of his being the court painter, but of course, he also could have wanted another opportunity to enjoy drinking and merrymaking. Lee Gwang-seop was Lee Deok-mu's distant nephew, and although he was a military officer, he was well versed in writing and music. The Seowon Gathering was a very significant elegant gathering in that the three guests who had gathered at Lee Deok-mu's house four years previously met again, with all of them having different titles.

The gathering is supposed to have taken place right after Lee was appointed *byeongsa*, which is recorded as the 5th of the 9th lunar month of 1792 in the *True Record of the Joseon Dynasty*. The gathering must have been sometime in the 9th lunar month. Lee was supposed to have been in his thirties but he was actually forty-three years old; this explains why the 63-year-old Hwang Un-jo was reluctant to come even after receiving a letter from Lee.

The problem was the uneasy relationship between Lee Hyeong-won and Lee Gwang-seop. When Lee Gwang-seop was coming to his new post, in Chungcheong, he had personally ordered the beatings of several petty officials at stations along the way. Governor Lee Hyeong-won opposed this, and in the 12th lunar month he reported it to the central government. The issue was resolved, but in the 5th lunar month of 1793, another incident occurred. A former Busa Gu Sun reported a theft and wrongly accused his archrival Kim Myeong-sin; this ended with Kim's death. Lee Gwang-seop became involved in the affair; Lee Hyeong-won filed a brief against him and had him dismissed from office. Many innocent people lost their lives over this matter, and the damage spread like wildfire as Lee Gwang-seop egregiously punished the lower ranking officials who were working under Governor Lee Hyeong-won. Lee Hyeong-won got the upper hand in the battle, and Lee Gwang-seop was exiled to Yeongdong-hyeon; however, the incident also resulted in Lee Hyeong-won's dismissal. He was soon reinstated and he continued to be governor even after Kim Hong-do was dismissed from his *hyeongam* post in 1795. Kim Hong-do was friends with Lee Gwang-seop and voluntarily greeted him when he was appointed. They all partied at the Seowon Gathering and made no secret about it, so it must have been awkward for Kim to handle the conflict between the two Lees. Hong Dae-hyeop, who had been dispatched to Chungcheong Province to investigate the whole affair, was the official who accused Kim of misgovernment later on. In 1793 and 1794, the Chungcheong, Jeolla and Gyeongsang area, which included Yeonpung, suffered consecutive droughts. There was a bad drought in1792 when Kim was appointed to his office, and the crops were very bad the following two years. Many people starved, *wiyusa*[82] were dispatched from the central government and governors were busy writing and submitting status reports.

In 1793, Kim Hong-do was forty-nine years old. The entry dated 24th of the 5th lunar month in *The Record of Daily Reflections* mentioned Chungcheong Governor Lee Hyeong-won's establishing Jinhyulcheo[83] and writing a report after the relief efforts.

> Chungcheong Governor Lee Hyeong-won wrote in the report, "The crops were very bad last year, but the king has been munificent enough to provide the people of the region with food aid and *naetangjeon*[84]. He has done everything within his power to relieve the people is suffering. Relief work was completed in each administrative district and the reports have all arrived. Village heads who have displayed excellent achievement and relief and who have 'saved for a

82 A temporary post for an official who assisted the local population in times of a natural disaster.
83 An agency that fed the hungry people during years of bad harvest
84 Money directly managed by the royal government.

rainy day,' villagers who gave voluntary donations, and private benefactors who have contributed more than fifty *seok*[85] of rice shall be mentioned in a separate report according to the rule. Gongju and Yeonpung were each struck by first and second-degree natural disasters. Gongju Pangwan Lee Jong-hwi and Yeonpung Hyeongam Kim Hong-do did not depend on government relief because they were self-sufficient in distributing grain and cooking porridge. They closely followed the procedure and were able to save the starving population."

The same day's article of *The Record of Daily Reflections* describes in detail Kim Hong-do's achievements.

> Yeonpung-hyeon: Twelve inspections were made from the 1st lunar month to the 4th lunar month. There were 3,060 starving people and they were provided with the following rations: One hundred and sixty *seok* and 10 du of millet was distributed, of which 110 *seok* 10 *du* were from Kim Hong-do and the rest from the office. Thirty-one *seok* 1 *du* of barley, 5 *seok* 1 *du* of porridge rice, 2 *seok* 11 *du* of soy, 3 *seok* 5 *du* of salt and 46 *dan* 2 *juji* of beans were given by Kim Hong-do.
>
> The previous year, 239 starving people were relieved and they were saved with 14 *seok* 13 *du* of millet donated by Kim Hong-do.
>
> An ad hoc inspection round discovered that 241 people were starving, and they were given 16 *seok* 4 *du* of millet, 6 *du* of porridge rice, 7 *du* of soy and 2 *dan* 7 *juji* of beans.

Three thousand out of five thousand people in Yeon-pung went hungry, which indicates the severity of the famine. The evaluation on the above relief work is written in an article of the same day, "Voluntary Donors and Private Benefactors were Rewarded Accordingly."

> Village heads, whose names were recorded on separate records and in books, and frontier-generals who had prepared for natural disasters in advance must be

85 *Seok*, *du*, *dan* and *juji* are all units of volume.

classified and be awarded accordingly. Voluntary benefactors who gave cash, in-kind donations and grains must be awarded according to the amount of donation given. Yeongchun Hyeongam Lee Myeong-seong and Yeonpung Hyeongam Kim Hong-do only donated between 100 and 400 units from their personal stocks. The contribution was minimal and thus their relief is not worth rewarding.

A review of Chungcheong Governor Lee Hyeong-won's status report tells us that the 1793 relief work in Chungcheong area took place from the 1st lunar month to the 4th lunar month. The previous year, Kim Hong-do had prayed for rain but to no avail. Yeonpung Hyeongam Kim Hong-do did not depend on public grain provision and tried to make do with his personal provisions to help the hungry in the village. His achievement, however, was considered insignificant, and he was excluded from government compensation. Considering the small population and production volume of Yeonpung, he could not have received a favorable review of his work when compared to heads of larger villages if the evaluation was solely based on the absolute amount of relief aid given. It is only natural that village heads who had given out large amounts of foodstuffs received high recognition in times of natural disasters.

In 1794, when Kim Hong-do was fifty years of age, he was still *hyeongam*, and the drought continued. On the 22nd of the 6th lunar month, King Jeongjo sent the list of Gyujanggak court painters to the central government. He commented on Byeon Gwang-bok possessing the same level of skill and sophistication as Kim Hong-do. He gave Byeon a job as public servant and ordered that he be exempt from the *chwijae* (screening) test. The entry of *Gyujanggak Daily Journal* dated 22nd of the 6th lunar month of 1794 recorded the following.

King Jeongjo decided on the list of court painters and announced it to the central government. He said, "Byeon Gwang-bok is as skilled and sophisticat-

> ed as Kim Hong-do. Give Byeon a government officer title and excuse him from taking the *chwijae* exam. In the future, he is to paint an 8-fold screen every month for the evaluation. The canvas and paint shall be provided to him. During the summer and winter seasons, he is to paint two sheets to be put up on the wall every month.

This shows that King Jeongjo had not forgotten about Kim Hong-do, although he was serving outside the palace.

By the year-end in 1794, three consecutive years of drought had dealt a heavy blow to the Chungcheong, Jeolla and Gyeongsang region. The central government dispatched *wiyusa* again to each province, and Chungcheong Wiyusa Hong Dae-hyeop (1750–1801) wrote a negative report about Kim Hong-do that later served to dismiss him from his office.

Kim Hong-do was 51 in 1795 and was in his third year as *hyeongam*. On the 7th of the 1st lunar month, he was removed from office by order of the king. The same day is entry of *The Record of Daily Reflections* has the following article entitled "The King Invited the Chungcheong, Jeolla and Gyeongsang Wiyusa to the Royal Palace."

> The king asked, "So how are things in Yeonpung?" Hong Dae-hyeop answered, "I was unable to see for myself, but rumor had it that the government order was in terrible shape." The king said, "The village heads of Yeonpung and Sinchang shall be the first ones replaced."

The bad state of affairs in Yeonpung that Hong had only heard of was specifically detailed in the entry of *The Record of Daily Reflections* on the same day under the article entitled, "Chungcheong Wiyusa Hong Dae-hyeop's Report and Separate List."

> I submit my report in writing. I received orders on the 4th of the 11th lunar month last year and went to the assigned region as Chungcheong *wiyusa*. Ac-

cording to my observations, Yeonpung Hyeongam Kim Hong-do has done nothing good since he has been in office. For several years, the only thing he has done as village head was to act as a matchmaker and threaten petty officials to pay in livestock. If they did not obey, he became furious and inflicted severe punishments. There is a rumor that Kim requisitioned the soldiers garrisoned in town for hunting trips. He counted the soldiers who did not show up and the number of days and levied rice tax accordingly. Everyone is in contempt of Hyeongam Kim. I interrogated the *hyeongam*'s secretary to verify the matter, and his confessions showed all rumors to be true. Such a public enemy must be appropriately punished.

According to Hong Dae-hyeop, Kim Hong-do, as a *hyeongam* who enjoyed the benefits of his position, harassed villagers, plundered his subordinates of livestock and used the excuse of a hunting trip to levy higher taxes. The above was not directly observed by the *wiyusa*, but rather confirmed by the confessions of the secretary of Yeonpung *hyeongam* under interrogation. There is no way to discover if Kim Hong-do mismanaged government affairs, or whether the secretary was plotting against Kim or whether Hong Dae-hyeop personally disliked Kim. At any rate, this incident led to Kim's dismissal and replacement, by Song Ji-gyeong. For reference, Song lasted less than two years in the post.

According to King Jeongjo's verbal order, Kim Hong-do was discharged from office on the 7th of the 1st lunar month. The next day, an article entitled, "Bibyeonsa's Comments Attached to Chungcheong Wiyusa Hong Dae-hyeop's Report and Separate List appeared in *The Record of Daily Reflections*."

Yeonpung Hyeongam Kim Hong-do plundered his subordinates of livestock, inflicted unheard-of harsh punishments, requisitioned soldiers for his hunting trips and levied rice tax on those who did not obey. The villagers were in contempt of Kim. Such a man of humble origin never thought of repaying

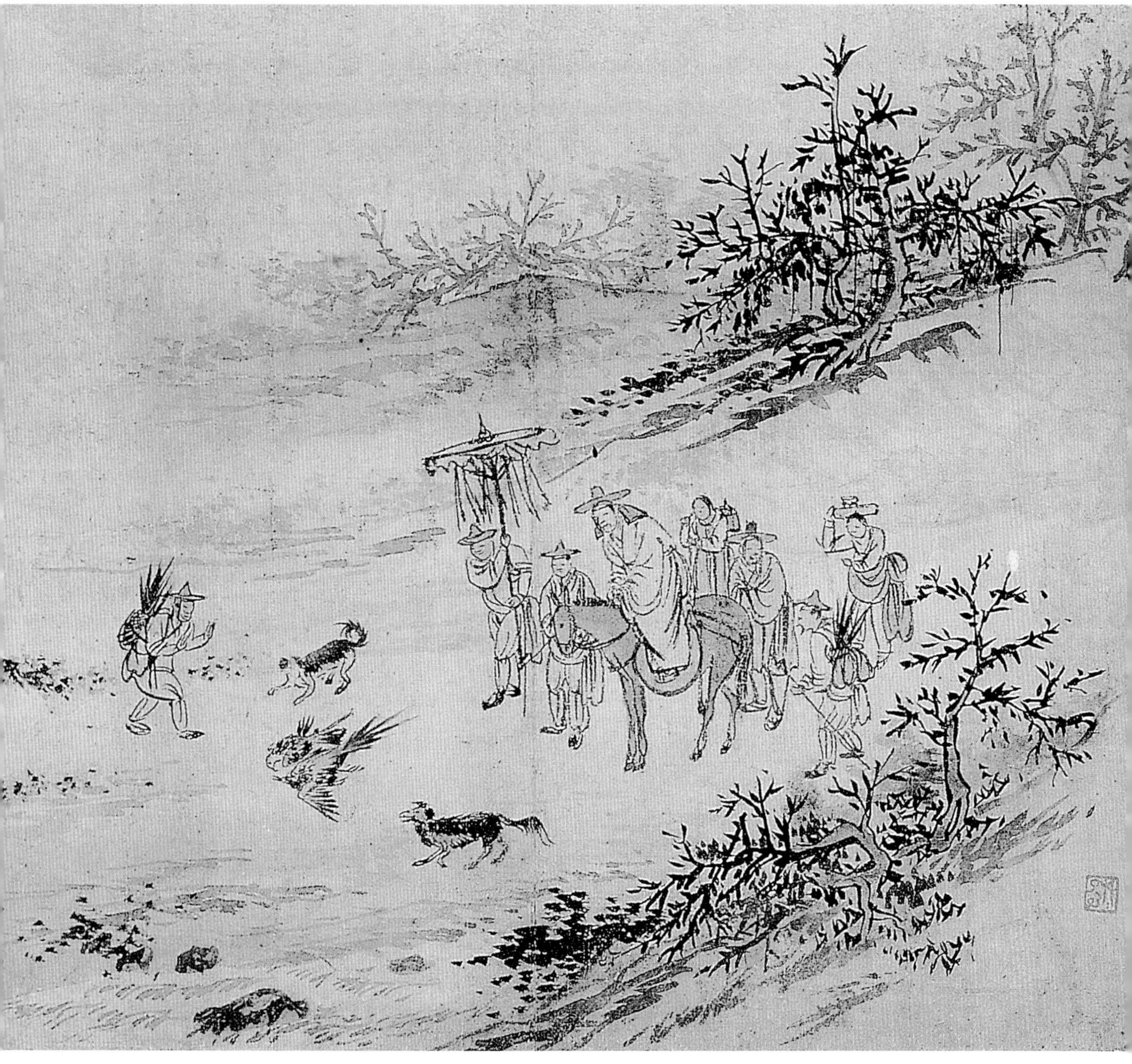

77 *Falcon Hunting*

Ink and color on paper. 28 × 34.2cm. Kansong Art Museum.

Kim Hong-do probably painted this when he served as *hyeongam* in Yeonpung. As if to defend himself from the accusation of [requisitioning] soldiers for his hunting trips and [levying] rice tax on those who did not obey, Kim painted the scene of a falcon-hunting trip. The hyeongam wears protective headgear under his hat, which indicates early winter and occasional snow. There are seven other people in the company: a man holding the reins, a man carrying a parasol, a secretary, an errand boy, a woman carrying drinks on her head and two porters. The falcon is chasing a pheasant on the ground as the porter hurries to separate them. Only the secretary is looking in a direction different from the rest. The hunting dog barking at the falcon is almost audible in the cold winter air.

the king's kindness but committed hideous crimes. It is not enough to dismiss him from office. An order must be issued to the relevant department to keep him in custody, interrogate him and bring his crimes to light. How about rounding up Kim and Sinchang Hyeongam Kwon Sang-hui together and have them interrogated too?" The king agreed.

Kim Hong-do committed serious crimes and he could not be let off with just a dismissal. It was requested that he be punished by the Uigeumbu,[86] and King Jeongjo gave his permission. There is no record, however, of the Uigeumbu ever interrogating Kim because King Jeongjo pardoned him only ten days after he ordered him taken away. The 18th of the 1st lunar month's entry of *The Record of Daily Reflections* reads

> The criminals who were not yet sent to Uigeumbu and who were given amnesty included Im Bung-han, Kwon Sang-hui, Kim Hong-do and Sim In. They were released.

Kim Hong-do was pardoned even before he was escorted to Hanyang. These are the series of events purporting Kim Hong-do's corruption, his dishonorable dismissal from his office and his amnesty. The interpretation of these events is important. Let us examine Hong Dae-hyeop, whose accusations led to Kim's dismissal. His family was from Namyang, his grandfather was Daesaseong Bongjo, his father was Ik (birth father Eok), and his cousin was Damheon Hong Dae-yong, a *bukhak* scholar. In other words, he comes from a renowned *noron* family. Kim Hong-do had the full support of Kang Se-hwang who belonged to the *namin* faction of *sobuk* line. Kim's artistic skills were enough to win King Jeongjo's approval. The office of *hyeongam*, a post reserved only for nobles and envied by the middle class, had gone to Kim Hong-do. This alone would have been enough for Hong to dislike Kim. If Kim did have a stain on his governance, then Hong would have pounced on it whenever the opportunity arose. It is interesting that

86 The supreme investigation and prosecution office.

Chungcheong Wiyusa Hong Dae-hyeop was the Chungcheong Royal Investigator who had been dispatched at the time of the former Busa Gu Sun's incident two years earlier. In 1792, Kim Hong-do received support from Chungcheong Governor Lee Hyeong-won regarding the restoration of Sangamsa Temple, and the two were on good terms. Kim was also close to Byeongsa Lee Gwang-seop–so much so that he greeted Lee immediately after he was appointed. He also enjoyed Lee's company at the famous Seowon Gathering at the *byeongsa* office in Cheongju that fall. Kim had met with Byeongsa Lee four years before when they both were invited to attend the birthday party for Lee Deok-mu's father. The 12th lunar month of 1792 marked the beginning of the conflict between Lee Hyeong-won and Lee Gwang-seop, and in the 5th lunar month of 1793, former Busa Gu Sun wrongfully accused his archrival and had him killed. This led to a full-fledged battle between the two Lees. It ended in Byeongsa Lee Gwang-seop's exile and Governor Lee Hyeong-won's temporary dismissal. Hong Dae-hyeop was the royal investigator dispatched from Hanyang to investigate the case. His report was a vital source of information for handling the situation. It is believed that Hong's real father Hong Eok was in the same political camp as Lee Hyeong-won. Hong Dae-hyeop would have sided with Lee Hyeong-won, and the Gu Sun case was ruled in favor of Hyeong-won largely because of Hong's report. The evaluation of Hyeongam Kim Hong-do was the responsibility of the governor. Even if the *wiyusa* had accused Kim, if his immediate boss Governor Lee had objected, the impeachment process would not have gone smoothly. Considering the circumstances, it is possible that Kim Hong-do was a victim who was caught in the struggle between the governor and *byeongsa*.

Regardless of what lay underneath, King Jeongjo removed Kim from office and gave permission for him to be interrogated by the Uigeumbu. It was also King Jeongjo, however, who gave Kim amnesty only ten days later. Regardless of how petty the government post was, it would be difficult to plot against and falsely accuse someone whom the king himself had appointed. The author is unable to verify the nature of Kim's dismissal and near interrogation at Uigeumbu; it is unclear whether Kim Hong-do was at fault, as the record seems to indicate, or whether he fell victim in the power struggle that went on between Governor Lee Hyeong-won, Byeongsa Lee Gwang-seop and Wiyusa Hong Dae-hyeop. A minor mistake that would ordinarily have been overlooked may have been amplified because of the complex dynamics among these powerful individuals. At any rate, three years as *hyeongam* was an appropriate length of time and longer than the average term.

The atmosphere in the royal palace may have had something to do with Kim Hong-do being exonerated in just ten days, and before he was escorted to Uigeumbu. The year 1795 was significant because King Yeongjo's second wife Queen Jeongsun turned fifty-one, Lady Hong turned sixty-one as would have Crown Prince Sado had he lived, and it was the twentieth year of King Jeongjo's reign. The palace was planning a politically significant parade to Hyeonryungwon, and King Jeongjo's main project, construction of the Hwaseong Fortress, was underway. Talented painters were in demand. In a year like this with many things to celebrate, convicted prisoners were often released unless they were serious felons. It was only natural to grant Kim Hong-do amnesty because he was not yet convicted and had a lot to contribute to the royal palace.

In the year prior to Kim's dismissal, Yeonpung had seen severe damage, as it had suffered several years of drought. Kim's term in office was far from comfortable. He must also have been uncomfortable because his immediate supervisor Governor Lee Hyeong-won and his acquaintance Byeongsa Lee Gwang-seop were not on good terms. Eventually, Wiyusa Hong Dae-hyeop reported how his relief efforts were negligible, and how he deprived the lower ranking officials and villagers of their property. He was dishonorably discharged.

On the bright side, however, Kim Hong-do finally sired a son, Yang-gi, while he was in Yeonpung. He toured the Danyang area and encountered beautiful sights. He painted pictures for King Jeongjo and felt the joy of creating something. As in the tale related earlier in this section, perhaps Kim Hong-do lived a happy and simple life in this small and warm village. The office building in Yeonpung has almost disappeared. The main entrance and the guesthouse remained until the Korean War, so what remains today are the main office building, Pungnakheon, which was relocated to where the *hyeongam*'s quarters were; the *hyangcheong*, which significantly changed because of its use as a Japanese patrol station and church during colonial rule; and the *hyanggyo* and lotus pond. Of the *hyanggyo*, only the *daeseongjeon*[87] is authentic. The rest of the *myeongryundang*,[88] *dongjae* and *seojae*[89] were burnt during the Korean War and rebuilt. Books, documents and other materials that were stored in the *hyanggyo* were lost, and there are no relics of Kim Hong-do. On the path next to the *hyanggyo*, there are a number of monuments commemorating good government; however since Kim was dishonorably dismissed there is no monument to him. In the playground of an elementary school in front of the main office building are two zelkova trees (Plate 78) that are 250 years old. They were young trees when Kim was *hyeongam* and must have seen everything, but they remain silent about the whole affair. While on a field trip to the area, the author was informed that when Kim Hong-do was leaving, he left two paintings of flowers and birds as a token of friendship to a Mr. Kim who was either a gatekeeper or someone who ran errands. They seem to be the only mementos the warm-hearted Kim Hong-do left behind.

87 A hall that housed a Confucian memorial tablet.
88 Students auditorium.
89 Students dormitories.

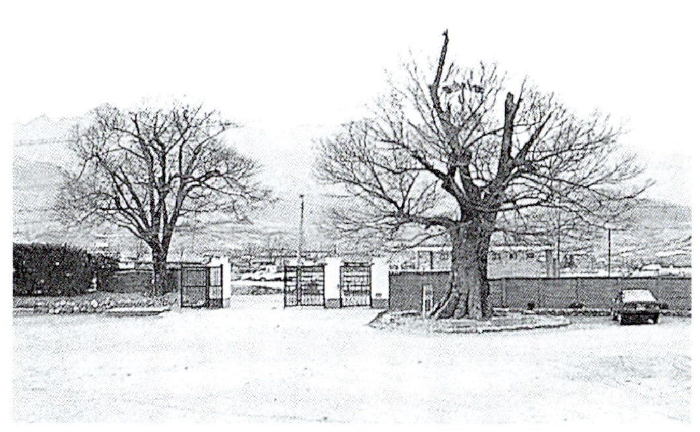

78 A zelkova tree standing where the government office used to be

The following section covers some materials that are relevant to Kim's tenure as *hyeongam*. Lee Gyu-sang, who told about

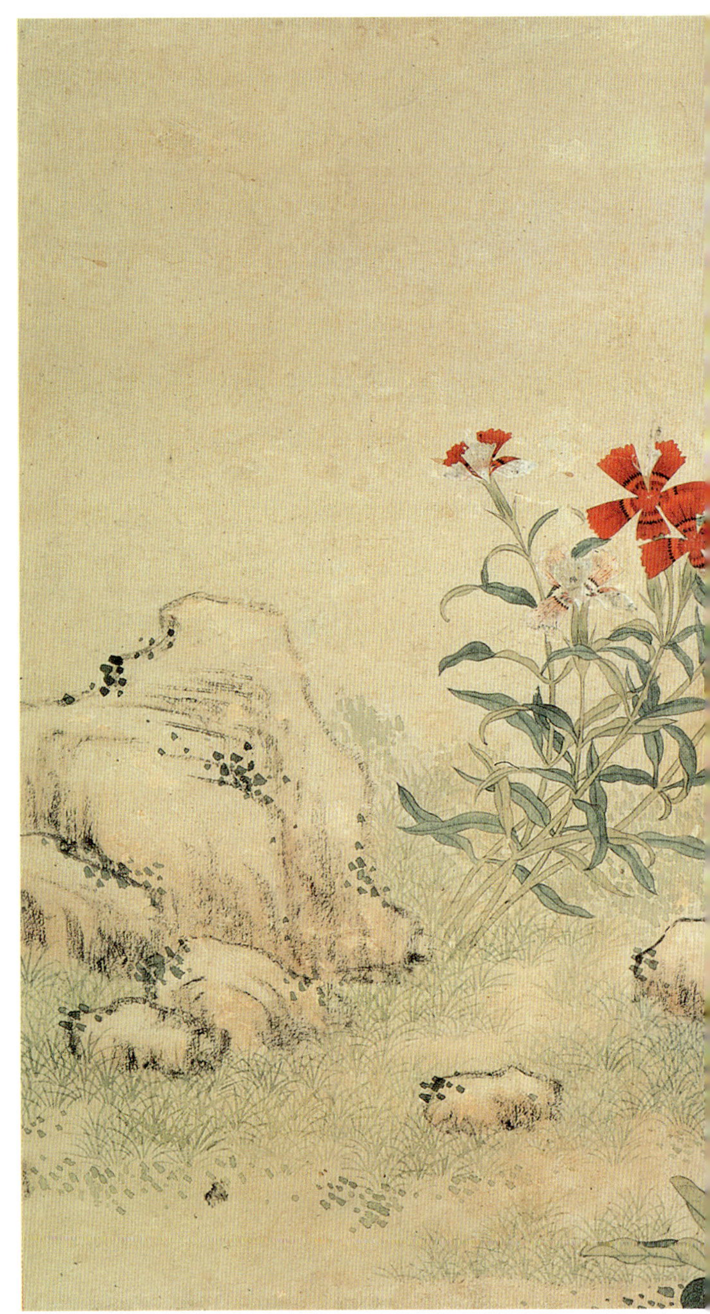

79 *A Yellow Cat and a Dark-colored Butterfly*
Color on paper. 30.1 × 46.1cm. Kansong Art Museum.
A small kitten is naively looking at a large spotted butterfly. The two animals, the pink Chinese flowers and pansies, are very realistic, and the colors are all splendid. In old paintings, a cat symbolized a septuagenarian, and a butterfly an octogenarian. The pink Chinese flower stood for youth, and stones of various sizes stood for longevity. This was painted for an old man.

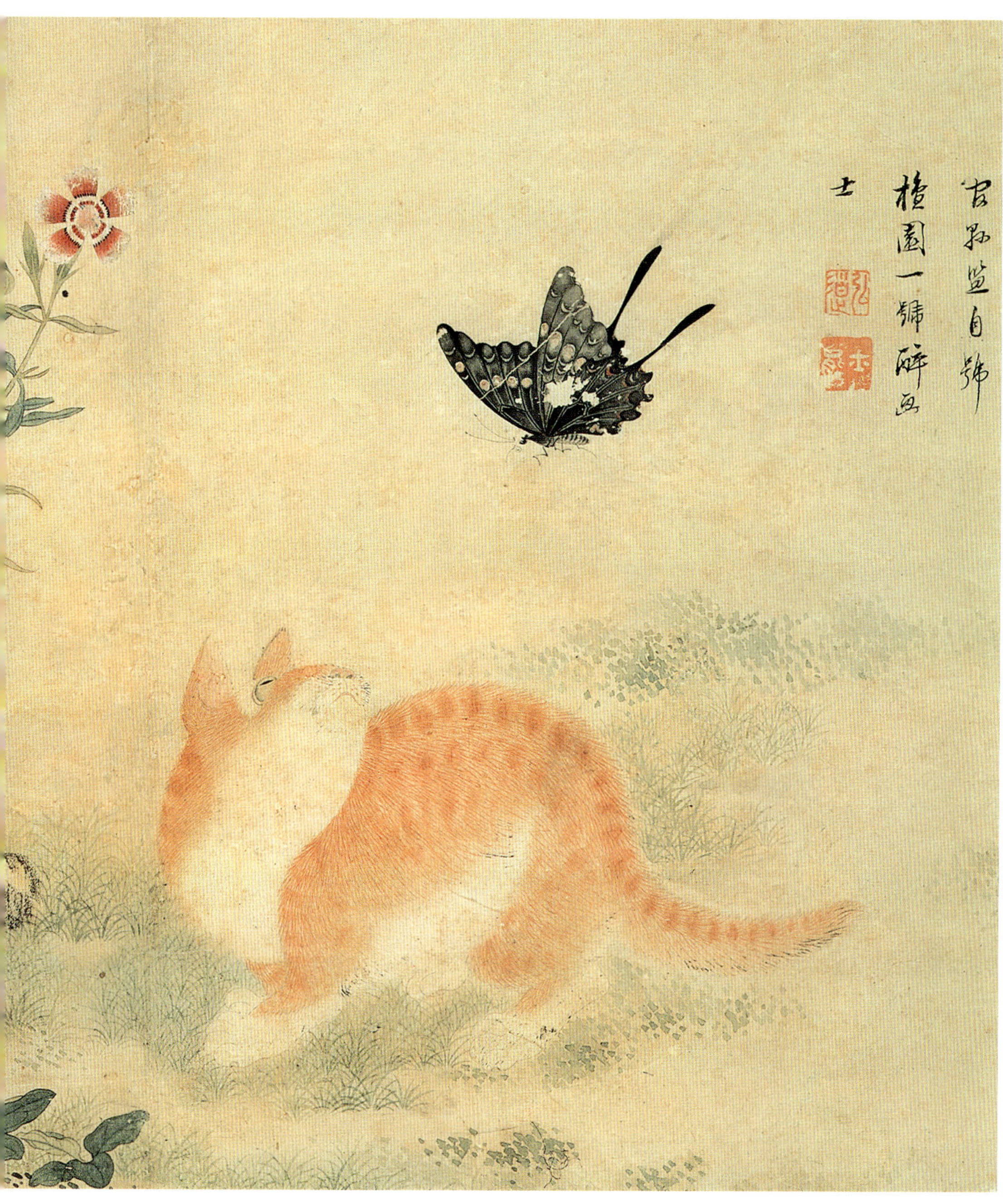

the Seowon Gathering episode, left the following record about the time Kim served as *hyeongam*.

> Kim Hong-do's courtesy name is Saneung, and his pen name is Danwon. He made his name in Dohwaseo, and now he is *hyeongam*. He is an excellent painter, especially of horses and customs. People called it genre painting. It follows the rules of painting, but the spirit is alive. He participated in the painting of the current king's portrait and in return, he was offered the *hyeongam* post. For the first time, Dohwaseo's painting copied the Western painting style of perspective. If you look at the finished painting with one eye closed, everything in the painting seems to be in perfect order. People called this type of painting a *chaekgeori*. The painting was always in color, and at one time, people of noble birth all decorated their walls with it. Hong-do was very good at this genre.

The Western art technique and the *chaekgeori* painting were previously mentioned in the section regarding the platform painting in Yongjusa Temple, as was the significance of the comment, "his painting followed the rules of painting, but the spirit was alive." The phrase, "people called it genre painting" implies that his works were considered an original style. None of the horse paintings are extant, but Seo Yu-gu's record reconfirms that he drew them. Kim Hong-do's work related to his *hyeongam* post is 'A Yellow Cat and a Dark-colored Butterfly' (Plate 79). The inscription, "The *hyeongam* has the pen name Danwon, and he is also called Chwihwasa," is written on the painting. The above "*hyeongam*," however, does not confirm whether it was painted during or after his tenure. The painting contains a cat, a butterfly, a pink flower and stones that are realistically painted in soft colors. The objects in the painting all symbolize longevity, so the painting must have been a birthday present for an elderly man, but the recipient is unknown. The author has also heard from Sin Eung-hyeon, who lives in Jincheon and is a descendant of Doksongjae Sin Jap (1541–1609), that two portraits of Sin Jap remain in Noeunyeongdang. Kim I-beon painted the original in 1607, and the other is a copy painted by Kim Hong-do. Doksongjae's grandchild seven generations later, Hansujae Sin Dae-gu (1745–1806), was the *gunsu* in neighboring Goesan when Hong-do was the hyeongam in Yeonpung, and had Kim copy it.

80 ***Hwaseong Secondary Palace*** **from** ***Wonhaeng-eulmyo-jeongri-uigwe***
King Jeongjo built this palace with the intention of spending his final years after his abdication in Suwon. Built in a large space at the foot of the eastern side of Paldang Mountain, it was originally designed to serve as the center of Hwa-seong. During the Japanese occupation, however, the conquerors destroyed the palace and constructed hospitals, police stations and schools instead. Only the Naknamheon still survives, and restoration work is under way.

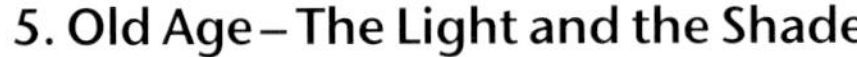

5. Old Age – The Light and the Shade

On the 28th of the 2nd lunar leap-month of 1795, a *uigwe* office was established in the royal printing house to publish *uigwe* concerning the Wonhaeng-eulmyo parade for the 61st birthday of Lady Hong, King Jeongjo's mother. The same day, Kim Hong-do was appointed to a fulltime military position so he could paint illustrations for the *Wonhaeng-eulmyo-jeongri-uigwe* (Plate 80).

The king called in Sim I-ji, Min Jong-hyeon, Lee Si-su,
Lee Ga-hwan, Seo Yong-bo and Yun Haeng-im,
the officers of the uigwe office, to Chundangdae
[backyard of Changdeok Palace]

The king said, "Publishing this *uigwe* will require a considerable amount of work … After good texts are selected for the book, they should be transcribed. Therefore, Jo Seok-jung and Hwang Gi-cheon, who were trained in Gyujanggak, shall be appointed as *nangcheong* to do the job." Yun Haeng-im responded, "Since there are already descriptions for the illustrations, it would be desirable to call in Kim Hong-do." The king said, "Do so."

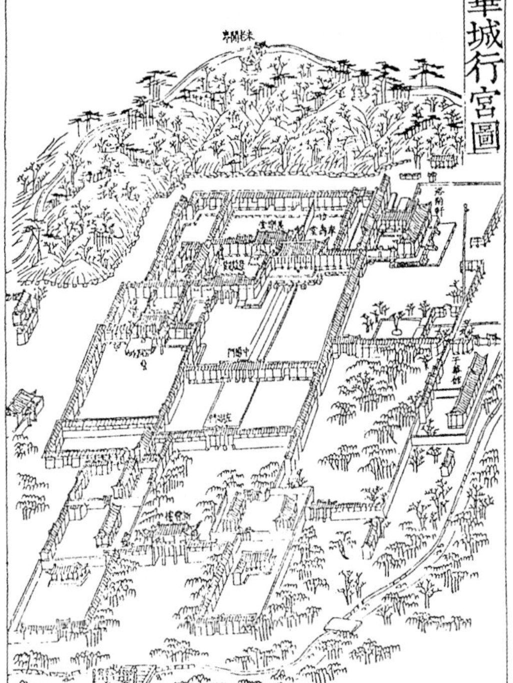

The king ordered the uigwe office to appoint
Jo Seok-jung and Hwang Gi-cheon,
who were trained in Gyujanggak, as nangcheong
and to appoint Kim Hong-do to a military position…

…Jo Seok-jung and Hwang Gi-cheon, who had worked hard before, were appointed as *nangcheong* in charge of proofreading. Kim Hong-do, the former *hyeongam*, was appointed to a military position by the relevant office to work on a full-time basis. The presentation of the book to the king was scheduled for the 13th of the 4th lunar month.

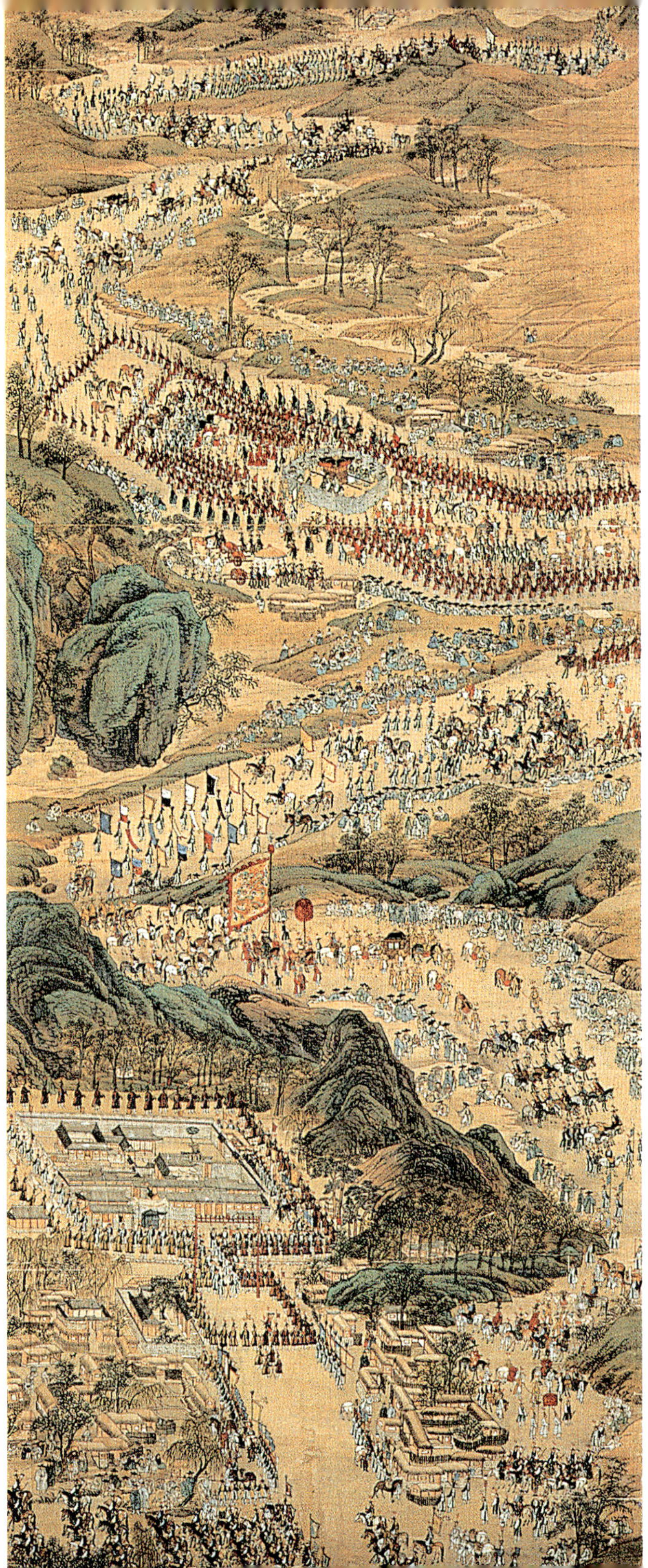

81 ***Royal Procession Back to Seoul*** **from *Wonhaeng-eulmyo-jeongri-uigwe***
Ink and color on silk. 142×62cm. Hoam Art Museum.
A large royal procession from Hwaseong arrives at Siheung Secondary Palace on the 15th of the 2nd lunar leap-month in 1795. The immense retinue, which includes at least 6,000 people and 1,400 horses, is tactically presented in a zigzag pattern. The free, peaceful attitude of the onlookers is especially impressive.

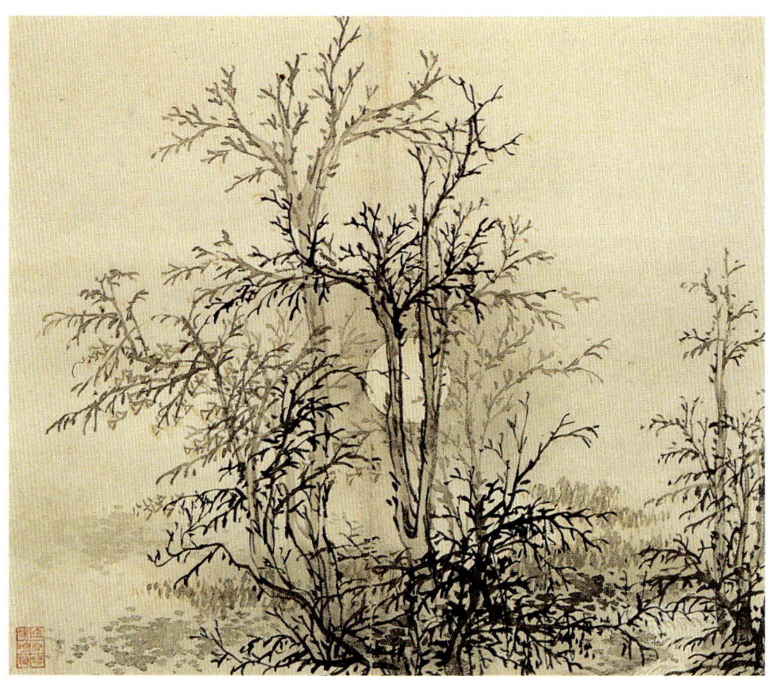

82 *Full Moon behind Leafless Trees* from *Danwon-jeolsebo Album*
1796. Ink and color on paper. 26.7×31.6cm. Hoam Art Museum.
The full moon slowly rises behind almost leafless trees on an unknown hill in autumn. Some of the leaves have fallen from the high branches, but the twigs and leaves in the lower branches retain the vestiges of the lingering summer. The casual-looking branches, which have grown on their own in the wild, are typical of the beauty of Korean nature. On the right side, below the straight tree, which is separated a little from the trees in the center, flows a small stream, around which small bushes are simplified as dots. The trees in the woods are shaded differently to express the depth of the space. A ring around the full moon highlights the woods existence. Kim masterfully depicted the calm and peaceful atmosphere of autumn by positioning the full moon in the background in the lower part of the painting.

This is also confirmed in the *Wonhaeng-eulmyo-jeongri-uigwe*. The famous 'Wonhaeng-eulmyo-uigwedo' (Plate 81) on on 8-fold screen was completed and distributed by Jeongriso, which was a temporary preparatory office for the Wonhaeng-eulmyo parade. Consequently, Kim Hong-do, who had been in charge of *Wonhaeng-eulmyo-jeongri-uigwe* with other court painters, is believed to have painted this painting.

In the 8th lunar month, Kim painted the *Eulmyonyeon Album*. Although only 'A Brave Eagle on a Rock in the Sea' (Plate 11), 'A Fawn under the Old Pine Tree' (Plate 83) and 'Chongseokjeong' (Plate 12) survived, they are all masterpieces, and show mature brushstrokes and artistic charm. 'Gyeongrim,' in the inscription, is the courtesy name of Kim Han-tae, who was a court interpreter and the richest man in town. According to *Danwon and His Housekeeping*, the unfinished work by Jeon Hyeong-pil (1906–1962), Kim Han-tae was Danwon's patron, who provided him with living

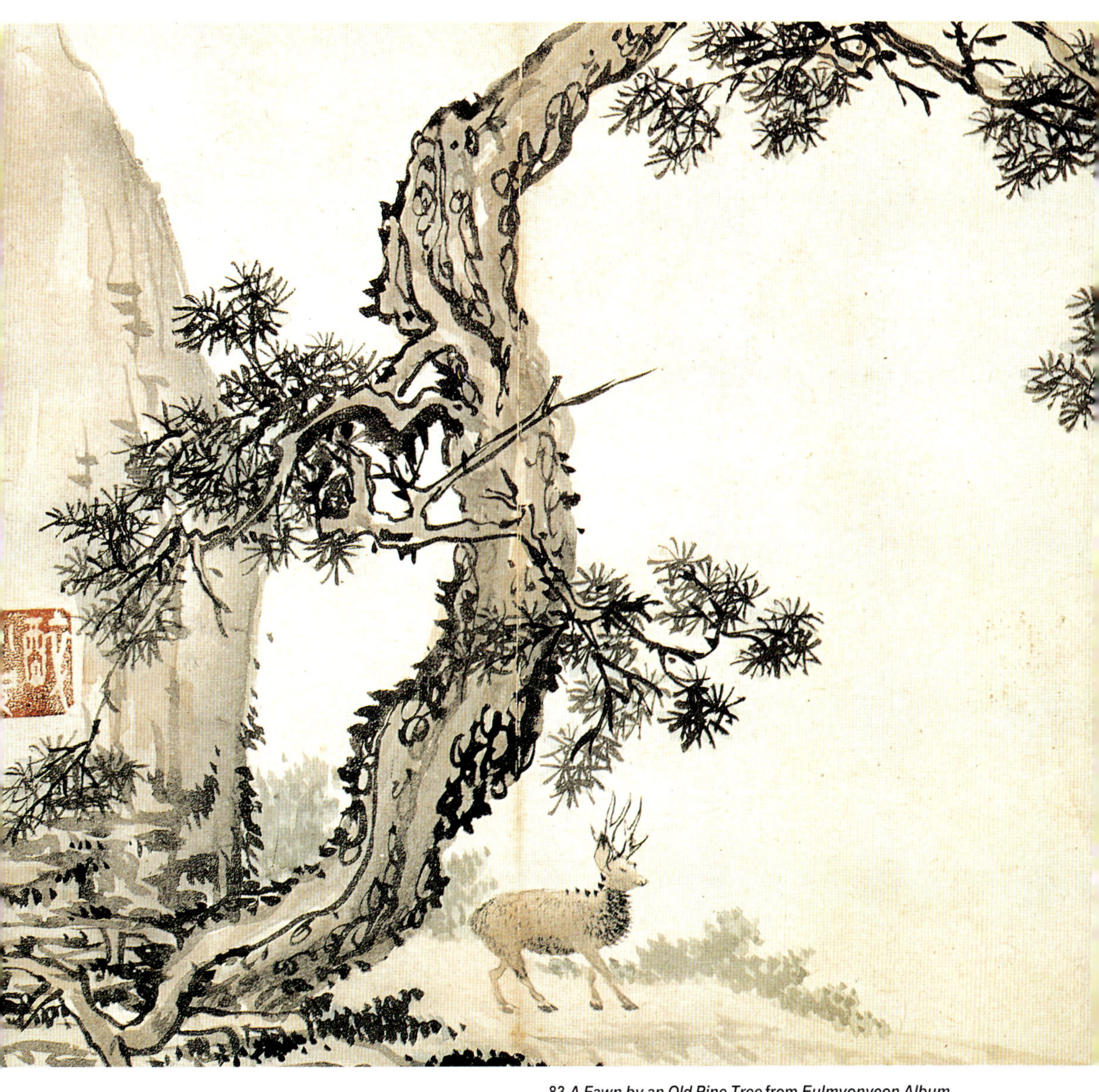

83 ***A Fawn by an Old Pine Tree*** **from *Eulmyonyeon Album***
1795. Ink and color on paper. 23.2×27.7cm. Private collection.
An innocent-looking fawn is passing under an old pine tree. The lines of its eyes and lips are interesting, and show almost no expression. The casual brushwork of the dots in the hair is also mature. The cliff on the left side is completed primarily by shadings. The affixed seal, Chwihwasa, was given by Kim Hong-do s teacher, Kang Se-hwang.

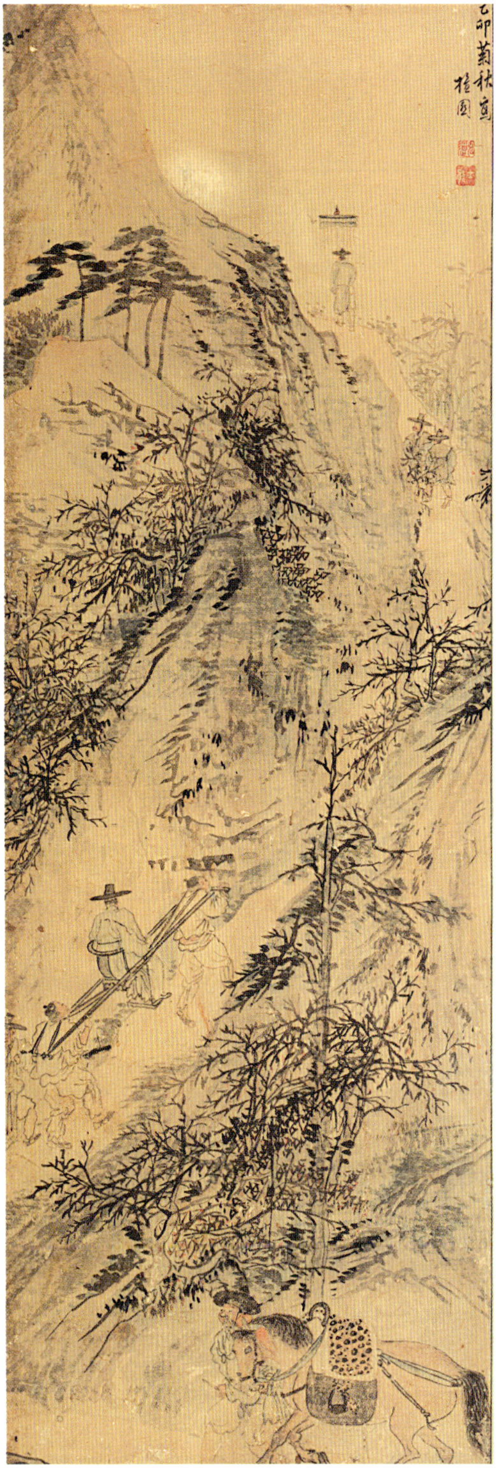

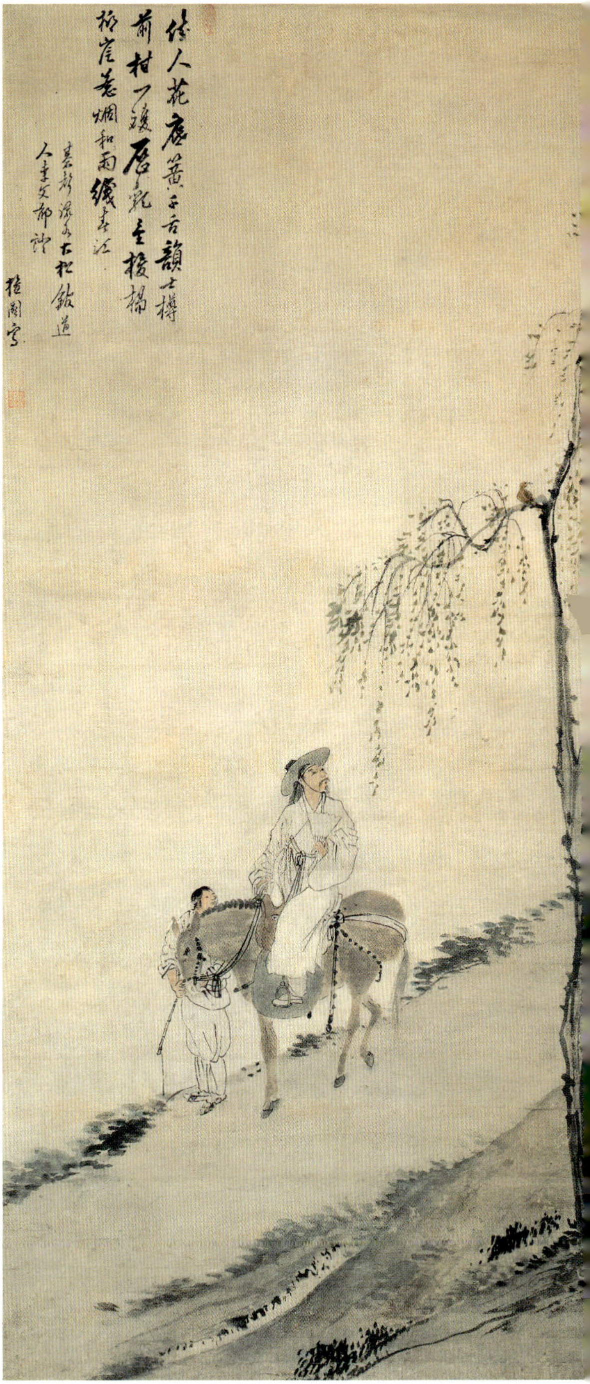

expenses as well as housing.

Kim Han-tae was wealthy, deeply interested in poetry, calligraphy and painting, and Danwon's close friend. He gave Danwon a house from among his holdings and provided everyday necessities so Danwon could focus on art. Given that Danwon was a free spirit who did not want to be bothered by mundane matters, he was lucky to have a good friend like Kim Han-tae. It has been a general opinion that Kim Han-tae owned Danwon's most remarkable works. Kim Han-tae's house was well built and until recently stood intact in Euljiro-2ga in Cheonggyecheon.

In the 9th lunar month, Kim Hong-do painted 'Genre Painting' on an eight-paneled folding screen (Plates 84, 86). This picture was discovered in 1995 while the author was preparing for a special exhibition on Danwon Kim Hong-do. The inscription reads, "Painted by Danwon in the 9th lunar month, 1795." Although this work was damaged and restored, the mature technique and Kim Hong-do's unique brushstroke reveal Kim's painting style at the time. Notably, 'Listening to the Nightingale While Riding on a Horse' on the fourth panel (Plate 86) shows the same subject as the painting with the same title in the Kansong Art Museum (Plate 85).

In the spring of 1796, at age 52, he painted the *Danwon-jeolsebo Album*, which is a collection of 20 paintings that shows the brushstroke and artistic charm of the *Eulmyonyeon Album*. 'Full Moon behind Leafless Trees' (Plate 82) in particular shows the characteristic beauty of Korea.

In the spring of the same year, King Jeongjo learned of *Daebobumoeunjungge*. Presumably, the king ordered Kim Hong-do to paint the illustrations for *Bulseoldaebobumoeunjunggyeong*. The *Eunjunggegaengjaechuk* of *Hongjaejeonseo* explains as follows.

> I was not familiar with Buddhist literature, but in the spring of 1796, I read *Daebobumoeunjungge*, which fascinated me with its focus on the importance of filial piety and ethics: the same teachings as Confucianism. Therefore, I issued an ordinance to print this on New Year's Eve and on *dano* [the 5th of the

84 *A Government Official on a Trip* from *Genre Painting*
1795. Ink and color on paper. 100.6×34.8cm. National Museum of Korea.
A village chief is traveling on a mountain road. A man with a sunshade and two duty officers whose hats are decorated with feathers are walking far ahead of the procession, while the village chief, in full-dress attire, is in a carriage over the mountain. The horse he rode over the flat ground is following behind. The straight, high-rising tree suggests the roughness of the mountain terrain. It is believed that Kim Hong-do depicted himself as the village chief.

85 *Listening to a Nightingale While Riding on a Horse*
Ink and color on paper. 117.2×52cm. Kansong Art Museum.
A traveler is fascinated by a pair of golden yellow nightingales in a drizzling rain. Kim Hong-do s poem describes the painting. A beautiful woman is playing a reed instrument beneath blooming flowers, but she feels dizzy as if a graceful nobleman has put a pair of tangerines in front of the wine cup. That golden-yellow shuttle of the loom going back and forth along the shore with weeping willows has woven silk gauze with fog and rain!

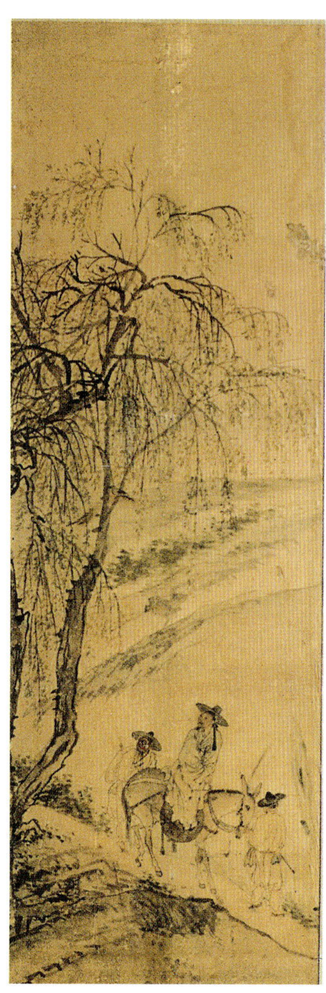

86 ***Listening to a Nightingale While Riding on a Horse*** **from** ***Genre Painting***
1795. Ink and color on paper. 100.6×34.8cm. National Museum of Korea.
This painting is similar to the one in Plate 85, but the left and right sides are reversed. In addition, this painting is quite descriptive, and has many branches and a background, whereas Plate 85 offers a more sentimental approach by treating the margin as the background. Unfortunately, the faces of the men and the nightingales on the tree are seriously damaged.

5th lunar month], which will then be attached on the lintel and replace the talisman distributed by the *gwansanggam*. In addition, I showed good stories from the book to several subjects, fourteen of whom then composed poetry in response.

As the aforementioned text concerns only *Daebobumoeunjungge*, so it is different from the entire *Bulseoldaebobumoeunjunggyeong*. Furthermore, there is no solid evidence that Kim Hong-do painted the illustrations for *Bulseoldaebobumoeunjunggyeong*; however, the work shows Kim's characteristic style, so it is probably Kim's work, and the author inserted the text. In the 5th lunar month, the king ordered that *Bulseoldaebobumo-eunjunggyeong* be printed and the engraving block stored in Yongjusa Temple.

That summer, Kim painted 'The Portrait of Seo Jik-su' (Plate 87) with Lee Myeong-gi. Seo Jik-su was in charge of managing Crown Prince Sado's cemetery in 1790 when Danwon and Lee Myeong-gi were painting the Buddhist pictures for Yongjusa Temple. Their acquaintance at that time led Kim to paint Seo's portrait. Seo Jik-su wrote the following inscription.

Lee Myeong-gi painted the face and Kim Hong-do painted the body. Reputable painters though they are, they did not succeed in expressing the spirit. Alas! Why didn't I go to the mountains and study instead of wasting my time wandering about beautiful mountains and appreciating miscellaneous art? Looking back on my life, at least I didn't fall into worldly ambition. Sibuheon, an old man aged 62, comments on himself on one summer day in 1796.

It appears that Kim's role in portrait paintings was to paint the body since he had fulfilled that role three times in painting the king's portrait. 'The Portrait of Seo Jik-su' is a further example of this.

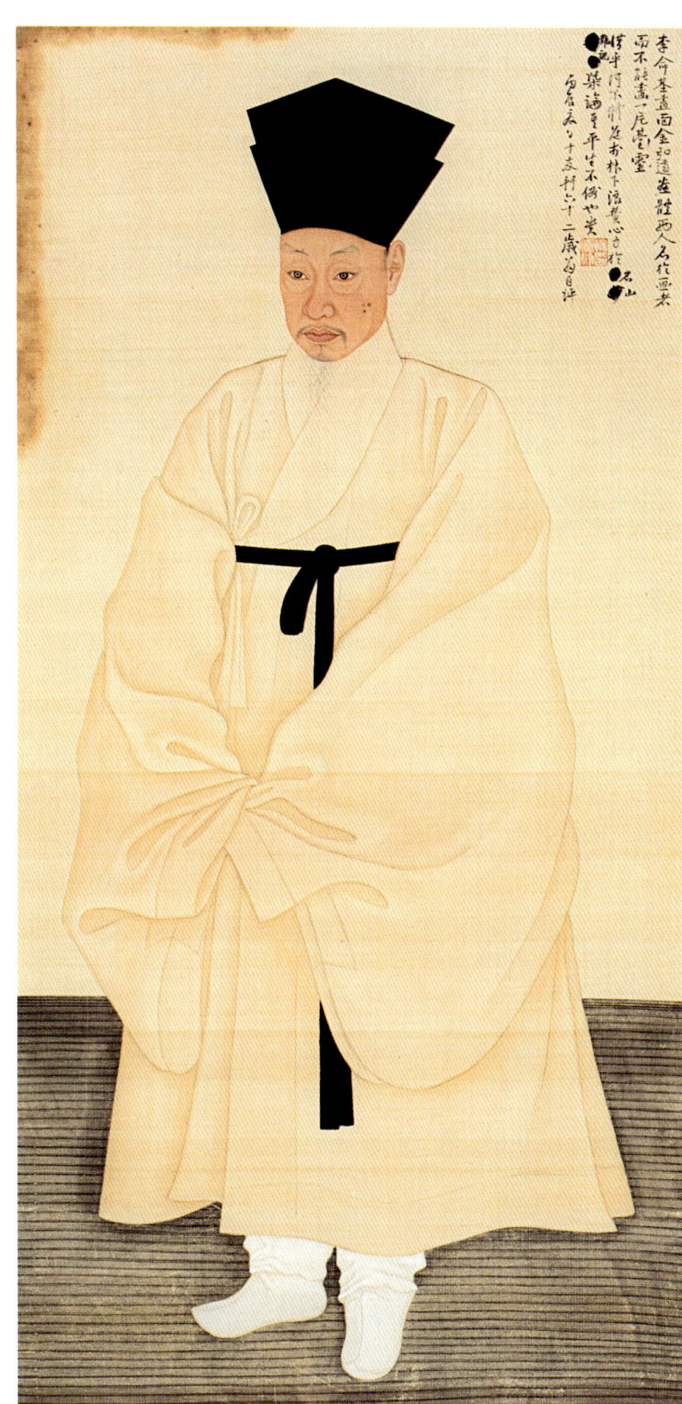

87 Kim Hong-do and Lee Myeong-gi. *Portrait of Seo Jik-su*

1796. Ink and color on silk. 147.9×73.2cm. National Museum of Korea.

Seo Jik-su is wearing a hat, an overcoat, a belt and socks. The dignified lines, wide sleeves and shading maintain the elegance of the painting. The black and white contrast of hat, belt and socks is outstanding, but the feet that float in the air represent a flaw. Seo s inscription, Reputable painters as they are, they did not succeed in expressing the spirit, is too negative, but he may have wanted his portrait to assume a virtuous air.

In the beginning of 1797, when Kim Hong-do was 53, King Jeongjo ordered Sim Sang-gyu and others to publish *The Five Morals with Illustrations*, which was actually printed on the 20th of the 7th lunar month. Although there is no solid evidence that Kim painted the illustrations for the book, it seems probable that Kim played a leading role in completing them, given the importance of the book and analysis of the work (Plate 88).

In 1798, when Kim was 54, he painted 'Banghwasuryudo,' using Danong as his seal. The author has seen neither the actual painting nor the photo, but considering the title of the painting, I only assume that he must have painted Banghwasuryujeong, which was regarded as one of the most beautiful scenes in Hwaseong, Suwon.

In the spring of 1799, when Kim was 55, an epidemic swept the country and killed 120,000 people nationwide. In a letter dated 8th of the 6th lunar month in *Danwon's Posthumous Works*, Kim wrote that he was still in great pain from the disease.

> I assume that you received my letter that I asked the papermaking monk to deliver to you. How have you been in this sizzling weather? This foolish person dares to console you. Since I am still suffering from the disease, I have nothing special to say except that I am worried. I am very frustrated with money-related matters at the paper shop. I wish you all the best. Please understand the lack of courtesy in my writing.
>
> On the 8th of the 6th lunar month of 1799, your sick friend, Hong-do.

The manuscript of *Eojeongdaehakryuui* was completed between the 27th of the 10th lunar month and the 5th of the 11th lunar month. This book is the result of King Jeongjo's lifetime study of *The Great Learning*, which he began studying before he was invested as the crown prince. The manuscript was completed about a couple of months before Kim presented the king with 'The Meanings of Chu Hsi's Poems,' which was painted on a folding screen, and whose subject matter was the teachings of *The Great Learning*

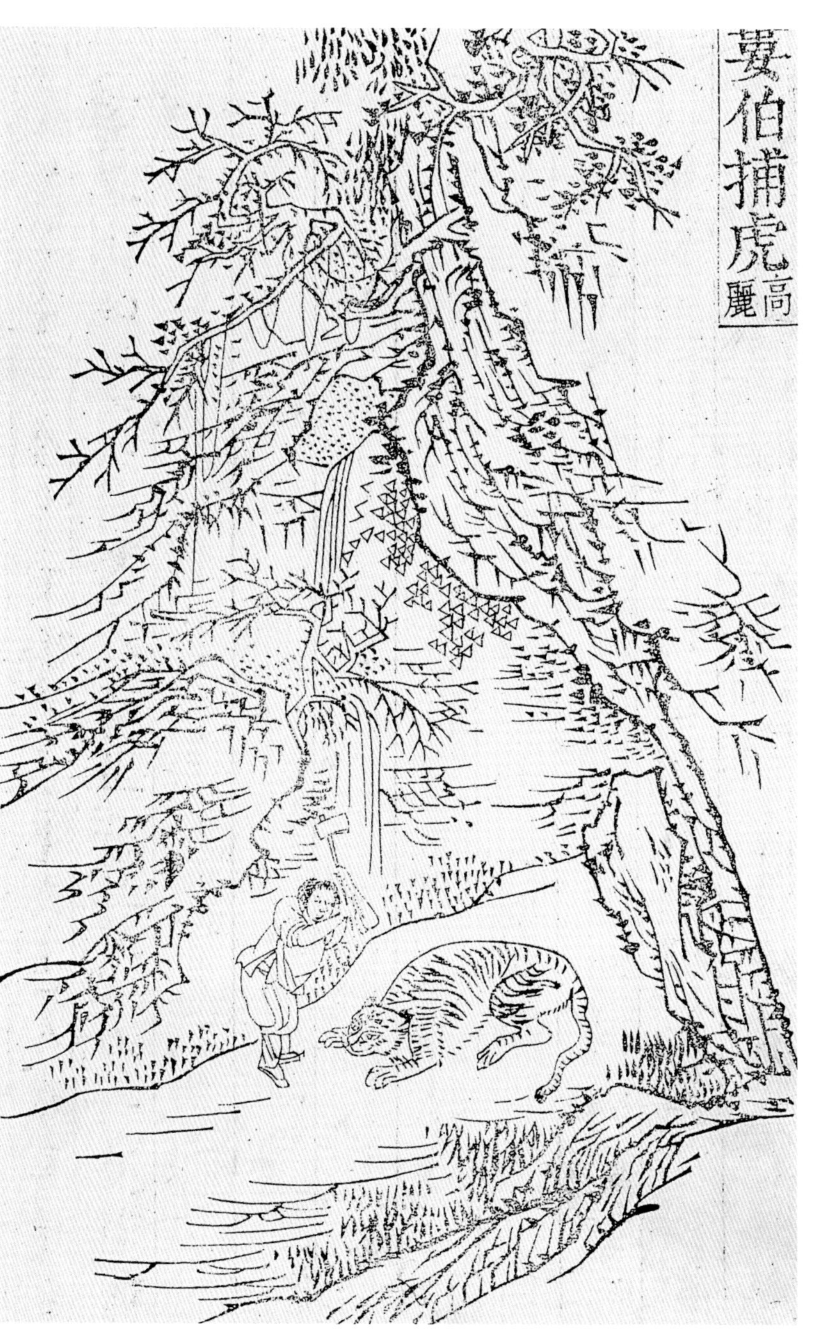

88 ***Nu-baek Captures the Tiger*** from ***The Five Moral Rules with Illustration***
One day, during the Goryeo Dynasty, a pious son named Choi Nu-baek from Suwon heard that his father was caught by a tiger. Although he was only 15 years old, he immediately took an ax and killed the tiger. After Nu-baek avenged his father s death by killing the tiger, which was asleep with a full stomach, he performed his father s funeral, put the tiger s meat in a large jar and buried it in a cool spot by the brook. After three years of mourning, he dug up the tiger meat and ate it all. *The Five Moral Rules with Illustrations* is an illustrated book about the noble deeds of 150 ancestors and features 7 themes: pious sons, loyal subjects, chaste women, brotherly affection, family, friendship and master-disciple relationships.

(Plates 89, 90).

On New Year's Day in 1800 when Kim Hong-do was 56, King Jeongjo ordered that his eldest son be invested as crown prince. According to the custom of court painters, Kim Hong-do presented an eight-paneled screen painting to the king on this day entitled 'The Meanings of Chu Hsi's Poems.' The subject of the painting was the eight pieces of poetry by Chu Hsi mentioned in *Hongjaejeonseo*. This screen consists of the eight steps in *The Great Learning*: investigation of things, extension of knowledge, sincerity of the will, rectification of the mind, cultivation of the personal life, regulation of the family, national order and world peace. It is believed that the screen was painted in direct relation to *Eojeongdaehakryuui*, the transcript of which had been completed about two months before.

As for 'The Meanings of Chu Hsi's Poems,' King Jeongjo wrote, "I was deeply touched by the teachings of Chu Hsi, so I composed eight poems. I will always look at the painting to remind myself of the teachings." In addition, the king recollected that he had known Kim Hong-do for a long time and that he had ordered Kim to preside over all court paintings for the past 30 years.

On the 2nd of the 2nd lunar month, the ceremonies for coming-of-age and title investment of the Crown Prince were held, and on the 28th of the 6th lunar month, King Jeongjo unexpectedly died. King Jeongjo was an enlightened monarch who dedicated himself to governing the people based on the wise, absolute ruler he learned about in *The Great Learning*. Furthermore, as the king himself was artistically talented in calligraphy and painting, he soon recognized Kim Hong-do's outstanding talent and had him involved in court paintings. Given King Jeongjo's patronage of Kim Hong-do, the king's sudden demise must have shocked Kim in many ways.

In the 12th lunar month of 1801, Kim was 57 and painted 'Landscape' (Plate 91) to celebrate King Sunjo's recovery from chicken pox that month. The inscription reads as follows:

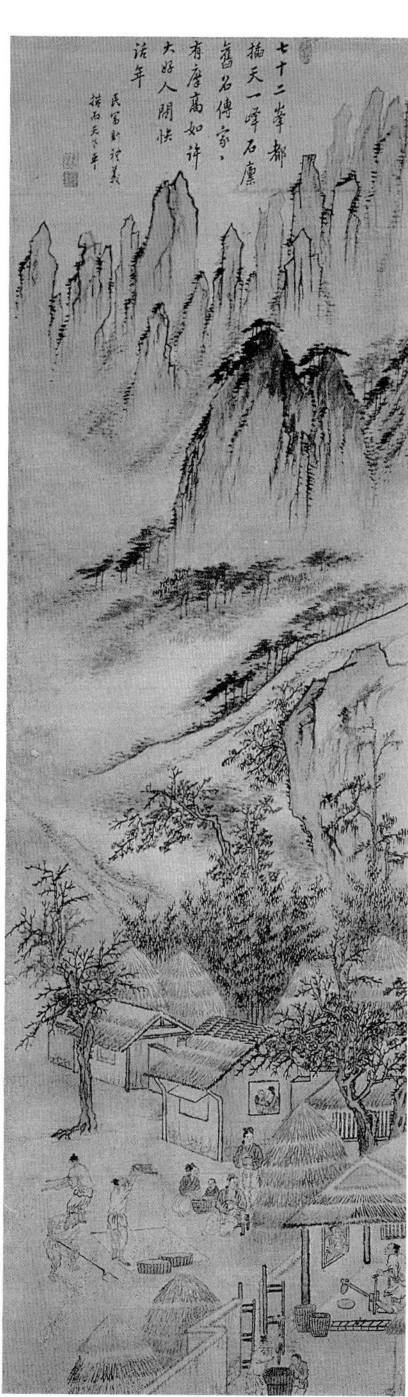

89

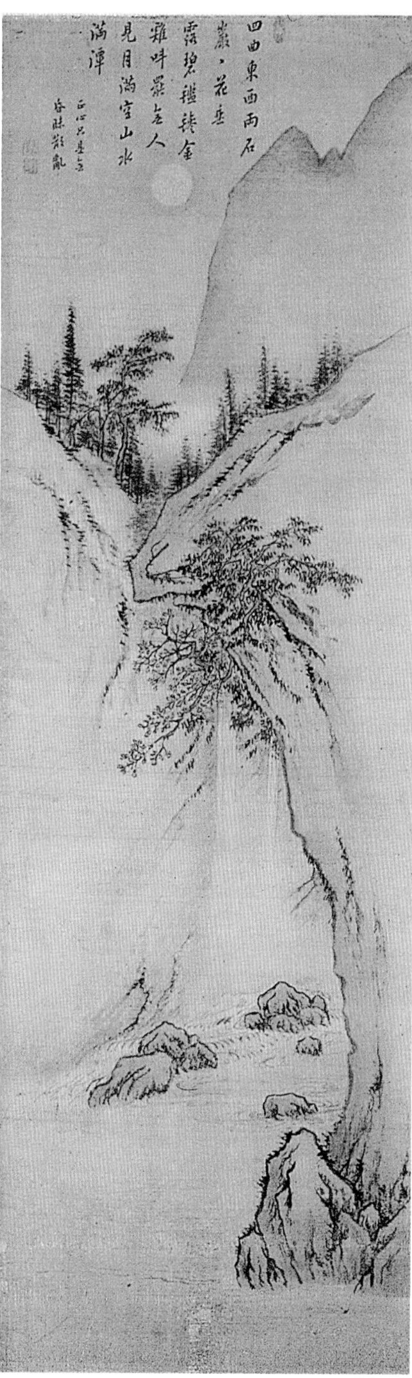

90

89 ***Stacks of Grain in Every Household*** **from** ***The Meanings of Chu Hsi s Poems***

1800. Ink and color on silk. 125 ×40.5cm. Hoam Art Museum.

This is the eighth painting of The Meanings of Chu Hsi s Poems under the theme, Make the whole world peaceful. People are the most important subject to a political leader, and eating is the most important activity for the people. Therefore, stacks of grain in a repository pacify the world. Even the peaks of the mountains resemble stacks of grain, and every household has stacks of grain in the courtyards, and is busy harvesting. The Z-shaped composition gives life to the merry atmosphere.

90 ***The Full Moon and a Valley Filled with Water*** **from** ***The Meanings of Chu Hsi s Poems***

1800. Ink and color on silk. 125 ×40.5cm. Hoam Art Museum.

This is the fourth painting of The Meanings of Chu Hsi s Poems under the theme, Right mind. Deep in the night, the full moon rises unseen and shines over the empty mountain. In the moonlight, cold clean water flows into the valley and fills it to the brim. This landscape represents the state of mind of a truthful man.

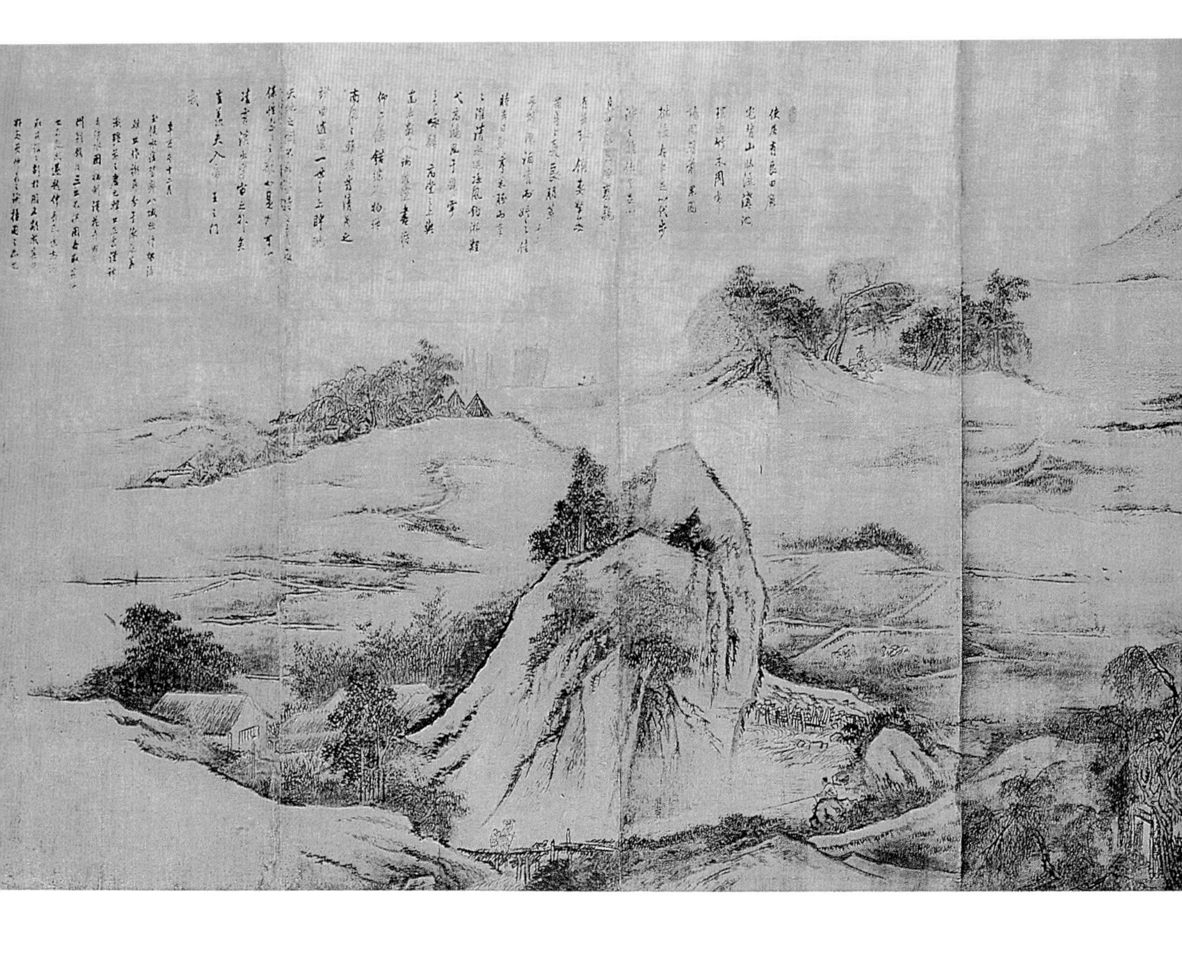

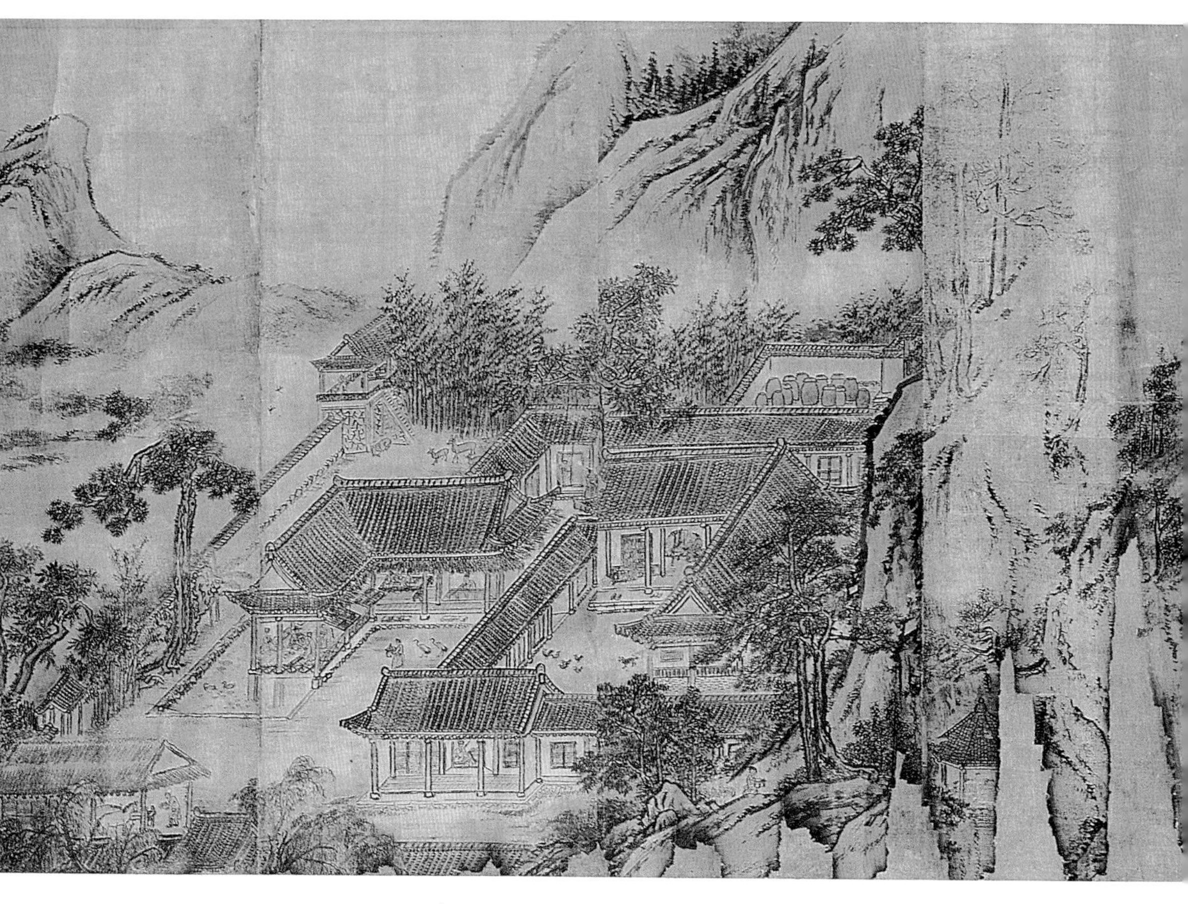

91 ***Landscape***

1801. Ink and color on silk. 133.7×418.4cm. Hoam Art Museum.

The original title of this painting, derived from a Chinese poem, *Poem on a Fishing Place* indicated that the Sung Dynasty poet Dai Fugu greatly preferred his idyllic life in nature to holding high government offices such as prime minister or deputy prime minister. The large river in the forefront, the immense mansion at the foot of the mountain and the rich field are shown in one view. The lower part of the first panel of the folding screen was damaged by fire. As for the composition, the right side is full and the left side is empty.

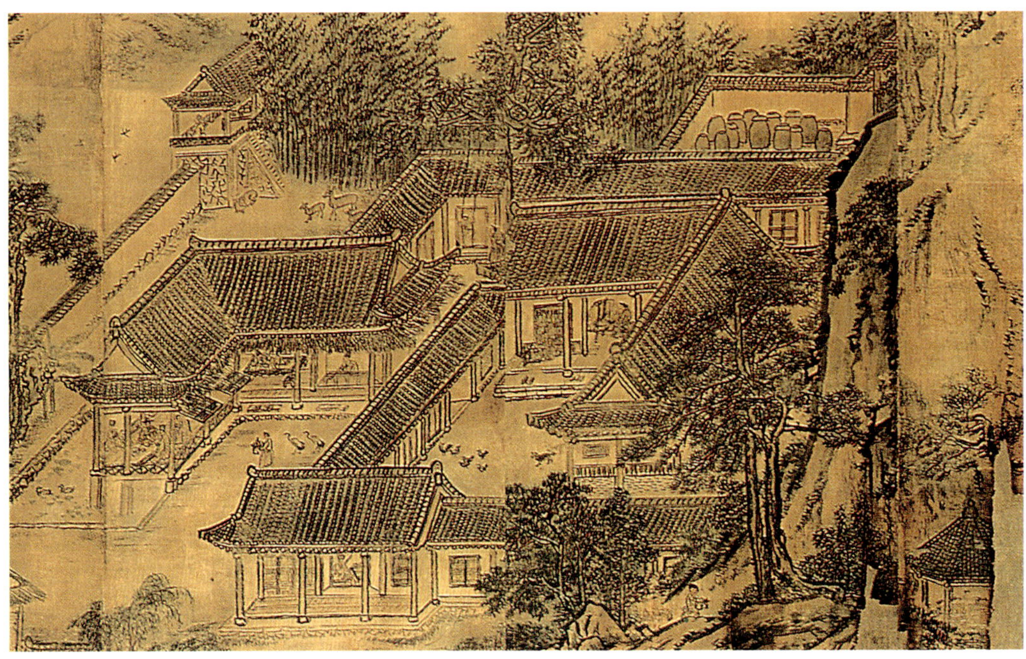

92 Detail of Plate 91
Although the title is derived from a Chinese poem, the painting clearly depicts the architecture and customs of Joseon. In the large tile-roofed house with its beautiful eave line, each family member is enjoying a peaceful time: playing the geomungo for a guest, reading a book while lying on a wooden bed, or studying with a tutor. The scene suggests the idealist life that men of ancient times desired. The densely placed crocks are familiar to Korean eyes even today.

In the 12th lunar month of 1801, the entire nation celebrated the king's recovery from chicken pox. Yuhu Han distributed folding screens with commemorative paintings to his subordinates. Han and I got 'Sinuchisudo,' the *chongje* got 'Flowers and Animals' and the *jupan* got 'Landscape.' As the painting was already completed, relevant phrases from *Nakjiron* by Jungjang were selected as the inscription on the painting. I hope that each one will accomplish their wishes and honor the lessons expressed in Danwon's painting.

Ganjae Hong Ui-yeong wrote the inscription on 'Landscape,' painted by Danwon.

In the aforementioned text, the sentence, "Yuhu Han distributed folding screens with commemorative paintings to his subordinates" deserves attention. *Yuhu* is another title for *yusu*. A government official surnamed Han was *yusu* toward the end of the year. Han Man-yu (1746–1812) was appointed *yusu* in Ganghwabu on the 9th of the 5th lunar month of 1801 and is probably being referred to here. If so, the owner of 'Landscape' would be his subordinate, who would be a *jupan*. However, there is no further evidence. Despite the Chinese literary theme, 'Landscape' shows the unique Joseon style of Korean landscape and customs and is a masterpiece of Kim's later works.

The same year, while Sim No-sung was exiled in Gyeongsang Province, he left a diary entitled *Sanhaepilhui*. In it, he compared Kim Hong-do's genre painting to *paesasopum*[90] writing style, which was popular at the time.

> The writing style can be divided into the high and the tasteful spirits. The high spirits are shown in the books of the *Hundred Schools of Thought* and biographies, while the tasteful ones are in *paegailpa*. *The Romance of the Western Chamber* and *Jin Ping Mei* are the masterpieces of *paegailpa*. My younger brother, Taeseom [Sim No-am's courtesy name] did not agree with me because he had not read them. I said, "If you read them, you would be like the monk in the old tale that went up to the shrine to eat Buddha when he knew the taste of meat." We laughed aloud together.
>
> Now that I read his diary, he writes that he borrowed *Jin Ping Mei* from Yun, but that he returned it after one night and wrote, "The book is like Kim Hong-do's genre painting." He teases me saying that I like *paesasopum* prose. Although I told him, "You will know the taste of the book once you read it," he does not recognize the taste even after reading it. That is as if a precious antique were set upon shabby clothes. In my loneliness far away from home, I smile at this.

A strong character himself, Sim No-sung highly praised "the masterpieces," *The Romance of the Western Chamber* and *Jin Ping Mei*, which ordinary nobles would not have openly read. In contrast, his younger brother, who was rather solemn and fond of classics, constantly teased his elder brother's worldly taste in literature, saying that, "It [was] like Kim Hong-do's genre painting." However, Sim No-sung compared Danwon's genre painting to a precious antique and his younger brother's low regard for it to

90 Early novels; also known as *paegailpa*.

shabby clothes.

Such comments as "*Jin Ping Mei* is like Danwon's genre painting" and "he said that my poetry is like Kim Hong-do's genre painting" were merely playful remarks between the Sim brothers, however, and cannot be evidence that Danwon frequently painted genre pictures, or was noted for doing so in 1801. Nevertheless, it is interesting that Kim Hong-do's genre painting was compared to *The Romance of the Western Chamber* and *The Four Great Ming Novels*, which included *Jin Ping Mei.* In addition, it indicates that even though nobles disdained Kim's genre paintings, they were popular with the common people.

On the 22nd of the 6th lunar month of 1802, when Kim Hong-do was 58, the court granted the lithograph and relief of *Bulseoldaebobumoeunjunggyeong* to Yongjusa Temple. On the 23rd of the 7th lunar month, Kim calligraphed ten poems by Byeokokran and affixed his seal, Nonghan.

> On the 23rd of the 7th lunar month, in the autumn of 1802, Nonghan wrote the poems by Byeokokran Lee Seon-bo.

Lee Seon-bo in the aforementioned text is presumed to be Lee Yugyeom. Lee Deok-mu wrote in the preface of *Byeokokransigo* that the anthology's author was a younger brother of Lee Yu-su (1721–1771). (Lee Yu-su had three younger brothers.) Because Yu-nyeon, his immediate younger brother, died young, the author is thought to be either Yu-gye or Yu-gyeom. However, since Lee Seon-bo was renowned as an adolescent poet in 1778 when Lee Deok-mu visited Yenching, he is thought to have been born around 1760. Consequently, Lee Seon-bo is probably Lee Yugeom, Lee Yu-su's youngest brother.

The pen name Nonghan, which Kim Hong-do used in 1802, is similar in meaning to his other pen name, Nongsaong, which means an old farmer; his seal reads, "As an old man, I became a farmer, which is an important job." Probably, Kim was living in the countryside at the time because there is no record of his whereabouts or activities between the 23rd of the 7th lunar month of 1802 and the 5th of the 5th lunar month of 1804, when he was first recruited as *jabidaeryeong* painter under Gyujanggak, other than the following records in his paintings.

In the late part of the 9th lunar month, Cheopchwiong painted 'The Blue Ocean.'

In the 12th lunar month, Danwon painted 'An Old Monk Looking at the Waves.'

Painted 'Returning Fish.'

There is no record for 1803, when Kim was 59.

On the 5th of the 5th lunar month of 1804, at age 60, Kim was recruited as *jabidaeryeong* painter in Gyujanggak for the first time. According to the *Gyujanggak Daily Journal*,

> The king issued an ordinance to appoint court painters Kim Hong-do and Park Yu-seong to vacant positions. If there was no position available, they should work as supernumerary staff. The king made the decision considering the list of proposed candidates, Kim Hong-do and Park Yu-seong, the *jabidaeryeong* painters.

On the 22nd of the 6th lunar month, as a *jabidaeryeong* painter in Gyujanggak, Kim Hong-do took his first government exam to paint for the court. He scored first for his genre painting with a high save in the third exam of *naechudeung nokchwijae*.

> In the third exam of *naechudeung nokchwijae* for *jabidaeryeong* painters on the 22nd of the 6th lunar month, the applicants were asked to paint genre paintings on whatever subject they wanted. Kim Hong-do, Kim Jae-gong and Lee Myeong-gyu scored high, Sin Han-pyeong, Heo Yong and Park Yu-seong scored medium and Kim Deuk-sin, Park In-su and Kim Myeong-won scored low.

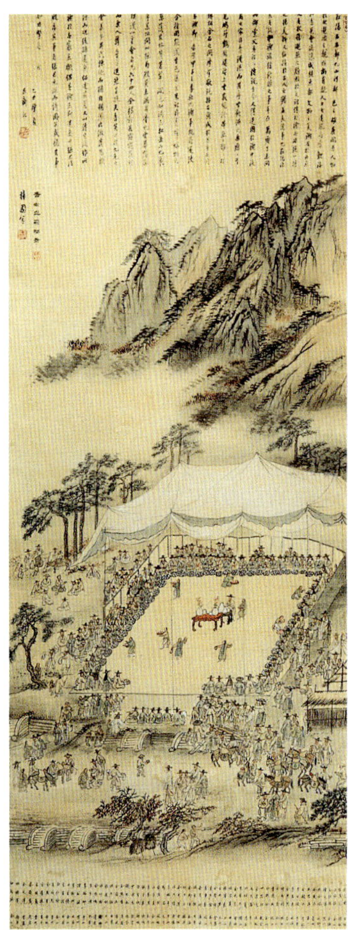

93 *Giroseryeongyedo*
1804. Ink and color on silk. 137×53.3cm. Private collection.
The painting is clean and in good condition. It depicts a fraternity gathering of old men in Gaeseong that was held in the 9th lunar month of 1804 at Manwoldae in honor of a two-century-old tradition. The site is an old palace at the foot of Songak Mountain. Sixty-four old men sit under the large marquee. The white vases on the large red table serve as the center of the space. The long inscription in the upper portion reads, In the famous old city of Gaeseong, the mountains, rivers and buildings are grand and splendid, and the people are well dressed and stylish because the city retains the elegance of the old capital. The script in the lower portion lists the 64 participants and their family origins.

After the 9th lunar month, Kim Hong-do painted 'Giroseryeongyedo' (Plate 93). The following is part of Hong Ui-yeong's inscription.

It was in the 9th lunar month of 1804 during the incumbent king's reign that this social gathering was held again. As the event was ending, Danwon Kim Hong-do was asked to paint the scene and I was asked to record the event for the painting.

Like 'Landscape' (Plate 91), 'Giroseryeongyedo' is one of Kim Hong-do's later masterpieces that embodies the Korean landscape and lifestyle painting. In the first exam of *geumdongdeung nokchwijae* on the 10th of the 10th lunar month, Kim ranked second for his genre painting, 'Competing Archery at the Pavilion,' with a second grade high.

In the first *geumdongdeung nokchwijae* exam, the applicants were instructed to paint a genre painting with the title, 'Competing Archery at the Pavilion.' Kim Jae-gong got a first grade high, Kim Hong-do a second grade high, and Park Yu-seong a third grade high. Park In-su got a first grade medium, Kim Deuk-sin a second grade medium, and Lee In-mun got a third grade medium. Lee Myeong-gyu got a first grade low and Kim Myeong-won got a second grade low.

In the second *geumdongdeung nokchwijae* exam, on the 12th of the 10th lunar month, Kim came out on top with the highest score for his figure painting, 'Cutting through the Dragon Gate with a Big Ax.' The motif is thought to be the same as that of 'Sinuchisu-do,' which is mentioned in the inscription on 'Landscape.'

In the second *geumdongdeung nokchwijae* exam, on the 12th of the

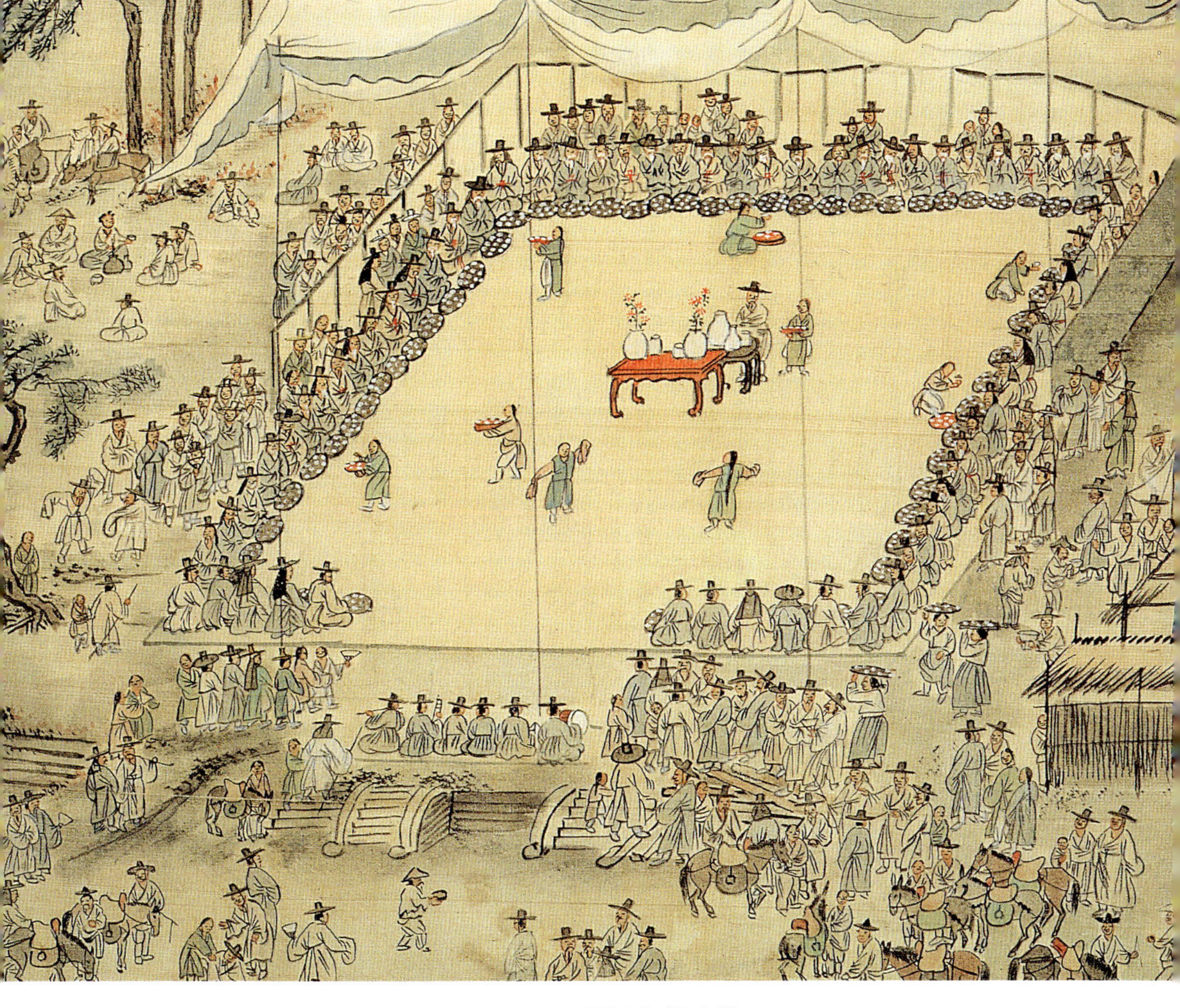

94 Detail of Plate 93

Two children dance face to face to the tune of an orchestra. In the upper left portion, a woman is selling wine to sightseers; below her are two old men dancing in the excess of their mirth. A drunken man by the horses cannot keep himself steady. In addition, old bachelors with pigtails have just put down their firewood ricks and hurry to go to the gathering. On the right side, a man in the house is dismissing a beggar.

10th lunar month, the applicants were told to paint a figure painting with the title, 'Cutting through the Dragon Gate with a Big Ax.' Kim Hong-do scored high, Kim Jae-gong scored first grade medium, Lee Myeong-gyu was second grade medium, Lee In-mun was third grade medium, and Kim Myeong-won scored the fourth-grade medium.

In the third *geumdongdeung nokchwijae* exam, on the 15th of the 10th lunar month, Kim took first place over other painters for his genre painting with a first grade high.

In the third *geumdongdeung nokchwijae* exam on the 15th of the 10th lunar month, the applicants were instructed to paint a genre painting with a title chosen from 'Every Shop Advertises Curious Products,' 'Storing Rice in the Shed,' or 'Rich Family Receives a Son-in-law.' Lee In-mun, Kim Deuk-sin, Lee Myeong-gyu, Park In-su, Kim Jae-gong, Kim Myeong-won, Kim Hong-do, and Park Yu-seong scored high.

In the comparative exam of *geumdongdeung nokchwijae* on the 21st of the 10th lunar month, Kim ranked sixth for his genre painting with a first grade low, and ranked second, together with another painter with 10 *bun* in the *dogyehwabang* evaluation held on the same day.

In the comparative *geumdongdeung nokchwijae* exam for *jabidaeryeong* painters on the 18th of the 10th lunar month, the applicants were asked to paint a genre painting, choosing a title of 'Establishing Pillars for the Royal Audience Chamber' or 'Practicing Military Arts in the Yard outside the Palace.' Kim Jae-gong scored first grade high, Park In-su: second grade high, Kim Deuk-sin: third grade high; Park Yu-seong: first grade medium; Kim Myeong-won: second grade medium; Kim Hong-do: first grade low; Lee In-mun: second grade low; and Lee Myeong-gyu: third grade low.

The final results of *geumdongdeung nokchwijae* for *jabidaeryeong* painters

> on the 18th of the 10th lunar month are as follows: Kim Jae-gong got 11 *bun*. Park In-su, Kim Deuk-sin, Park Yu-seong, and Kim Hong-do received 10 *bun*. Kim Myeong-won and Lee In-mun received 8 *bun*. Lee Myeong-gyu received 7 *bun*.

On the 20th of the 12th lunar month, Kim Hong-do painted 'Zhizang Riding a Horse' (Plate 95) in Park Yu-seong's Seomukjae. The inscription reads, "Painted by Dangu on the 20th of the 12th lunar month of 1804." His brushstroke gives the impression that he painted it when he was drunk. Park Yu-seong was the same age as Kim Hong-do. As mentioned earlier, both appreciated Kim Eung-hwan's 'Landscape' together in Sibudang in the 12th lunar month of 1788, and they were recruited together as *jabidaeryeong* painters in Gyujanggak. They were close friends during this period in particular.

In 1805, Kim Hong-do turned 61. On the 12th of the 1st lunar month,

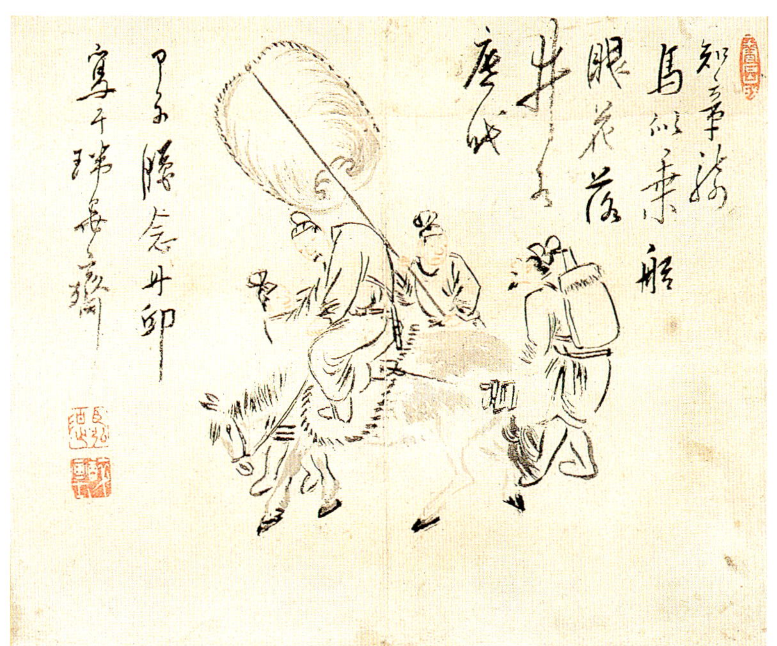

95 ***Zhizang Riding a Horse***
1804. Ink and color on paper. 25.8×35.9cm. National Museum of Korea.
The scene depicts the first line of Du Fu s *The Eight Drunken Immortals,* a poem that was adored by tipplers of the time. He Zhizang rides the horse as if he rides a boat. / If he fell into a well, he would just fall asleep there! Danwon, a wine lover himself, painted this at year-end after drinking with his friends. Interestingly, the brushwork, especially of the feet of the men, is almost croquis-like.

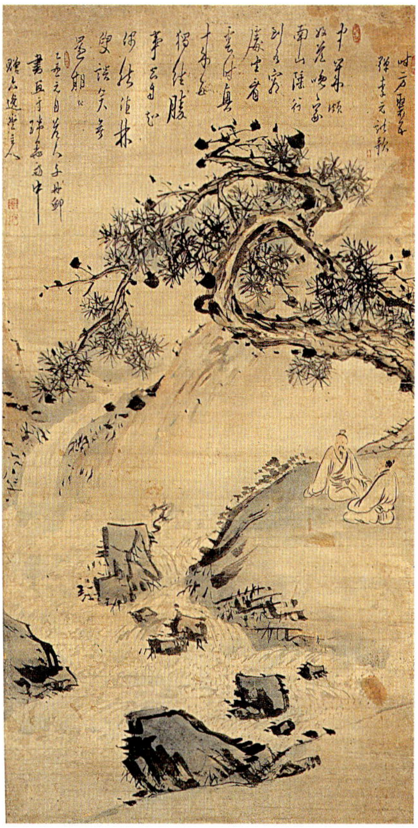

96 Kim Hong-do (Calligraphy) and Lee In-mun (Painting). ***Chatting under a Pine Tree***

1805. Ink and color on paper. 109.3× 57.4cm. National Museum of Korea.

The painting shows lively brushwork rarely seen in the works of Lee In-mun, who was renowned for his meticulous painting. Danwon s calligraphy in the upper portion suggests the effects of heavy drinking. He wrote the Wang Wei poem, *My Retreat at Mount Zhongnan*, in a continuous extended script with some lines out of sequence and some characters added later. The two 60-year olds must have had a pleasant time together at the beginning of that year. The two men sitting across from each other in the semi-circular composition of the old pine tree and flowing stream might be Kim Hong-do and Gosongyusugwandoin Lee In-mun, who shared their joys and sorrows together throughout their lives.

King Yeongjo's second wife Queen Jeongsun, who had been supporting the arbitrary power of *byeokpa* (Party of Principle), passed away. Also, in the same month, a gathering was held again in Park Yu-seong's Seomukjae, where Kim painted 'Chatting under the Pine Tree' (Plate 96) together with his close friend, Lee In-mun. They gave this painting to the owner of Yugildang. Lee In-mun took part in painting, and Kim Hong-do did the calligraphy, which is also believed to have been completed while he was drunk.

In the morning of the 22nd of the 1st lunar month of 1805, Kim copied Wang Duo's letter and gave it to his son, Kim Yang-gi (Plate 97).

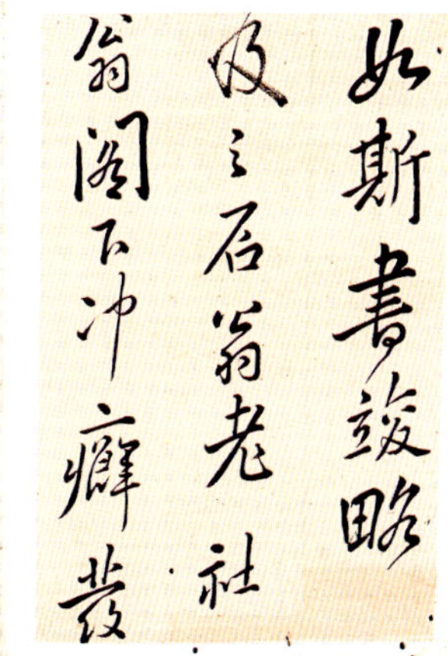

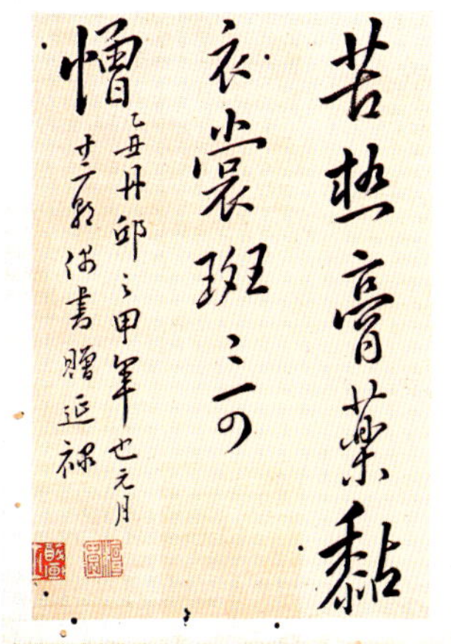

97 Wang Duo s letter from *Danwon s Posthumous Works*
Ink on paper. Album leaf 29 ×19.5cm. National Museum of Korea.
This neat, stylish calligraphy is one of Kim Hong-do s masterpieces. The phrase by chance from writes this by chance and gives it to Yeon-rok had been used by calligraphers to describe an unexpectedly good work since *The Preface to the Lanting Collection of Poems* by Wang Xizhi. The last phrase of the letter confirms Kim Hong-do s birth year as 1745.

Wang Duo writes in the withering shade of trees by the pond near the western peak of Huashan on the 3rd of the 6th lunar month.

Suddenly the capital is noisy, which is worse than when it was in peace. How can I put this surprise into words? Are you already aware of the details of this matter from the official gazette? As some of the facts are confidential, it is hard to explain in the letter. Many surprises crop up when one is a government official. I mentioned a little bit of the issue in the last part of this letter. Lao Sheweng is suffering from the heat from his chronic disease and his clothes are tainted with the medicine. I feel sorry for him.

In the morning of the 22nd of the 1st lunar month of 1805, Dangu, who turns 61, writes this by chance and gives it to Yeon-rok.

According to the letter, the capital is suddenly noisy, and many surprises crop up when one is a government official. Although the letter is an excerpt from the letter of Wang Duo from China, one can imagine that Kim Hong-do wrote this with the commotion revolving around the entreaty of Kim Dal-sun(1760–1806) to the king in mind.

On the 15th of the 4th lunar month, Kim received a *geup*[91] of salted *coilia ectenes* and a *geup* of large-eyed herring, which were granted to court painters. A week later, Kim received a *geup* of *coilia ectenes*, which were granted to seven court painters. On *dano* [the 5th of the 5th lunar month], Kim received two fans, which by custom were granted to the 13 court painters.

On the 12th of the 6th lunar leap-month, Kim Hong-do ranked second for his 'Su Dongpo Watches a Baduk game in Baekhakgwan' with the second grade high as a *jabidaeryeong* painter in the first *geochundeung nokchwijae*

91 A unit of counting fish.

exam. 'Su Dongpo Watches a *Baduk* game in Baekhakgwan' is a painting of an old story, in which Su Dongpo went to a Taoist monastery and became fascinated by *baduk*.

> In the first exam of *geochundeung nokchwijae* for *jabidaeryeong* painters, the applicants were instructed to paint a figure and landscape painting with the title, 'Su Dongpo Watches a *Baduk* game in Baekhakgwan.' Lee In-mun scored first grade high; Kim Hong-do: second grade high; Kim Deuk-sin: third grade high; Lee Myeong-gyu: first grade medium; Kim Jae-gong: second grade medium; Heo Yong: third grade medium; Kim Myeong-won: first grade low; and Sin Han-pyeong: second grade low.

In the second *geochundeung nokchwijae* exam, on the 14th of the same month, Kim Hong-do came out on top for his genre painting with the highest score.

> In the second exam of *geochundeung nokchwijae* for *jabidaeryeong* painters, the applicants were told to paint what they wanted. Kim Hong-do scored high; Kim Myeong-won: first grade medium; Kim Deuk-sin: second grade medium; Sin Han-pyeong: third grade medium; Heo Yong: fourth grade medium; Lee Myeong-gyu: fifth grade medium; Kim Jae-gong: first grade low; and Lee In-mun: second grade low.

In the third *geochundeung nokchwijae* exam, on the 16th of the 6th lunar leap-month, Kim Hong-do came out on top for his genre painting with the highest score. In the *dogyehwabang* evaluation on the same day, he was ranked highest with 9 *bun* and became *sagwa*.

> In the third *geochundeung nokchwijae* exam for *jabidaeryeong* painters, the applicants were told to paint a genre painting with any title they wanted. Kim Hong-do received first grade high; Kim Deuk-sin: second grade high; Kim

Myeong-won: third grade high; Kim Jae-gong: first grade medium; Lee Myeong-gyu: second grade medium; Heo Yong: third grade medium; Sin Han-pyeong: first grade low; and Lee In-mun: second grade low.

The final results of the *geochundeung nokchwijae* exam for *jabidaeryeong* painters are as follows: Kim Hong-do received 9 *bun*; Kim Deuk-sin: 8 *bun*; Kim Myeong-won, Lee Myeong-gyu and Heo Yong: 6 *bun*; Kim Jae-gong and Lee In-mun: 5 *bun*; and Sin Han-pyeong: 4 *bun*.

In the first *geohadeung nokchwijae* exam, on the 17th of the 6th lunar leap-month, Kim ranked fifth for his 'Lotus flower Blossoming in the Clean Water,' with a fifth grade medium. In the second *geohadeung nokchwijae* exam of the same day, Kim ranked first for his figure painting with a first grade high.

In the first *geohadeung nokchwijae* exam for *jabidaeryeong* painters, the applicants were instructed to paint a painting entitled, 'Lotus Flower Blossoming in the Clean Water.' Lee Myeong-gyu received first grade medium; Kim Deuk-sin: second grade medium; Heo Yong: third grade medium; Kim Jae-gong: fourth grade medium; Kim Hong-do: fifth grade medium; Kim Myeong-won: sixth grade medium; Sin Han-pyeong: first grade low; Park In-su: second grade low; and Lee In-mun: third grade low.

In the second *geohadeung nokchwijae* exam for *jabidaeryeong* painters, the applicants were instructed to paint a figure painting with any title they wanted. Kim Hong-do got the first grade high, Sin Han-pyeong the second grade high, Lee Myeong-gyu the third grade high, Kim Deuk-sin the first grade medium, Lee In-mun the second grade medium, Park In-su the third grade medium, Heo Yong the fourth grade medium, Kim Myeong-won the first grade low, and Kim Jae-gong the second grade low.

On the 20th of that month, Kim Hong-do ranked first for his genre painting, along with other painters, and scored low.

In the third *geohadeung nokchwijae* exam for *jabidaeryeong* painters, the applicants were instructed to paint a genre painting with any title they wanted. Sin Han-pyeong, Lee In-mun, Kim Deuk-sin, Lee Myeong-gyu, Park In-su, Heo Yong, Kim Jae-gong, Kim Myeong-won and Kim Hong-do all scored low.

On the 23rd of the month, 15 *sajagwan* and court painters who took the *nokchwijae* exam were granted five *doe*[92] of black pepper.

In the *geumhadeung nokchwijae* comparative exam the next day, Kim ranked sixth for his genre painting with a third grade medium. In the *dogyehwabang* evaluation on the same day, he ranked first, with 8 *bun*, and became *sagwa*.

In the comparative exam of *geumhadeung nokchwijae* for *jabidaeryeong* painters, the applicants were told to paint a genre painting with any title they wanted. Park In-su received first grade high; Kim Jae-gong: second grade high; Lee In-mun: third grade high; Heo Yong: first grade medium; Kim Deuk-sin: second grade medium; Kim Hong-do: third grade medium; Kim Myeong-won: first grade low; Lee Myeong-gyu: second grade low; and Sin Han-pyeong: third grade low.

The final results of the *geumhadeung nokchwijae* exam for *jabidaeryeong* painters are as follows: Kim Hong-do received 8 *bun*; Park In-su, Kim Jae-gong, Lee In-mun, Heo Yong, Kim Deuk-sin and Lee Myeong-gyu: 7 *bun*; Sing Han-pyeong: 6 *bun*; and Kim Myeong-won: 5 *bun*.

In the first *naechudeung nokchwijae* exam on the 26th of the month, Kim Hong-do ranked third and scored low for his 'Following the Example of Li Gonglin's Hyeonido.'

In the first *naechudeung nokchwijae* exam for *jabidaeryeong* painters, the applicants were told to paint a genre painting entitled 'Following the Example of Li Gonglin's Hyeonido.' Park In-su received first grade high; Kim Deuk-sin: second grade high; Kim Hong-do: medium; Kim Jae-gong: first grade low; Lee

92 A unit of volume.

Myeong-gyu: second grade low; Heo Yong: third grade low; Kim Myeong-won: fourth grade low; and Lee In-mun: fifth grade low.

In the second *naechudeung nokchwijae* exam on the twenty-eighth, Kim Hong-do ranked first with a first grade low for his figure painting, 'Lee Gwang Shoots an Arrow into the Tiger-shaped Rock.'

In the second *naechudeung nokchwijae* exam for *jabidaeryeong* painters, the applicants were told to paint a figure painting entitled, 'Lee Gwang Shoots an Arrow into the Tiger-shaped Rock.' Kim Hong-do received first grade low; Kim Myeong-won: second grade low; Heo Yong: third grade low; Park In-su: fourth grade low; Kim Jae-gong: fifth grade low; Kim Deuk-sin: sixth grade low; Lee Myeong-gyu: seventh grade low; and Lee In-mun: eighth grade low.

In the third *geumchudeung nokchwijae* exam on the 19th of the 8th lunar month, Kim Hong-do ranked second. In the *dogyehwabang* evaluation on the same day, he became *sajeong* with 8 *bun*.

In the third geumchudeung nokchwijae exam for jabidaeryeong painters, the applicants were told to paint one of the following: a figure, a palace, an insect, stationery, a plum tree and bamboo or a genre painting. Park In-su received superior-high; Kim Hong-do: superior-medium; Kim Myeong-won: superior-low; Kim Jae-gong: high; Lee In-mun: medium; Heo Yong: first grade low; Kim Deuk-sin: second grade low; and Lee Myeong-gyu: third grade low...

The final results of the *geumchudeung nokchwijae* exam for *jabidaeryeong* painters are as follows: Park In-su: 10 *bun*; Kim Hong-do: 8 *bun*; Kim Myeong-won: 6 *bun*; Kim Jae-gong and Kim Deuk-sin: 5 *bun*; Lee In-mun: 4 *bun*; and Heo Yong and Lee Myeong-gyu: 3 *bun*.

The article dated the 19th of the 8th lunar month is the last public record of Kim Hong-do because Kim became sick in the autumn and was ap-

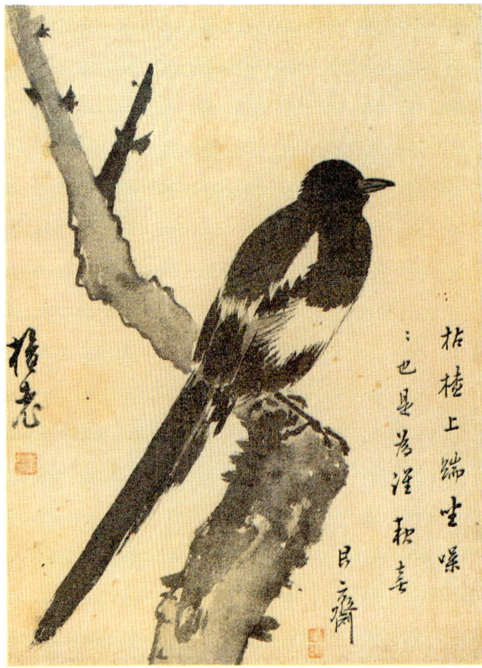

98 *A Magpie*
Ink on silk. 27.2×20.2cm. Seoul National University Museum.
The magpie looks morose. Because of the ink spread around the eye, one cannot tell what it has in mind. The painting is filled with the solemnity of motionlessness, absolute solitude and mysterious melancholy. Why did the old Danwon paint such a picture? Hong Ui-yeong wrote in the bottom right-hand corner, For whom does it herald pleasant news? At first glance, he seems to have misunderstood the painting. However, since a sinuous lifeline is added to the branch as though water is rising up through it, possibly the disconsolate magpie is waiting for hope.

proaching death as shown in a letter dated 29th of the 11th lunar month in *Danwon's Posthumous Works.*

Please deliver this letter to the room where a guest named Saengwon Kim is staying.

His friend Sorim Kim wrote to him. Formalities omitted.

As snow covers the windows of the house, my longing to meet people grows deeper. Your letter was a pleasant surprise. I am so grateful that you asked after my health. And I would like to praise you for traveling safe and sound in this freezing weather. Your foolish friend has experienced several life or death moments and has been in pain since autumn. Now that the end of the year is nearing, all kinds of worries grieve my heart. I feel sorry for myself and can do nothing about it.

I would like to congratulate your son on his passing the government exam. I also appreciate the fine-tooth bamboo comb that you sent me. I am sorry that I bothered you. I wonder when you will visit Hanyang. I hope I can meet and talk to you. I wish you all the best.

The 29th of the 11th lunar month, 1805. Kim Hong-do.

Kim had stopped working as a *jabidaeryeong* painter since autumn. In the above letter, the following sentences are worth a noting: "Your foolish friend has experienced several life or death moments and has been in pain since autumn. Now that the end of the year is nearing, all kinds of worries grieve my heart. I feel sorry for myself and can do nothing about it. " The inscription on Kim's last work, 'Ode to the Sound of Autumn' (Plate 99), contains the same words. The following is part of the inscription to 'Ode to the Sound of Autumn,' which was painted three days after the winter solstice:

Alas! Although trees and grass do not have emotions, they shed leaves against the wind when the time comes. Unlike other animals, man has a soul. All kinds of worries grieve my heart, and everything pains my body. A movement in one's heart must shake one's soul. Therefore, if one thinks of that which he can do nothing about or worries about things that he cannot solve even if he used all his wisdom, his rosy cheeks will wither like a thin tree, and his black hair will turn silver in no time. Why would I compete with trees and grass for prosperity? Who kills and hurts them? Why do I lament the sound of autumn?

The young boy is sleeping; his head is drooping and he doesn't answer. It seems that only the insects making sounds inside the walls join me in my lamentation.

Dangu writes three days after the winter solstice, 1805.

While writing, "one thinks of that which he can do nothing about or worries about things that he cannot solve even if he used all his wisdom," Kim Hong-do, now a sick old man, is in all likelihood concerned about the future of his only son, Kim Yang-gi, who was about 14 years old at the time.

In the letter dated the 19th of the 12th lunar month of 1805, Kim Hong-do suggests that he is leading a miserable life: he is over 60 years, sick and worried about tuition for his young son.

Dear my son Yeon-rok,

How are you doing in this cold weather? Are you keeping up with your studies? I have already told your mother about my disease in detail, so I won't repeat it to you here. I guess Kim Dong-ji also spoke to you in person about the matter. I lament that I could not send the tuition for your teacher. I feel dizzy now, and I cannot continue writing anymore.

Your father wrote on the 19th of the 12th lunar month of 1805.

Presumably, Kim Hong-do died in 1806 when he was 62, as his physical status related to his disease and the aforementioned letter being the last

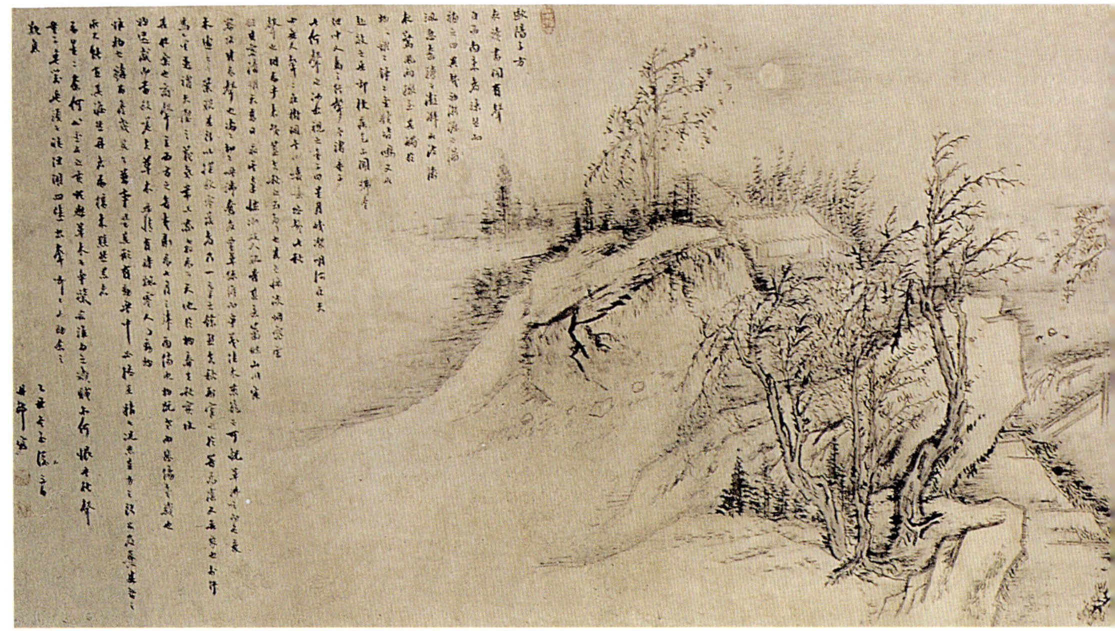

page of *Danwon's Posthumous Works* indicate. Above all, there is no remaining record of his activities or works after 1806. Even if he had lived longer, things were changing more rapidly than they did during the reign of King Jeongjo.

Kim Hong-do's young son, Kim Yang-gi, did not have ample time to learn painting from his father. That is probably why he and his friend Jo Hui-ryong joined the *chusa* painting school, following the contemporary art trend. Although Chusa Kim Jeong-hui left no comment on Kim Hong-do, the great painter of the time, he wrote a poem that highly praised Kim Yang-gi's painting in *Wandangjip* [Wandang and Chusa are Kim Jeong-hui's pen names], the literary collection of his works. Concluding this study of Kim Hong-do's life in chronological order, I would like to take a brief look at his final years, based on the recently-discovered *The Preface to Danwon's Landscape Painting on 6-paneled Screen*, which is included in *Uijaejip*, the literary collection of Nam Ju-heon (1769–1821; pen name Uijae).

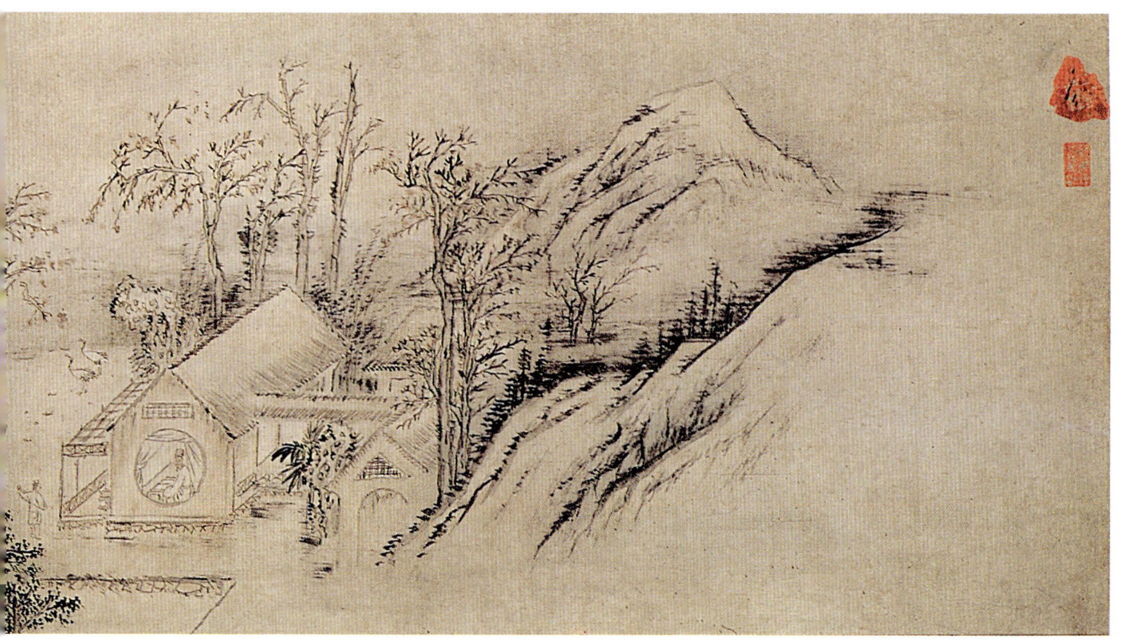

99 ***Ode to the Sound of Autumn***
1805. Ink and color on paper. 56×214cm. Hoam Art Museum.
Ouyang Xiu, a Chinese scholar-poet, who was old and nearing the end of his life, was reading a book alone at night in autumn when he heard a strange sound from outside. He sent a servant boy into the yard. The servant pointed at the sky and said, There is no one around. Only the stars and the moon are shining brightly. The sound comes from the trees. The trees against the wind in the cold moonlight recall the sadness of old age. The wind continues to blow against the rough and leafless branches. As though the moon were brushed with the wind, the painting is tinted with gloomy gray. The wind blows from left to right and into the painter s heart. A dry brush swept across the painting like an empty yard swept with a dry broomstick; everything has lost its liveliness, and only the sound of autumn resonates in the ears.

Danwon Kim Hong-do loved painting so much that he could not reject requests to paint pictures. Consequently, the entire nation had a great number of his works. I knew him for several years, and I used to decide whether to obtain a painting only after I sought his advice. That is why I have seen many good paintings although I do not have an eye for art. He compared my admiration for paintings to Wang Huizhi's love for bamboo. Once I had a folding screen made for my bedside and asked him to paint a landscape for the screen. He willingly consented, but did not start working on it for three months. When I urged him to hurry, he smiled and said, "How can I paint without feeling excited? I am only waiting for the excitement to come."

One day, when he was very drunk, he ground the ink stick himself and stopped for a moment to think before sweeping the brush. Then, a certain high-ranking official sent a horse for him. He threw away the brush, turned the courier out of the house and said, "What kind of an undignified noble is ruining my pleasure of painting?" Suddenly, he sat down and began to paint. At his will, the sweep of the brush created lofty mountains, the wide ocean behind them, grass, trees, birds, animals, clouds and the moon in the shimmering, and he put them all together to reflect the changes of morning and evening throughout the four seasons. The painting was so touching that one felt one's heart fully cleansed. It took but a moment to complete the painting, and the sun was still shining brightly.

I said jokingly, "Your painting is possessed with a spirit. I will write *Biography of a Painter* for you in the future." He courteously declined my offer and said, "Please don't say that. What is better: your writings or my paintings? Everyone knows about my paintings now, but I've heard from noblemen that your writings are refined classics. Would you please write an inscription on this painting for me?" I promised I would.

He left for the other world soon after that episode; this world lost a great painter. Now I am honoring my longstanding promise on this six-paneled folding screen.

In the preface, Nam Ju-heon writes that Danwon's deep love for painting is the reason "the entire nation had a great number of his works." However, Kim did not paint for just anyone at any time. Nam cites the example of Kim Hong-do's rejection of the invitation of a high-ranking official to show Kim's great pride as an artist.

Nam Ju-heon seems to have been a close friend of Kim Hong-do during Kim's late life. He was the eldest grandson of Geumreung Nam Gong-cheol, a renowned collector and art appreciator. He had been a local magistrate since he passed the first-level government exam in 1798; he rose through the ranks to become the Chuncheon *busa* after passing the second-level government exam in 1814. Although he came from a noble family, he was 25 years younger than Kim Hong-do was and was only a local magistrate when Kim, who had been a *hyeongam*, was alive. They were sincere friends, so Nam probably volunteered to write Kim's biography.

After Kim's death, Nam Ju-heon wrote, "Now I am honoring my long-standing promise" in his inscription on Kim Hong-do's painting. He promised to write an inscription, rather than a biography because Kim Hong-do had declined the offer. If Kim Hong-do had allowed Nam Ju-heon to write his biography, we may have had a good record of the great artist. In *Uijaejip*, there are several biographies, but none of Kim Hong-do.

The great painter said, "Everyone knows about my paintings now." Maybe he thought that a painter's life is told through his paintings. However, out of the thousands of paintings he had painted throughout his life, only a few works survived. I want to fill this void in the heart by citing Nam Ju-heon's beautiful inscription.

> For the first painting,
> The cold pine tree in the cliff is like a hidden scholar
> The tall tree near the village is like a mountain pheasant with a long tail
> The rocks and forest are secluded and the stony slope has ups and downs
> Where do you live?
> It's where deer live under the green bush and red walls.
>
> For the second painting,
> The moon flows down to the stream
> The moon stops, but the stream does not
> In the middle of the pond shines the moon
> The pond stops, but the moon does not
> Moving and calm, but there is only one moon
> Depending on its being the stream or the pond, the moon flows or stops.

For the third painting,
The stone gate is solemn and dark
The first rain goes past by the western peak
In the old valley, birds sing
They flutter away to gather in the deep forest
Then reverberating in the whole forest is the sound of a wind-bell
Against the shadow of the pine tree, the lamp offered at the Buddhist altar is growing dim.

For the fourth painting,
Hey, boy, who is leading a donkey,
The grass on the riverside is green
Hey, boy, who is holding a liquor jar,
The cloud over the river is white
A Taoist Immortal in hemp-cord sandals and headdress
looks at the Three Holy Mountains from a lonely boat
As the light of the Three Holy Mountains is empty now, he just sadly watches autumn
The geese sing in the wind
The evening glow in the field of reeds.

For the fifth painting,
A *baduk* board,
A fishing rod,
When the wine cup of the poet looks dizzy and
The old fisherman in conical bamboo hat returns,
Under the green cliff
On the red water-pepper
They meet at dusk
And feel unconcerned and think of nothing.

For the sixth painting,

A large fish is under the water
A small fish is near the waterside
Among reeds move the crabs along the riverside
Near the sail and oars floats the water-shield plant
How many people in this world know this pleasure?

Conclusion

Koreans have existed for generations by engaging in agriculture in a blessed natural environment. Nature has always felt like a cozy, warm home. The change of seasons in its periodical cycle has silently taught us to live reasonably and humbly. Therefore, it is no wonder that the most outstanding aspect of the Korean art that matured in this environment is its natural characteristic. Although time has altered this character somewhat, and differences exist depending on the genre and artist, this natural characteristic continues to be the main characteristic of Korean art. The natural characteristic is in contrast with artificial features such as exaggeration, sensationalism and decorativeness. The natural characteristic of Korean art does not immediately draw attention from observers, but it gradually makes them feel familiar and eventually fills their hearts with warmth. Above all, the natural characteristic provides calm and true energy from somewhere deep inside.

The works of the great artist Kim Hong-do embody the Korean features of this natural characteristic, a familiarity and calm energy. That reflects the well-rounded personality of the artist, the peaceful time he lived in and the spirit of the king who supported him. However, not everyone saw him in that light. Sim Jae (1721–1784), who died when Kim Hong-do was 40, commented on Danwon's early works in his *Songcheonpildam* as follows.

> Byeon Sang-byeok's cat painting and Kim Hong-do's genre painting are verisimilar, but both of them only focus on the external form, not the spirit.

How could he make such a direct remark belittling the best portrait painter in King Yeongjo's reign and the greatest artist in King Jeongjo's reign? In fact, it was merely a denouncement of 'painters of humble origin' from the perspective of Chinese paintings in the manner of artistic *literati*. The reason that I included the aforementioned text in concluding a book on the great painter Kim Hong-do is to show Sim's bigoted opinion.

> As writings and paintings of our country have imitated those of the Great China, we do have some great artists. However, compared to the works of the great country, they are like imitation jade when compared to the genuine and a dull lead blade against a master crafted sword. This is probably because our culture is different from Chinese culture and the energy of our natural features is limited.

To Sim Jae, in addition to painters like Byeon Sang-byeok and Kim Hong-do, the entire culture and natural features of Joseon had problems. Hong Yang-ho wrote the following about this kind of narrow-minded elitism.

> Painting is one of the six categories of Chinese characters and its origin is in pictographs. However, paintings deliver divinity whereas writings carry truth. Although they are eventually different, they have some principles in common. In many cases, good calligraphers are also good painters, and good calligraphers can evaluate good paintings. One can therefore say that they merely have different expertise. I have been to China twice, and all the poets and men of refined tastes that I met there appreciated both calligraphy and painting. Only in this eastern country do the noble men disdain painters who engage in miscellaneous art. Consequently, even if someone were so talented that he is good at

painting without studying it, these individuals would only mock him. It is because they do not understand the origin of pictographs. What a pity is their bigotry!

The last sentence looks as if it is directed at Sim Jae. Hong Yang-ho also wrote the following inscription on Kim Hong-do's painting.

On Kim Hong-do's Painting on a Fan

The sun is so hot that it feels as if you are sitting beside a large stove. It must be exactly the same situation as in the phrase, "Wearing stays maddens me. I could scream with anger" in Du Fu's "*High Fever*." I gained a piece of a bamboo painting where a cool whirlwind blows past the stretched stems and sparse leaves and into my arms and sleeves. I feel so fresh. Now I know. This bamboo does not surrender to frost and allows one to avoid the heat! However, if the spirit had not accompanied the tip of the painter's brush, how could the painter have expressed the true character in the fantasy world? Danwonja has truly achieved the blissful state of spiritual concentration of Gu Kaizhi.

Hong Yang-ho called Kim Hong-do by the elegant nickname of Danwonja, which was used by those who understood art and respected artists. Additional data on Kim Hong-do exists, but it is not always accurate. In *Songnamjapji*, Jo Jae-sam (1808–1866) wrote the following.

On 'Savages Hunting'

According to *Gwonyurok*, Pungdan wrote Yu Yeo-gyeong's *Saesangsi* as follows.

"The whimpering arrow is soaring straight upward one thousand *cheok*
The sound of it is so dry in the calm sky with no wind
Three hundred savage soldiers with blue eyes riding horses
All look towards the clouds, holding golden bits."

This story is about how the Jin and Yuan Dynastics brought calamity upon

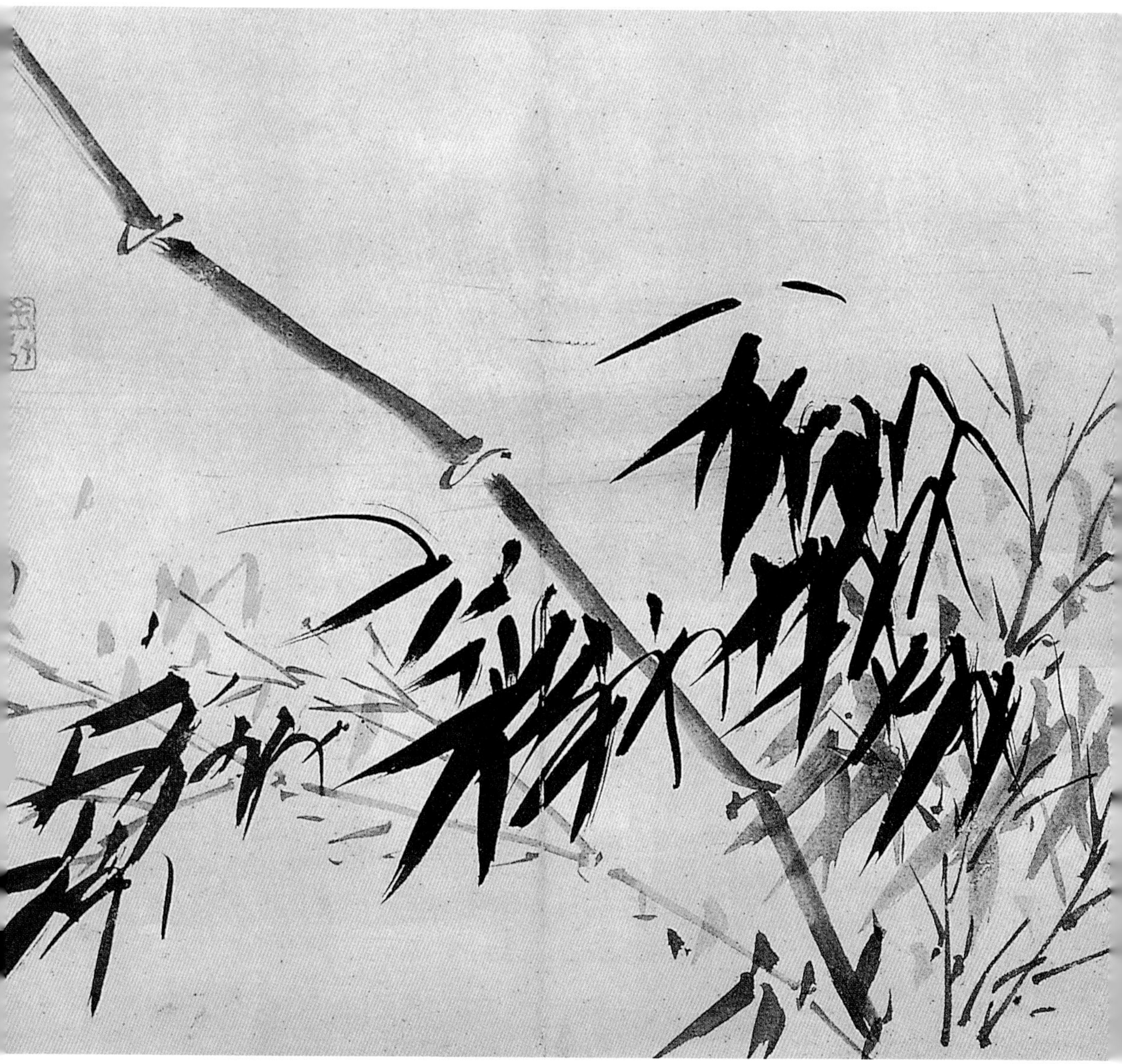

100 *Ink Bamboo*

Ink on paper. 23×27.4cm. Kansong Art Museum.

With dim air as background, a sudden shower pours down on bamboo. Danwon painted the bamboo leaves so fast that one can hear the sound of the raindrops. While orchids represent happiness, bamboo often symbolizes wrath. If Kim Hong-do felt wrathful at the time, he must have forgotten it when he finished this painting.

the world, and it deserves to be painted on a folding screen. Kim Hong-do was the first in our country to paint this painting, and it became highly renowned, together with Wu Daozi's 'Ten Thousand Horses.'

Obviously, Kim Hong-do was not the first one in Joseon to paint 'Savages Hunting'; however, it serves to show that Kim Hong-do's 'Savages Hunting' was excellent. Perhaps, the mistaken belief arose from the fame of Kim Hong-do's 'Hunting,' which Kim Hong-do prided as his masterpiece. Seo Yu-gu wrote the following.

On 'Hunting'

My family has owned Kim Hong-do's 'Hunting' for a long time. It is painted on an eight-paneled silk folding screen. Savages are pulling their bowstrings, running and chasing around an empty field where the wild grass looks so vivid that it seems alive. Kim Hong-do said that it was his masterpiece and that if he saw copies of other painters, he could tell them at once just as he can tell the eyes of fish and a gem emitting light in the dark.

In another misleading historical record, Kim Hong-do was described as authenticating a senior painter's work. According to this record, Kim wrote the following inscription on Sim Sa-jeong's painting.

This is 'Sangeodo'(山居圖) that Sim Sa-jeong painted for Sanggodang Kim Gwang-su by following the method of Chou Ying. I have seen this on an eight-paneled folding screen, but I do not know who removed the painting from the first panel and made it into a scroll. There is no record and seal here because they were on the last panel of the screen. I am worried that future generations might doubt who the painter was, so I am writing some lines here. However, those with the eye for art do not have to read my inscription for confirmation. Danwon Kim Hong-do authenticates this painting by writing an inscription.

However, it is believed that the aforementioned Sim Sa-jeong's painting and Kim Hong-do's inscription are forgeries. Another record is believed to have been written on Kim Hong-do's painting, although there is no solid evidence. That is the inscription entitled *On the Genre Painting on Eight-paneled Folding Screen*, 1781, which is found in the writings of Yu Han-jun (1732–1811).

A Wayfarer

For which village is the man bound north headed
What is the man bound south going to do?
Although a man's lifetime is less than one hundred years,
He spends the half of it hesitating in the crossroad.

Making a Twig Gate

Very humble, but the work itself has substance. Very tough, but the meaning has truth. As the world is full of lies, one seeks substance and truth in this field.

The Smithy

Heroes and great men always like to hide. They hide making straw sandals or casks. Perhaps, there might be a person named Hyegang in this tavern.

A Boy Playing Flute on the Back of a Cow

A weeping willow is drooping,
Drooping on the cattails and reeds
They are in the distant river and sky
Distant is the bright sunset glow
The sunset glow, bright and broad!
If it touches nothing, that's it, but
If it touches something,
That must be that boy playing flute on the back of a cow

Watching Weeding

When the lunch delivery boy is gone and the weeding man starts to work, a man holding a cane listens to water flowing in the rice field. I first thought that the man was Tao Yuanming, but now I know that he was not. How? For the thing on the head is worldly.

A Tavern in the Road

A thirsty man comes back to this place
A hungry man runs to get here
Who would know the credit for saving the men
Lies with the old lady of the tavern by the brook with weeping willows on the side?

A Crab-selling Woman

Between Incheon and Bucheon live small crabs, as the land is close to the ocean. Women living here gather the crabs, with which they go to Hanyang in groups to buy new clothes. This has been the custom in Incheon and Bucheon.

Riverside Hill

When I lived on the riverside, I wrote a poem to give to a fisherman, and said, "Fisherman, fisherman, as foreign troubles come from all things, if you kill living things, there will be many troubles. This fishing you do is worse than plowing the field on the hill." Someone agreed that it made sense.

There is no solid evidence that the aforementioned genre paintings are the works of Kim Hong-do. However, the description in the text almost matches Kim's 'Haengryeopungsokdo,' which was painted on an eight-paneled folding screen in 1778. Furthermore, in 1781 when the above text was written, Kim Hong-do was 37 and painting many genre paintings. Therefore, it is highly likely that this text is referring to Kim Hong-do's paintings. *The Smithy* in particular might be referring to Kim Hong-do's 'A

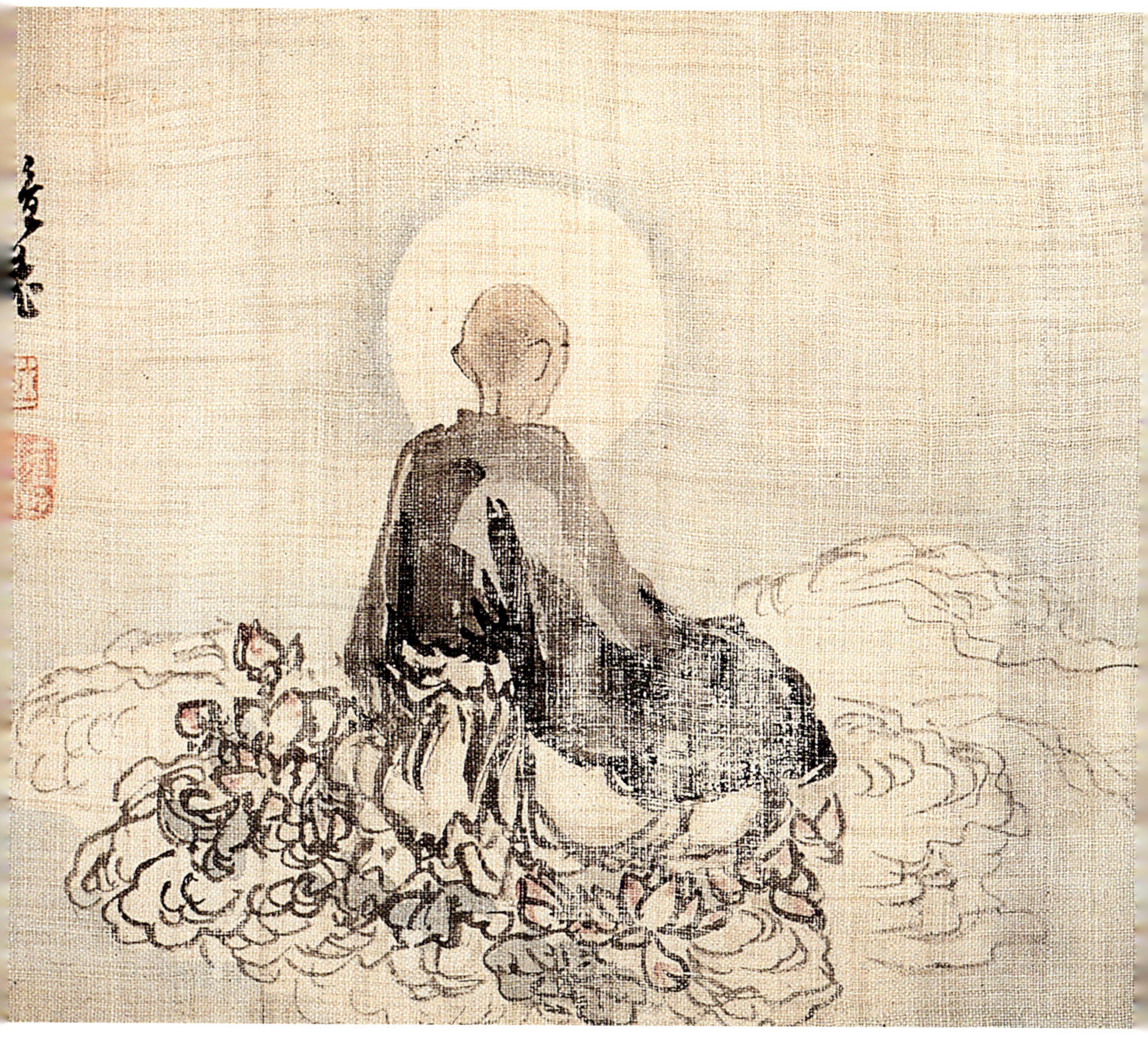

101 ***A Buddhist Monk Flying West***

Ink and color on ramie. 20.8×28.7cm. Kansong Art Museum.

The neat, pale back of the old monk s head looks so clean that it dazzles the eye. He is sitting squarely in a robe that reveals the shape of his thin shoulders. In the western sky, he is riding something that resembles a cloud or a lotus leaf. The bright light from his head, or from the full moon, fills the fine ramie. In many cases, art is art and religion is religion, because neither one is real art or real religion. Therefore, art and religion sometimes do not correspond to each other. However, once a certain state is achieved, art becomes religion, religion becomes art, and, together, art and religion become life.

Forge.' However, some records that have been introduced as pertinent to Kim Hong-do are more likely to be false than true.

Comments on Kim Hong-do by his contemporaries are in the prologue and epilogue of the famous *Danwon's Posthumous Works*. As the texts were written at the request of Kim Hong-do's son for a memorial work to his late father, they all praise Kim's paintings. However, the authors of the texts could not have fabricated the stories. Hong Seok-ju wrote as follows in the prologue.

> I have known Danwonja for a long time. However, my knowledge of him was limited to his genre paintings. Only after I saw 'The Ocean and the Mountain', after he passed away, did I realize that his talent reached far beyond genre paintings. Now that I see his album, I understand that his art is not limited to paintings, either. Calligraphy and paintings are seen on the outside, so they are relatively easy to understand. Nevertheless, some parts cannot be fully understood, such as in this case. Then, how can I easily say that I know a person? Danwon's son Yang-gi has carefully guarded this album, which bequeathed his father's art, and attained fame on his own. Danwon did many good deeds that live on through his son. This is what people know so far. Yang-gi has more things to do. He should make the next generations continue talking about Danwon and help them understand Kim Hong-do's unknown sides.
>
> Yeoncheon Hong Seok-ju wrote this on the 9th of the 1st lunar month, 1828.

The eminent writer Hong Seok-ju wrote this important record. It is also noteworthy that Hong Seok-ju called Kim 'Danwonja' as did Hong Yang-ho. Above all, the record comments that Kim Hong-do produced excellent calligraphy. This comment is repeated in the following prologue written by Sin Wi.

> The figures, birds, animals and other objects that Danwon painted all show that his talent was well above average: his works are all masterpieces. Although he would not have exerted as much effort for his calligraphy as he did in

paintings, his calligraphy is also excellent. This indicates that his talent in writing was better than ordinary. Yang-gi, Danwon's son, ardently beseeched me to write for this album because I have known Danwon longer than anyone in the art circle. I remember how we used to discuss the six canons of Chinese paintings and experimented with them with ink sticks and brushes on a desk made of *torreya* wood under the bright window, oblivious of worldly affairs. How can I experience such pleasure? Once again, caressing this book, I am saddened for him.

Old Man Jaha Sin Wi wrote this.

A great hand at calligraphy himself, Jaha Sin Wi highly esteemed Kim Hong-do's writing. He had studied painting together with Kim Hong-do under the guidance of Kang Se-hwang, so he reminisced about the days he spent with Kim Hong-do. Unfortunately, there is no record of what their relationship was like.

The first and second articles of the epilogue were written by Goengadanghakin in the late spring of 1818, and by Jijiong in the winter of 1827, respectively. They both praise Yang-gi for managing his late father's works and encourage him to follow his late father's example. Hong Gil-ju and Hong Hyeon-ju, the younger brothers of Hong Seok-ju and Hong U-geon, who was Hong Gil-ju's son, wrote the following three articles of the epilogue. Hong Gil-ju's article reads as follows.

Danwon's son Yang-gi, whose courtesy name is Cheonri, owns an album of his father's. Although Danwon's paintings are regarded as precious art, his calligraphy is not admired as much. Now that I look at this book, the large characters are as grand as if they are paintings of high mountains and large rocks, and the small characters are deep and beautiful like the painting of a small bird sitting in the young grass. Regular scripts are angular and solid like a painting of a palace, and the cursive scripts glance off the page like a painting of orchids or bamboos. In brief, everything about Danwon's painting is concentrated here. Even if Kim's writing were artless, Yang-gi would have to preserve his father's works. Now this masterpiece calligraphy is not only the treasure of Kim's family.

Pyoronggakchwein wrote this two days before the New Year's Eve in 1827.

The above article describes Kim Hong-do's writing and highlights that painting and writing are one thing. The subsequent article by Hong Hyeon-ju reads as follows.

The Diamond Sutra reads, "If Buddhist men and women receive a saguge [a poem on reaching nirvana] out of this sutra, they will know it. All heaven, humans and ghosts will respect the pagoda preserving Buddha's relic." Likewise, Geungwon [Kim Yang-gi's courtesy name] should respect this album. In addition, the Diamond Sutra reads, "If Buddhist men and women read and memorize this sutra, they will all be able to infinitely accumulate virtuous deeds." Likewise, Geungwon should also do the same thing with this album.

In the 1st lunar month of 1828, Haedoin wrote this for *Danwon's Posthumous Works*, which is owned by Geungwon.

Here, it is emphasized that Kim Yang-gi should keep this album in the same manner that he would keep a Buddhist sutra; he should find profound meaning in it. Hong U-geon wrote the last article in the epilogue.

Danwon's Posthumous Works is an album of the late Kim Hong-do's works that was put together by his son Yang-gi, and will be handed down for posterity. One day, Yang-gi brought this album to me and asked me to write an article for it. "Your father and uncles all wrote for this book. Why don't you add your writing to theirs?" I knew that I could not refuse his request, so now I hold the brush to write. Alas! Why do people only know that Danwon was good at painting, but are left in the dark as to his calligraphic talent? It is because many have seen his paintings, but only a few have seen his calligraphy Danwon attained fame for his paintings, so when one acquires a work by Kim, he treasures it and would not exchange it for a thousand pieces of gold. That is why more people have seen his paintings than his calligraphy. Although Su Dongpo was a good painter, he was not on the same footing as Yan Liben or Gu Kaizhi because of his writing. Although Wang Xizhi was a talented poet, he was not on the same footing as Tao Yuanming or Xie Lingyun, because of his calligraphy. Danwon is not renowned for his writing for the same reason.

However, people do not realize that in nature calligraphy and painting are not really entirely different genres. Here is a man. He cleans a room, puts a table on a blanket, grinds a pitch-dark ink stick, spreads a sheet of silk as white as snow, puts the ink stone and brushes in disorder on the right and left sides, dips the brush in the ink and then stares hard for a long time. Alas! I cannot tell if this man is an outstanding calligrapher like Zhao Mengfu and Dong Qichang, or a master painter like Ni Zan and Shen Zhou! It is only after a man sweeps the brush, scatters the ink like rain driven by the wind, throws away the brush, stands up and looks around that I can tell calligraphy from painting. Likewise, how can one say that calligraphy and painting are that distant from each other? Furthermore, if the brush moves in a circle, it creates a point, and if it moves straight, it creates a stroke. I know that they make a character, but the technique of painting is close to this. If the brush moves horizontally, it creates a mountain, and if it moves vertically, it creates a tree, so I realize that they make a painting. A stroke of the brush to write a character is not that different from this. Therefore, if one is good at calligraphy, but not at painting, it is bigotry; and if one is good at painting, but not at calligraphy, it is baseness. Is Danwon the only master of both? If so, all the landscapes, birds and animals in Danwon's paintings can be called the strokes of characters. Likewise, this album can be called a collection of Danwon's paintings.

Woncheongeosa Hong U-geon, a native of Pungsan, wrote this in the late spring of 1829.

The aforementioned articles all praise Kim's calligraphy, because the authors wrote them for an album of Kim's writings. Danwon's representative calligraphy is shown in the poems written on each panel of 'The Meanings of Chu Hsi's Poems,' which Danwon presented to King Jeongjo in the 1st lunar month of 1800. King Jeongjo highly praised the work (Plates 89, 90): his brush strokes are similar to the elegantly composed style of Kang Se-hwang and Sin Wi. In fact, it was widely known that Kim Hong-do wrote masterfully. A newly discovered record, Lee Yong-hyu's *Daeuamgi,* mentions the following.

> Kim Hong-do wrote 'Daeu' (對右), framed it, and hung it on the wall in his house. It means 'face to face with respect.' The Chinese characters come from the phrase, "Look down on painting and respect writing (左圖右書)." Painting and writing have been separated for a long time, but now they are reunited. It is time that they were in accord and respected each other.

This indicates that Kim's calligraphy was already recognized by a renowned figure, Lee Yong-hyu. A nephew and disciple of the great scholar Seongho Lee Ik (1681–1763), Lee Yong-hyu won the highest literary fame of Lee Ik's disciples. Jeong Yak-yong wrote in his *Yeoyudangjeonseo*,

> Since he became *jinsa*, Lee Yong-hyu stopped taking government exams any more, and only focused on literature....His sentences are strange, new and witty....He was the most renowned literary man in the late period of King Yeongjo's reign. ...Although he was not an influential government official, he enjoyed 30 years of literary power. It was an unprecedented case.

Lee Yong-hyu was not only a great literary man but also a renowned scholar of *namin*, one of the four political factions at the time. Along with Kang Se-hwang, Yu Gyeong-jong, Chae Jae-gong, An Jeong-bok, Sin Gwang-su and Heo Pil, he was a member of the 15 Scholars of Ansan in the Ansan region. It is only natural that Lee Yong-hyu, who studied under

Kang Se-hwang, left many records about Kim Hong-do, the great figure in the art circle. However, there is no in–depth research on this matter. As research proceeds, more information on Kim Hong-do's background and early training is expected to emerge.

Twelve years after Kim Hong-do died, Lee Hyeong-bu (1782–1851), a great grandson of Lee Gyu-sang, saw Kim's work in the Yeonil Jeong family home near Nuam-seowon.

> On the 26th of the 3rd lunar month of 1818, I dropped by Jeong's farm… saw a painting owned by Jeong. There was a genuine Dong Qichang calligraphy on patterned silk, which I believe was a work of his late years. Attached on the head of *The Eight Drunken Immortals,* handwritten on silk by Zhu Yunming, was a painting of eight Taoist Immortals by a reputable painter, Kim Hong-do. They are all rare treasures.

The aforementioned work of Kim Hong-do's does not exist today. In fact, most of Kim Hong-do's paintings, calligraphy, poems, prose and the elegant melodies he floated away into the air have not survived. What we see today is only a fraction of his art. Interestingly, a certain record used to be regarded as proof that Sin Wi, who was one of the authors of the inscriptions in *Danwon's Posthumous Works*, disparaged Kim's ability to paint portraits. That record is the following poem in the *Maekrok of Gyeongsudang-jeongo: From the 3rd Lunar Month to the 7th Lunar Month of 1818.*

> When I was a *busa* in Chuncheon, I used to walk in Suchun, Gokun and Seorak Mountain, feeling as if Samyeon Kim Chang-heup were still alive. Thus, it occurred to me that Chusa Kim Jeong-hui had once said, "The portrait of Samyeon in Seoksil-seowon looks similar to you in terms of its spiritual and mysterious atmosphere. This could be the draft of your future portrait." Recollecting this comment, I composed four poems to laugh about it later on.
>
> Wang Zaiqing painted a horizontal painting whose brushstrokes were no good,

The portraits by two Lees and Danwon are not similar to their real appearance.

[Lee Myeong-gi and Kim Hong-do, the court painters, and Lee Pal-ryong, a painter from Pyeongyang, painted my portraits, which I am afraid are not similar to my real appearance. As for the horizontal portrait that Damgye Ong Bang-gang recently asked Zaiqing Wang Ruhan to paint, only the clothes of our country look similar.]

Someone says that the draft of my portrait was painted a hundred years ago.

He says that my spiritual and mysterious atmosphere is similar to this old man.

This record was thought to be a complaint about Kim Hong-do's portrait because the aforementioned poem was mistranslated without knowing the title. The poem is talking about three portraits: one by Wang Zaiqing, one by Lee Myeong-gi and Kim Hong-do, and one by Lee Pal-ryong. As for the joint work of Lee and Kim, it is highly likely that Lee Myeong-gi painted the face and Kim Hong-do painted the body, as they did in the royal portraits and 'Portrait of Seo Jik-su.' Therefore, Sin Wi's comment that the portrait is unlike the real appearance indicates that Sin Wi was dissatisfied with the face, which Lee Myeong-gi would have painted: the comment does not reflect on Kim Hong-do. In general, rarely was the subject of a portrait satisfied with his portrait. In fact, as shown in the following comment by Lee Yu-won, Kim Hong-do's portraits were highly regarded by later generations.

Recent Good Portrait Painters

Lee Myeong-gi, Kim Hong-do, Kim Geon-jong and Lee Pal-ryong, a native of Pyeongyang, are the portrait painters with the most illustrious talent I have ever seen. The Chinese painter, Wang Zaiqing painted a portrait of Damgye Ong Bang-gang, of which the clothes were described as being of the Joseon style and resembling the real appearance. However, the formalities are not as elegant. Yu Seok-ryeong attached a footnote to his poem on 'Eoyangseonyeol-do,' which reads, "Jeonyanggong once said that he had seen a portrait of Su

> Dongpo that resembled the real appearance." Indeed, men of the past are greater than are men of the present.

Sin Wi's portrait is no longer extant.

Kim Hong-do was a well-rounded person with many friends. One of his closest friends was Lee In-mun, a court painter who was the same age as Kim and renowned for his landscapes, representing King Jeongjo's court painters. That is proven by the inscription in the works of the two painters. The following are a few examples.

Lee In-mun painted two paintings at Kim Hong-do's house. The first one is 'Songseokwon Literary Gathering,' which presumably was painted in 1791. Its inscription reads, "Gosongyusugwandoin Lee In-mun Munuk painted this in Danwon's house." The second is 'A Small Cottage,' whose inscription reads, "Several cottages make up a village. Gosongyusugwandoin painted this in Danwon's house and gave it to Baekha-Sindong." In addition, the two painters jointly completed Lee In-mun's 'Chatting under the Pine Tree' (Plate 96) about a year before Kim Hong-do passed away. The inscription reads, "In the 1st lunar month of 1805, Doin Lee In-mun and Dangu Kim Hong-do wrote and painted in Park Yu-seong's Seomukjae and gave it to the owner of Yugildang."

Furthermore, at least three paintings by Kim Hong-do have traces that indicate that Lee In-mun saw them. First, in 'The Old Man of the South Pole Star' (Plate 43), it reads, "Gosongyusugwandoin saw this." Second, in 'Danwon, the Garden of Birch Trees' (Plate 40), it reads, "Gosongyusugwandoin Munuk Lee In-mun saw this." Third, in the famous 'Listening to the Nightingale While Riding on a Horse' (Plate 85) it reads, "Giseongyusugosonggwandoin Munuk Lee In-mun attests to this." A record also indicates that in the 12th lunar month of 1788 Kim Hong-do and Lee In-mun jointly appreciated 'Landscape' by Kim Eung-hwan, who was their senior court painter.

We cannot know what friendly talks the two artists had, but we can imagine how close they were as artists since they were the same age and were distant relatives. Jaha Sin Wi, the greatest poet of the time, wrote the following short poem, thinking about Lee In-mun painting alone after Kim Hong-do's death.

On the Painting of Lee In-mun

Among the court painters who served kings
Master hands were you and the old Danwon
Now that Danwon is not to be seen like shimmering clouds before my eyes,
Sitting alone in his studio, Doin still lives on in this world.

Chronology

1745/Yeongjo 21st/1

Date of birth: Unknown. Family origin: Gimhae. Grandfather's name: Suseong. Father's name: Seok-mu. Name: Hong-do. Courtesy name: Hamjang, Saneung. Pen name: Seoho, Chwihwasa, Gomyeongeosa, Danwon, Danno, Danong, Dangu, Cheopchwiong, Nonghan, Nongsaong. Studio name: Daeuam, Osudang.

1751/27th/7

Learned painting from Kang Se-hwang (1713–1791)

1765/41st/21

Painted 'Gyeonghyeondangsujakdo' on the 11th of the 10th lunar month, but the painting is not extant.

1772/48th/28

Bokheon Kim Eung-hwan drew 'Full-view Painting of Mount Geumgang' for him in the spring.

Imunjil of *Uigwe Record on Restoration Work of Yeonghuijeon* on the 28th of the 6th lunar month indicates that Kim Hong-do, along with other painters, was rewarded for his painting during the restoration work at Yeonghuijeon.

93 The first date given here is the year in Kim Hong-do s life. The second name and date shows the king of the time, and the year of his reign. The third number shows Kim Hong-do s age.

According to *King Hyeonjong-chujonho King Yeongjo-sajonho Sang-hodogam-uigwe*, Kim Hong-do painted *banchado* on the 18th of the 11th lunar month. At the time, he was the *busagwa*, who served as a court painter under the direction of the *ilbang*. He was rewarded with rice and cloth for his work.

1773/49th/29

From the 7th to 22nd of the 1st lunar month, as an associate painter Kim Hong-do participated in painting portraits of King Yeongjo and King Jeongjo, who was the eldest grandson of King Yeongjo. He was promoted to *byeolje* of Saposeo for his contribution. In the 8th lunar month, he painted 'A Taciturn Man', on which Kang Se-hwang wrote the inscription, and gave it to Jeong Beom-jo.

1774/50th/30

Included in the record of personnel appointments dated the 20th of the 5th lunar month as the third most qualified candidate. Appointed Saposeo *byeolje* on the 14th of the 10th lunar month. Worked alongside his mentor Kang when he was appointed to the same post on the 27th of the 10th lunar month. Hong Sin-yu wrote in *Bokheon and Baekhwa's Album* that Kim gained fame for his art before he turned 30.

1775/51st/31

Possible death of his parents.

1776/52nd/32

Painted 'Immortals' in spring. King Yeongjo passed away on the 5th of the 3rd lunar month. Painted a decoration on the cloth which covered the king's coffin.

Painted and submitted to King Jeongjo 'Gyujanggak' in the 7th lunar month.

1777/Jeongjo 1st/33

Kang Se-hwang wrote the inscription for 'The Gathering in the Western Garden' in the 7th lunar month. Kim was commissioned to paint public and private paintings together with his colleagues Sin Han-pyeong, Kim Eung-hwan, Lee In-mun, Han Jong-il and Lee Jong-hyeon at Kang Hui-eon's house in Jungbudong. At the time, Kim was *byeolje* and was acquainted with Ma Seong-rin, who frequented the house to appreciate the paintings and write inscriptions. The signature affixed to 'Haengryeopungsokdo,' which was painted the next year, suggests that this gathering of painters continued into early summer of the next year.

1778/2nd/34

In spring, painted 'The Gathering of Four Taoist Immortals' on a folding fan for Ma Seong-rin. In the 4th lunar month, painted the eight-paneled folding screen 'Haengryeopungsokdo' at Kang Hui-eon's house. On a rainy summer day, painted 'The Gathering in the Western Garden', a folding fan painting for Lee Yong-nul. In the 12th lunar month, painted 'The Gathering in the Western Garden' on a six-paneled folding screen.

1779/3rd/35

In the 8th lunar month, Kim asked Hong Sin-yu for a poem in *Bokheon and Baekhwa's Album*.

In the 10th lunar month, painted 'Taoist Immortals' on an eight-paneled folding screen. Painted 'A Pine Tree and the Moon'.

1780/4th/36

Possible trip to China as part of delegation to congratulate the emperor Qianlong on his 70th birthday.

1781/5th/37

On the 1st of the 4th lunar month, Kim held a gathering called *jinsolhoe*, together with Changhae Jeongran and Kang Hui-eon, at his house. Painted 'A Beauty' in the same month. On *daeseo* [July 23 by the solar calendar], Seo Yu-gu wrote the inscription on Kim Hong-do's 'Segeomjeong Gathering'. This inscription provides the earliest recorded use of the pen name Danwon. On the 26th of the 8th lunar month, participated as associate painter in painting the portrait of King Jeongjo. Han Jong-yu, Sin Han-pyeong and Kim Hong-do each drafted a painting of the king. On the 3rd of the 9th lunar month, a draft portrait of the king in his royal crown and formal garments was painted. The next day, the royal portrait was reproduced on silk. On the 16th of the 9th lunar month, the completed portrait was placed in Juhapru. The king issued an ordinance to appoint Kim Hong-do to a *sanjik* in *ijo* or *byeongjo*, which later served as a basis for his appointment to Angi *chalbang* on the 28th of the 12th lunar month of 1783.

1782/6th/38

Yu Gyeong-jong's poem on the 4th of the 4th lunar month reveals that Kang Se-hwang and Kim painted a tiger side by side. In autumn, painted 'Butterflies' on a folding fan and 'The Old Man of the South Pole Star'. Writings by Lee Sang-hyu, who died this year, confirm that Kim used the studio name Daeuam before 1782.

1783/7th/39

On the 21st of the 11th lunar month, the *jabidaeryeong* court-painter system was launched in Gyujanggak, from which Kim was exempt. Appointed to Angi *chalbang* on the 28th of the 12th lunar month.

1784/8th/40

Began his post in the 1st lunar month. Enjoyed *jinggakajip* in the summer at Governor Lee Byeong-mo's house with Seong Dae-jung and Hong Sin-yu, the painting of which is not extant. On the 17th of the 8th lunar month went to Mount Cheongryang with Governor Lee and *hyeongam* of many regions to enjoy poetry and music. Painted 'Bamboo flute played in Mount Cheongryang'. Supposed to have left *Cheongryangcheop* but only a partial copy remains. On the 12th of the 10th lunar month, Kang Se-hwang left for Yenching [Beijing] as a government envoy. Two days after *ipchun*, Kim Hong-do painted 'Danwon, the Garden of Birch Trees' for Jeongran.

1785/9th/41

Served as *chalbang*. Governor Lee left office in the 2nd lunar month, succeeded by Jeong Chang-sun.

1786/10th/42

Eclipse on the 1st day of the 1st lunar month. The king issued ordinances to 363 government officials to report on the evils of the times and took relevant measures to correct them. On the 1st of the 4th lunar month, Jo Su-sam saw a painting of 12 Buddhist gods in *Danwon's Album of Buddhist Paintings* at Dasangwan. Kim returned to work at Dohwaseo after his term as Angi *chalbang* expired in the 5th lunar month. As he completed his term, he painted a calligraphy that reads 'Damrakjae' on a tablet in Chehwajeong, which was hung in the *sarangbang* of a house in Pungsan-eup, Andong-gun. He also engraved a monument to Governor Kim Sang-cheol and Governor Lee Byeong-mo on a huge rock. Soon after returning to Hanyang, Kim met with Kang Se-hwang, and asked him for *Danwongi*. In the 6th lunar month, Songseokwon Literary Club, a literary club of the *jungin* class, was established. Painted 'Anreungsinyeongdo' in autumn, but the original is not extant.

1788/12th/44

Kim and 14 others held a gathering at Great Eunam with Gyeongsan Lee Han-jin present, which was painted by Kim. The painting is not extant. At the 71st birthday celebration for Lee Deok-mu's father held, on the 3rd of the 4th lunar month, Kim painted pictures of a plantain, chrysanthemum, plum, bamboo and the god of longevity. On the 13th of the 9th lunar month, he left for Mount Geumgang from the Hoeyang office to carry out King Jeongjo's orders to paint the mountain. Before that time, he had already sketched the famous sights of nine counties in the northeastern part of the peninsula. On the evening of the 14th of the 9th lunar month, Park Hwang and Jeongran joined them at Jangansa Temple. The following day, Kim sketched the vicinity of the temple. On the 16th, he sketched the area around Baektapdong, sleeping at Pyohunsa Temple. On the 17th, he left for Yujeomsa Temple. At the end of the sketch travel, Kim stopped by the Hoeyang Office and showed Kang Se-hwang what he had drawn. He returned to Hanyang with a piece of writing from Kang, *Seeing off Chalbang Kim Hong-do and Chalbang Kim Eung-hwan*. Kim Hong-do's 'Mount Geumgang' in the form of a 50-meter colored scroll does not exist today. Kim Hong-do went to Chungryeolsa Temple in Chungju on the 20th of the 11th lunar month. From the 21st of the 11th lunar month to the 14th of the 12th lunar month, he copied the portrait of General Im Gyeong-eop, which when completed was moved to the temple on the fifteenth. In the earlier part of the 12th lunar month, Kim and his friends gathered at Sibudang and appreciated 'Landscape,' which was copied and painted by Kim Eung-hwan in 1779. The epilogue mentions that the plums were in blossom.

1789/13th/45

In the 7th lunar month, King Jeongjo decided to move Yeonguwon, the grave of his father Royal Crown Prince Sado, to Suwon and rename it Hyeonryung-won. On the 14th of the 8th lunar month, Kim Hong-do and Lee Myeong-gi accompanied Minister Lee Seong-won on his trip to China and returned in the 2nd lunar month the following year. According to records, including *Genealogy of the Kims*, there was an album in the palace consisting of paintings that Kim and Kim Eung-hwan had drawn while traveling in the southeastern part of the country, and there were comments referring to Eung-hwan being the more talented one. The two Kims were on a royal mission to draw a secret map in Tsushima Island. Eung-hwan died on the way in Busan, Hong-do took care of the funeral arrangements and completed the mission on his own. He probably stopped by Gangjin County in Jeolla Province.

1790/14th/46

Groundbreaking for the reconstruction of the Yongjusa Temple on the 19th of the 2nd lunar month.

1791/15th/47

Mentor and lifetime supporter Kang Se-hwang died at the age of 79 on the 23rd of the 11 lunar month. Painted 'Nightly Gathering of the Songseok-won Literary Club', which depicts scenes from the gathering held on the 15th of the 6th lunar month. On the 19th of the 6th lunar month, Sim No-sung wrote *The Prologue to the Poem about the Trip to the West* which mentions Kim Hong-do's genre paintings. On the 22nd of the 9th lunar month, the king named Lee Myeong-gi the chief painter of the portrait and Kim Hong-do the associate painter. *The Diaries of the Royal Secretariat* mentions that Kim Hong-do held the title of Jangwonseo *byeolje* at the time. On the 28th of the 9th lunar month, his title changes to Binggo *byeolje*. On the 7th of the 10th lunar month, Kim was appointed to a new post in return for his service as associate painter. On the 22nd of the 12th lunar month, he was appointed Yeonpung *hyeongam*.

1792/16th/48

Served as Yeonpung *hyeongam*. Went to Sangamsa Temple at Mount Jo-ryeong to pray for rain, as Yeonpung suffered from a drought that year. Found the temple holy and prayed for a son, donating a hefty sum to have the Buddhist statue gilded and a Buddhist painting created. On the 5th of the 9th lunar month, Lee Gwang-seop was appointed Chungcheong *byeongsa,* and he hosted the Seowon Gathering in Cheongju and invited Kim Hong-do, Lee Han-jin and Hwang Un-jo. Kim had a son, Yang-gi, either this year or the next.

1793/17th/49

On the 11th of the 5th lunar month, Byeongsa Lee Gwang-seop was discharged after a conflict with Kim's direct boss, Governor Lee Hyeong-won. On the 24th of the 5th lunar month, Governor Lee wrote a report on his subordinate officials. Food relief efforts in Chungcheong Province continued from the 1st lunar month to the 24th of the 5th lunar month. Yeonpung had been struck with a second-degree disaster. Kim Hong-do did not depend on government relief but instead resorted to his personal means, but his deeds were evaluated as negligible. On the 13th of the 6th lunar month, Lee Gwang-seop was exiled and Lee Hyeong-won discharged from office, but the latter was reinstated on the 26th.

1794/18th/50

People suffered from a terrible drought. Yeonpung again was designated as a 2nd-degree disaster area. On the 22nd of the 6th lunar month, King Jeongjo sent the list of Gyujanggak court painters to the central government. He commented that Byeon Gwang-bok possessed the same level of skill and sophistication as Kim Hong-do, and gave Byeon a job as public servant, ordering that he be exempt from the *chwijae* (screening) test. Kim is supposed to have painting the Danyang area for the king, but the painting is not extant. Three pieces of work reflecting his experience at the time are included in the *Danwon-jeolsebo Album*. Kim Hong-do's work related to his *hyeongam* post is 'A Yellow Cat and a Dark-colored Butterfly'. The inscription, "The *hyeongam* has the pen name Danwon, and he is also called Chwihwasa," is written on the painting.

1795/19th/51

On the 4th of the 1st lunar month, Chungcheong *wiyusa* Hong Dae-hyeop accused Kim of misgovernment in his report, saying that Kim acted as a matchmaker, plundered petty officials and levied more taxes for his hunting trips. On the 7th, King Jeongjo ordered the replacement of Yeonpung *hyeongam* Kim Hong-do. On the 8th, Hong Dae-hyeop requested that Kim be punished at the Uigeumbu, and the king consented. On the 18th, the king granted amnesty to the criminals not yet sent to the Uigeumbu and ordered the release of Kim Hong-do. In spring there was a huge event celebrating King Yeongjo's second wife, Queen Jeongsun's, fifty-first birthday, Lady Hong's (King Jeongjo's mother) sixty-first birthday, as well as the twentieth year of King Jeongjo's reign. On the 28th of the 2nd lunar leap-month, a *uigwe* office was established in the royal printing house to publish *uigwe* concerning the Wonhaeng-eulmyo parade for the 61st birthday of Lady Hong. The same day, Kim Hong-do was appointed to a fulltime military position so he could paint illustrations for the *Wonhaeng-eulmyo-jeongri-uigwe*. In the 8th lunar month, Kim painted the *Eulmyonyeon Album* for Kim Han-tae. The 'Wonhaeng-eulmyo-uigwedo' on an eight-fold screen was completed. It is confirmed that he painted 'Eight Beautiful Scenes of Hwaseong in Spring and Fall' on a 16-fold screen (of which two panels remain) and 'The Golden Rooster.'

1796/20th/52

In spring, painted twenty paintings for the *Danwon-jeolsebo Album*. In spring, King Jeongjo was touched by *Daebobumoeunjungge* and presumably had Kim Hong-do paint the illustrations for *Bulseoldaebobumoeunjunggyeong*. In the 5th lunar month, the king ordered that *Bulseoldaebobumoeunjunggyeong* be printed and the engraving block stored in Yongjusa Temple. In summer, Kim painted 'The Portrait of Seo Jik-su' with Lee Myeong-gi.

1797/21st/53

On the 1st day of the 1st lunar month, King Jeongjo ordered the publication of *The Five Morals with Illustrations*, which was actually printed on the 20th of the 7th lunar month. Kim is supposed to have painted the illustrations for the book.

1798/22nd/54

Painted 'Banghwasuryudo'.

1799/23rd/55

In a letter dated the 8th of the 6th lunar month in *Danwon's Posthumous Works*, Kim wrote that he was still in great pain from a disease. The manuscript of *Eojeongdaehakryuui* was completed between the 27th of the 10th lunar month and the 5th of the 11th lunar month. This book is the result of King Jeongjo's lifetime study of *The Great Learning*, which he began studying before he was invested as the crown prince.

1800/24th/56

According to the custom of court painters, Kim Hong-do presented an eight-paneled screen painting to the king on New Year's Day entitled, 'The Meanings of Chu Hsi's Poems.' This screen consists of the eight steps in *The Great Learning*: investigation of things, extension of knowledge, sincerity of the will, rectification of the mind, cultivation of the personal life, regulation of the family, national order and world peace. It is believed that the screen was painted in direct relation to *Eojeongdaehakryuui*, the transcript of which had been completed about two months before. The king was deeply touched by the teachings of Chu Hsi, and he composed eight poems. He vowed to look at the painting to remind himself of the teachings. In addition, the king recollected that he had ordered Kim to preside over all court paintings for the past 30 years. On the 28th of the 6th lunar month, King Jeongjo unexpectedly died. Being artistically talented in calligraphy and painting himself, the king had recognized Kim Hong-do's outstanding talent and supported him.

1801/Sunjo 1st/57

In the 12th lunar month, painted 'Landscape' to celebrate King Sunjo's recovery from chicken pox. Sim No-sung mentioned Kim's genre paintings several times in his journal this year.

1802/2nd/58

On the 22nd of the 6th lunar month, the court gave the lithograph and relief of *Bulseoldaebobumoeunjunggyeong* to Yongjusa Temple. On the 23rd of the 7th lunar month, Kim calligraphed ten poems by Byeokokran and affixed his seal, Nonghan. In late 9th lunar month, painted 'The Blue Ocean.'In the 12th lunar month, painted 'An Old Monk Looking at the Waves.' Painted 'Returning Fish' this year.

1803/3rd/59

No record available. Possible residence in rural area.

1804/4th/60

On the 5th of the 5th lunar month, Kim was recruited as *jabidaeryeong* painter in Gyujanggak for the first time. Produced various paintings, for which he was evaluated. Painted 'Giroseryeongyedo'. On the 20th of the 12th lunar month, painted 'Zhizang Riding a Horse' in Park Yu-seong's Seomukjae.

1805/5th/61

In Park Yu-seong's Seomukjae, Kim painted 'Chatting under the Pine Tree' together with his close friend, Lee In-mun. They gave this painting to the owner of Yugildang. In the morning of the 22nd of the 1st lunar month, Kim copied Wang Duo's letter and gave it to his son Yang-gi. Continued to produce paintings as *jabidaeryeong* painter in Gyujanggak, for which he was evaluated. There is no mention of his name in the *Gyujanggak Daily Journal* from the 26th of the 9th lunar month. A letter dated the 29th of the 11th lunar month tells us of Kim's illness since autumn and his fragile condition. 'Ode to the Sound of Autumn' was painted three days after the winter solstice. Kim wrote in a letter dated the 19th of the 12th lunar month that he was sorry he could not pay tuition for Yang-gi and that he was still ill.

1806/6th/62

Possible year of death.

1809/9th

King Sunjo gave Kim's *The Ocean and the Mountain* as a gift to King Jeongjo's son-in-law, Hong Hyeon-ju. In the preface to *Danwon's Posthumous Works,* Hong's brother wrote in 1812 that he saw *The Ocean and the Mountain* after Kim's death. Kim is likely to have died before 1809.

1816/16th

Cheongguyeongeon (*Collection of Ancient Shijo*) edited by Lee Han-jin this year contains two verses by Kim Hong-do.

1818/18th

In the 3rd lunar month, Yang-gi put together his father's anthology and had the epilogue written by Goengadanghakin.

Index